ISBN 978-0-243-26929-7
PIBN 10763173

1 MONTH OF
FREE
READING

at

www.ForgottenBooks.com

By purchasing this book you are eligible for one month membership to ForgottenBooks.com, giving you unlimited access to our entire collection of over 1,000,000 titles via our web site and mobile apps.

To claim your free month visit:
www.forgottenbooks.com/free763173

EDWARD, FIFTH EARL OF DARNLEY

AND

EMMA PARNELL

HIS WIFE

ENMA, COUNTESS OF DARNLEY.
From the unfinished painting by Sir Thomas Lawrence, P.R.A.,
Now in the Walker Art Gallery, Liverpool.

Edward, Fifth Earl of Darnley

AND

Emma Parnell

HIS WIFE

THE STORY OF A SHORT AND HAPPY MARRIED LIFE

TOLD IN THEIR OWN LETTERS

AND OTHER FAMILY PAPERS

EDITED AND ARRANGED BY

THEIR DAUGHTER

LADY ELIZABETH CUST

AND

THEIR GRANDDAUGHTER

EVELYN GEORGIANA PELHAM

————

LEEDS :

RICHARD JACKSON, 16 & 17, COMMERCIAL STREET.

1913.

PREFACE.

A FEW years ago there came into my possession a bundle of letters and papers relating to the youth and short married life of my mother, Emma, Countess of Darnley, and incidentally of my father, Edward Bligh, Fifth Earl of Darnley. My mother, who was of the most retiring disposition, was in the habit of destroying all such papers, and the fact that these should have been preserved seems to prove that she was not unwilling that others should benefit by this record of her husband's singularly loveable and unselfish character. My daughter, the Hon. Mrs. Arthur Pelham, has assisted me in selecting and arranging these letters, and we have formed the opinion that this simple record of a married life in which loyal affection and fervent religious devotion played so large a part, might be received with sympathetic appreciation by a wider circle of readers than ourselves.

The story has been completed by letters and journals preserved by my uncle, Sir John Duncan Bligh, K.C.B., British Minister at Stockholm and Hanover. A few notes have been added to explain the allusions to social and political events of the period.

ELIZABETH C. CUST.

August, 1913.
MOORCROFT, MONMOUTH.

CONTENTS.

LIST OF ILLUSTRATIONS

CHAPTER I.

Emma Parnell.

A SHORT account of the ancestry and early days of Emma, Countess of Darnley, will be of use as a prelude to the letters preserved by her; it will also make known some details of family history which may otherwise be forgotten when those who knew her personally have passed away.

Emma Jane Parnell was the third daughter of Sir Henry Brooke Parnell, Bart., afterwards first Baron Congleton and his wife Lady Caroline Dawson, daughter of John, first Earl of Portarlington. The Parnells settled in Ireland about the middle of the 17th Century and came from Cheshire, where they lived at Congleton and at Astbury. At the latter place several of their monuments may be seen. Thomas Parnell, baptized at Astbury, 10th December, 1625, purchased land in Ireland which was inherited by his elder son, Archdeacon Thomas Parnell; this was the well-known poet, the friend of Pope, Addison and other literary men of his day, but as he left no surviving son, at his death in 1717, his property passed to his brother John, who in 1722 was appointed a Judge of the Irish Court of the King's Bench. John Parnell married Mary, sister of Lord Chief Justice Whitshed, and bought an estate at Rathleague in Queen's County, which still remains in the family.

Sir John Parnell, his only son, who succeeded him in 1727, was created a Baronet in 1766. He had married in 1744-5, Anne, daughter of Mr. Justice Michael Ward and sister of Bernard, First Viscount Bangor, and died 1782. Sir John Parnell, his only son, who succeeded him as second Baronet was M.P. for the Queen's County, from 1783 to his death in 1801. Sir John was Chancellor of the Exchequer, a Lord of the Treasury in the Irish Parliament, and vigorously opposed the Union in 1800. He married in 1774, Letitia Charlotte, one of the two daughters and co-heirs of Sir Arthur Brooke, Bart., by Margaret Fortescue, sister of the first Lord Clermont. She brought into the family a distinguished roll of ancestry, including a Royal descent from George, Duke of Clarence (brother of Edward IV) and his wife Isabel, daughter and co-heir of Richard Nevill, Earl of Warwick, the famous King-maker. Sir John and Lady Parnell had six children.

I. Sir John Parnell, Bart., a cripple and deaf and dumb, who died unmarried in 1812.

II. Sir Henry Brooke Parnell (father of Emma, Lady Darnley), born 1776, succeeded to his father's estates under a special Act of Parliament in 1801, and to the baronetcy at his elder brother's death. He sat as member of Parliament for Queen's County for many years, was created Baron Congleton of Congleton, in the United Kingdom in 1841, and died in 1842.

III. William Parnell, of Avondale, who assumed the name of Hayes, and married Frances, daughter of the Hon. Hugh Howard, by whom he had a son, John, father of the great agitator, Charles Stuart Parnell.

IV. Thomas Parnell (who often appears in this memoir as "Uncle Tom.") He died in 1867; aged 86.

V. Arthur, died young.

VI. Sophia, who married in 1805, George Evans of Portrane.

Henry Brooke Parnell, married in February, 1801, Lady Caroline Dawson, daughter of John, first Earl of Portarlington, and his wife, Lady Caroline Stuart, daughter of John, third Earl of Bute, K.G., and his wife Mary Wortley Montagu, created Baroness Mount Stuart in 1761.

Lady Caroline Dawson was descended from the Argyll Campbells and other great Scottish families, through the marriage of James, second Earl of Bute with Lady Anne Campbell, daughter of Archibald, eleventh Earl and first Duke of Argyll, and on the Wortley Montagu side she had also several interesting ancestors. Of these, perhaps the best known is Lady Mary Wortley Montagu, daughter of Evelyn Pierrepoint, Duke of Kingston, and wife of Edward Wortley Montagu, who had inherited a large property at Wharncliffe and Wortley in Yorkshire from his mother Anne, daughter and heiress of Sir Francis Wortley, Bart. Mr. Wortley Montagu was son of the Hon. Sidney Montagu, younger son of the well-known military and naval commander, Edward Montagu, Earl of Sandwich, who was killed in a sea fight with the Dutch in 1672. Lady Mary Wortley Montagu, after living for many years in the best London society of her day, parted from her husband and spent most of her life out of England. She was celebrated for her wit and literary powers, and for her delightful letters, many of which were written to her daughter Mary, Countess of Bute, who appears often in the memoirs of the 18th century as a great lady, much loved and respected. Her marriage with John, third Earl of Bute in 1737, was a runaway love match; as the alliance was not approved of by her parents, the young couple were at first rather limited in means, and lived very quietly near the Thames, in the village of Chelsea. Here they attracted the notice of the Prince and Princess of Wales, who were also living somewhat in retirement owing to being out of favour with the King (George II), and who were glad to find suitable companions near at hand for their card-table. After the death of Frederick, Prince of Wales, in 1751, Lord Bute became the chief friend and confidant of his son, and soon after George III's accession was appointed Secretary of State and Prime Minister. The friendship of the King, however, could not prevail against the ideas of the country; a combination of parties was made against Lord Bute, who was obliged to resign his position in the Government in 1763, and never again held office. He was a very intelligent and highly cultivated man, and in early life seems to have been sociable and agreeable ; his political misfortunes and the desertion of his royal friends were probably the cause of his somewhat unsympathetic character in later life. He always remained devoted to his wife though rather a stern and worldly father. They had eleven children, most of whom made advantageous alliances and were prosperous in after life ; the youngest, Lady Louisa Stuart, not being allowed to marry the man of her heart, remained unmarried, and died at the age of 94 in

1851. (The writer of this memoir well remembers her, and some of Lady Louisa's later letters mention visits from her greatniece, Lady Darnley and her daughters). The sister next above Lady Louisa in age, Caroline, Countess of Portarlington, (mother of Lady Caroline Dawson and grandmother of Lady Darnley), was Louisa's great friend, and though not her equal in intellect was noted for beauty and accomplishments ; while Louisa was the valued friend of Sir Walter Scott and corresponded with him on literary subjects, Caroline was the friend of Sir Joshua Reynolds and painted under his directions. The two sisters inherited much of their grandmother, Lady Mary Wortley Montagu's talent for correspondence ; their charming letters to each other have been edited by Mrs. Godfrey Clark.* Lady Louisa's letters to Sir Walter Scott and to Miss Clinton have also been published.

The marriage of Henry Parnell and Lady Caroline Dawson came about in this manner. In the autumn of 1800, he was on a visit to his uncle, Thomas, first Viscount de Vesci, at Abbeyleix, where he met Lady Portarlington and her daughters. He was then twenty-four, and being a very shy reserved young man does not appear to have talked much to the young ladies. However, he was so charmed with

* "Gleanings from an Old Portfolio," David Douglas, Edinburgh, 1895-98.

14

the good looks of the second girl, Lady Louisa, that he wished to marry her, and not long after wrote to Lady Portarlington to propose for her daughter's hand. Unluckily he worded his letter in such a way that she took his proposal to be for her eldest daughter Caroline, aged eighteen, Louisa, the one he admired, being still in the schoolroom. This we find recorded in the following letter to her sister Louisa:

Countess of Portarlington to Lady Louisa Stuart.

Cheltenham, 28th November, 1800.

My dear Louisa,

. . . . . You will be surprised when I tell you I do not know how long Caroline may keep the name of Dawson, as she has had a very agreeable proposal which she is inclined to accept. It is now time to tell you his name is Parnell, Sir John's eldest son, and if I were sure he would like her and make her a good husband, it is the match of all others I would have wished, as I have known him from a child, have a great regard for all his family and connections, and their house just half way between us and Lord de Vesci. He is remarkably handsome, very sensible and well-informed, and of a very active mind ; he was at Abbeyleix when we were there about a fortnight before we left Ireland. He did not seem to observe my girls, and has always

15

been more reserved to them than was natural, considering they used to play together as children. We thought all the admiration he had met with in Dublin had made him conceited, and that he was too fine to take notice of my shy timid girls. I have not yet written him an answer, as I hardly know what to say. Car. has no objection to make but the very natural one of not feeling sufficiently acquainted with him. By his letter (which is to me) it would appear that his father was not acquainted with his intentions, as he says, with our joint permission to acquaint his father, he has every reason to think he will act by him in the most liberal manner. He says that he has but a very small income independent of his father, but you know I cannot expect any great things for my daughters, who have so little to bring to a family. I can't tell you how happy this event would make me if I could think he had taken a fancy to her . . . . . If this event should take place, I suppose it will bring me to town sooner than I intended, for I conclude he will come over, and I could not make him stay in this place, where he would not have another man to speak to. Poor Caroline does not know what to think of it, she is so surprised, and indeed so are we all, for they have never been asked to think of husbands. Louisa and Harriet are as much children in their way as they were five years ago, and poor Car was only in the world for the small space of two months, half of which time being Easter, people went to the country and there was hardly anything going on, and she, not being forward or used to the ways of town misses, made very few acquaintances. If I dispose of her I believe I shall be tempted to bring out Harriet and Louisa together, as Harriet is more grown up in her person than Louisa, but she is very awkward, and it may take that off. The Duchess of Gordon admired Louisa, but I think Harriet will be thought the best looking. Caroline is certainly the least, so therefore it shows it is mere luck and not beauty that attracts husbands! I think I shall be very vain of my son-in-law if Henry Parnell becomes so, and I shall long to introduce him to you. Adieu, my dear sister. My mind is so occupied with this unexpected event I can think of nothing else.*

When Henry Parnell discovered that he was accepted by the wrong sister, he had not sufficient courage to explain matters, and his marriage with Lady Caroline Dawson took place on February 17th, 1801. The young couple seem never to have suited each other from the very first. Poor Lady Caroline, a warm-hearted, quick-tempered girl who would no doubt have been devoted to her husband had he taken any trouble to win her affections, was, as she afterwards told her daughter Emma, chilled by his coldness and indifference to her. Still, though never happy with each other, they

* "Gleanings from an Old Portfolio," iii, 68.

17

managed to get on pretty well for the next twelve years during which time they lived in London, Henry Parnell absorbed in his Parliamentary duties and political life, and she, a kind and watchful mother, devoting herself to the care of their seven children. Emma, Lady Darnley, long after this, wrote to her mother, then in Paris: " I have often felt myself excited to attend to my dear children's health and welfare by recollecting your great attention to us when we were all little children. I remember very well your coming to see us undressed and settled in our little beds, and your visits at night to the nursery to see that the nurses were taking proper care of us." Their first child, Caroline, afterwards the wife of Dr. Longley, later on Archbishop of Canterbury, and their second daughter Mary, who married Lord Henry Moore in 1824, were born in the same year, 1802. Emma, the subject of this memoir, was born April 7th, 1804, and John, afterwards the second Lord Congleton in 1805. Next came a daughter, Fanny, and then two more sons, Henry, the third Lord Congleton who died in 1896, and George, who took Holy Orders and died in 1882.

The death of her youngest daughter

Fanny, a charming child of five years old (buried in the cloisters of Westminster Abbey, where her memory is preserved by a tablet on the West wall) appears to have almost broken her mother's heart. She fell into ill health and felt herself unable to endure any longer her uncongenial home. Her mother and her sisters were much disturbed at her state of mind, and after Lady Portarlington's death in 1813, it was thought that a thorough change of scene might restore her health and spirits. Permission was thereupon obtained from the Emperor Napoleon to allow Lady Caroline Parnell to travel through France to Switzerland, on condition that no man or boy above the age of twelve should be of the party; a special favour at that time when no English were in France, excepting as prisoners of war. Taking with her the three girls and her younger sons, Henry and George, Lady Caroline went to Switzerland for a short time, and on her way back stopped in Paris. Here she made a number of friends whose society she found so agreeable, and her life in France so much pleasanter than in England that she could never afterwards make up her mind to return to her unloved home, and continued to live in Paris till her death in 1861. As in the similar case of her great-grand-mother, Lady Mary Wortley Montagu, no actual quarrel seems to have taken place between her and Sir Henry Parnell, who had succeeded his brother as fourth Baronet in 1812, but time wore on and Lady Caroline's return was continually postponed in spite of Sir Henry's remonstrances.

Emma, Lady Darnley, who was nine years old when she went to France, often entertained her children with reminiscences of her life there, which she seems to have greatly enjoyed. Emma remembered having seen Napoleon reviewing his troops, and what a pleasant house they lived in, and also the charming French officers who often visited them and made much of her and her brothers and sisters, and she had a vivid recollection of the hatred felt by them for the Allies when their beloved friends returned to them, maimed and wounded from some of Napoleon's battles. Lady Caroline was in Paris at the entry of the allied Sovereigns in 1814, and Emma remembered hearing the guns at Montmartre before the city surrendered. At the time of the battle of Waterloo they were living at Passy, then a village near Paris and now a large suburb; Emma well remembered what a pretty sight were the tents of the victorious English army encamped in the Bois de Boulogne during the following July.

Henry Parnell (afterwards third Lord Congleton), although five years younger than Emma, distinctly remembered a beloved French nurse who used to sing to him "Malbrook s'en va t'en guerre" and the fact that Napoleon was ungallant enough to requisition Lady Caroline's English travelling carriage for his own service. He used to say, in after life, that Napoleon's carriage at Madame Tussaud's which was captured after the battle of Waterloo was probably the one which had been taken from his mother.

After Waterloo Sir Henry Parnell was once more able to communicate freely with his wife. He desired that she should immediately return to England and when she refused to come he insisted that his children should be sent home. Lady Caroline preferring, it would seem, her liberty to either husband or children, declined to come herself but allowed the children to be sent to England.*

* Some account of Lady Caroline's life until her death in 1861 will be found in the Appendix.

By this time Sir Henry Parnell had lived so long as a bachelor and was so much occupied in parliamentary affairs that he felt himself unable to make a home for his children, and therefore placed them all in the charge of Dr. and Mrs. Crane at Brentford Rectory. Here they were very happy and Emma often afterwards spoke of the kindness with which they were treated by Dr. Crane and his family. Dr. Crane had at that time several youths of good birth as pupils, amongst whom Emma remembered the two sons of the Earl of Carlisle.

After some pleasant years spent at Brentford, the boys were sent to school and Emma and her sisters were placed with Mrs. Fowler at Derby, who also was very kind to them. She was a very religious woman, with strong Evangelical views and Emma under this influence became "converted" and ever after endeavoured to live up to her ideal of a truly religious life. A dangerous attack of inflammation of the lungs seems to have fixed her religious convictions and to have brought clearly before her the uncertainty of life and the necessity of always being prepared for death.

As the Misses Parnell grew up they

were allowed from time to time to visit their relations and friends, and Emma certainly often stayed with her great-aunt Lady Macartney at Chiswick and with Mrs. Puget, a kind old cousin of her father's who lived at Totteridge. Mrs. Puget, also one of the Evangelical school, talked much to her young cousin on serious subjects. Emma made great friends with her and was always much attached to her and her daughters, Mrs. Peter Browne, Mrs. James Browne and Lady Radstock. A little Testament, given to her in 1819 by Mrs. Puget was among the little treasures found in her desk after her death.

The two elder sisters, Caroline and Mary Parnell, left Derby before Emma and were planted out with relations in Ireland. Emma, as far as can be ascertained, left Derby when she was eighteen and at first stayed with her aunt Mrs. Evans at Portrane near Dublin; either here or on some other visit about this time she received an offer of marriage from Captain George Probyn, father of the present Sir Dighton Probyn, but she would not hear of it, thinking him much too stout and middle-aged. Emma did not care much for Mrs. Evans and was very glad when her uncle, Thomas Parnell, then a well-known religious leader in Dublin, took a great fancy to her and finding how much they had in common, took her with him to the North of Ireland to visit his great friends the Earl and Countess of Roden, also very religious people. The earliest preserved of Emma Parnell's letters were written from the Rodens' place, Tully-more Park, near Dundalk, to her brother John, then a student at the University of Edinburgh, in which town he and his brothers Henry and George had been for some time at school.

These letters are an interesting exposition of the doctrines held by seriously minded Christians of that day, written by a girl of eighteen to a boy of sixteen, evidently with sincere conviction.

The decade from 1820 to 1830 is remarkable for the momentous religions and political changes which were then maturing almost unseen. The Abolition of Religious Tests, Catholic Emancipation and the Reform Bill were the results in the political world and Emma's future husband and his father were much engaged at this time in promoting these measures. The revival of religious life naturally lies more beneath the surface, but is not less remarkable to the student of social changes. Pusey has dated its beginning from the first publication of Keble's "Christian Year" in 1827. But before this date the young Presbyterian minister Edward Irving, had been rousing the hearts of men and women of all classes of society by the thought of the Second Coming of Christ, and at Albury, near Guildford, Henry Drummond collected men of every variety of thought to discuss prophecy and the signs of the times. In Ireland also a great religious awakening was taking place which has been called the "Dublin Movement" in contradistinction to the better known "Oxford Movement." Space forbids us to enter more into detail or to attempt to trace the fundamental similarity and external differences of these various manifestations of the Spirit of God and the results in the century which followed. We can only here call attention to the fact that Emma Parnell and her brother John fell under the influence of these Irish pioneers of a vital religion and the bent then given to their minds proved no transient emotion but coloured deeply the whole of the remainder of their lives.

November 18th, 1822.

My dear John,

I was very glad to hear that you thought you should be comfortable in your new situation. You will have one great advantage over those who go to the English Universities, you will not have near so many temptations to idleness and extravagance, and all those foolish and wild ways in which I hear, most of the young men at Oxford and Cambridge spend their time, as you do not live among your fellow-students, and can therefore choose your own society. I think it often does young people harm to associate much with each other, I find it so when I associate with girls of my own age. My folly not being checked by any counteracting wisdom on their part, nor theirs by any on mine, we make each other worse than we were before, and encourage each other in our childishness and vanity.

I believe the people Uncle Tom has introduced you to are very nice people and have no doubt you will like them. Mr. Gray is a very clever accomplished man and I should think his acquaintance would be a great acquisition. We wish very much to have you in Ireland. Uncle Li* wants to teach you all your future duties as a country gentleman, and indeed, I think people ought to consider it as a serious duty to endeavour to make themselves acquainted with all the different ways and means in their power

* Hon. Lionel Dawson.

26

of doing good to the poor people around them. Only think how happy and comfortable all the tenants on an estate might be made by a little attention and kindness on the part of the landlord, and by his living among them, and helping them in the education of their children, and in all their hardships and difficulties, and what a pleasant reflection for one's self in such a case, to think one had been the means of lightening the misfortunes of so many fellow creatures, and of contributing to their happiness. I hope you will continue to endeavour to improve yourself, for nothing makes a man so pleasant or so useful as a good deal of information. In short, my dear John, I hope you will be everything that is excellent and delightful, not only as to this world but as to the next, for as this world *cannot* last for ever, surely it becomes a wise man to prepare for that world which lasts for ever and ever. This seems very reasonable but when we look at our own conduct and at that of others, I believe that we shall find that in general we hardly think at all of that future world which we are all hastening to. Even we who are so young might fall down dead in a moment, and then where should we go? Should we go to *heaven* or *hell*, for that is the question? There is no middle state, we must be either perfectly happy or miserable. The Bible says so and I dare not doubt the truth of what it says, for I have examined a great many times all the evidences of the Christian religion, and I have found them to be so clear and satisfactory that it was not because I was taught it as a child, or because it was the religion of my forefathers that I now profess it, but from a full conviction of its truth which I have obtained by diligent searching and enquiry in the most careful manner. Believing then the Bible to be the word of God, is it foolish then to be alarmed for one's eternal happening hereafter, when one reads that "without holiness no man shall see the Lord." And when one reads that it will not be enough to have called Christ, Lord, Lord, with our lips, that is, to have acknowledged him to be our Saviour to ensure our being saved, if we have continued to be workers of iniquity. Now are we not all workers of iniquity, do we not all commit sin in numerous different ways, every day? Read that part of the Bible, and tell me what you think of it. In short we have all reason to tremble for ourselves for we are all wicked, but yet we need not despair for "the blood of Jesus Christ cleanseth from all sin." You must forgive my writing in this way to you, for I have thought a good deal about myself lately, and this makes me feel anxious that you should think about yourself. I am beginning to find out that this world cannot make us happy, and then if we have no hope in the world to come, we are of all men the most miserable.

I find upon looking back that I have been particularly disobedient to one of God's commands namely, "Search the Scriptures." I have often spent days and weeks without hardly opening the Bible, take warning by me and do not neglect it, for it brings more happiness than any other way of spending your time. When I look back on what I have written, I am afraid you will call it a great preaching and think I am gone mad, but it is what everyone who thinks about their own souls and the word of God will tell you as well as me. So do not be angry with me, but think about these things. I and Uncle Tom are staying at Tullymore, Lord Roden's place, we leave it on Thursday when we shall have been here twelve days. They are delightful people and so very kind to me that I shall be ungrateful if I were not very fond of them. They have three children, who are always asking for stories, and put me in mind of Henry who used to make me tell him so many. The place itself is beautiful, when you come to Ireland I hope Lord Roden will ask you down here. He is a very handsome man as tall as Uncle Tom. Lady Roden is very like Aunt Louisa. I am to stay a week with Mr. and Mrs. Jocelyn, uncle and aunt to Lord Roden before I go back to Dublin. I shall be sorry to leave this part of the world, for I have spent my time very pleasantly here. Papa will be in Ireland in a day or two, so pray write to me and send it to him. Why did you not write to Uncle Tom, he is quite surprised you don't answer his letter? Give my best love.

Uncle Tom has got your letter. If you write soon you may direct under cover to Earl of Roden, Dundalk, as I am going to stay with them again for a little while.

Good bye my dear John.

Your affectionate sister,
EMMA.

EMMA PARNELL AT TULLYMORE, TO JOHN PARNELL
AT EDINBURGH.

December 1st, 1822.

My dear John,

I hope you got my letter to Mama which I
sent you. I am very much afraid she has thought
us unkind in not writing to her, but you know
we have to direct to her under a feigned name,
Madame Pearson. Now if we had sent a letter to
France with this direction everybody would know
that it was to Mama because we know no one else
abroad. And now, my dear John, you must
excuse me if I write upon a subject of which my
heart is full at present, namely of what the
scriptures tell us about our souls. Our souls will
live for ever and ever when our bodies will have
mouldered into dust is a truth which we all know
and believe, and we all believe also that there is
a Heaven and Hell, and that the wicked will go
to Hell. But now who are the wicked? Perhaps
you would be surprised if I said that I am one,
and that you yourself are one of the wicked. If
you will look at the Epistle to the Romans you
will find that "the wages of sin is death," 6th
chapter, 23rd verse, and in the 2nd chapter and
in the 8th and 9th verses you will find that in
the day of wrath and revelation of the righteous
judgment of God, who shall render to every man
according to his deeds; unto them that are con-
tentious and do not obey the truth, but obey
unrighteousness, indignation and wrath, tribulation
and anguish, upon every soul of man that doeth
evil. And again, "the wrath of God is revealed

from heaven against all unrighteousness and ungodliness of man," Romans i, 18. Maybe you never read this epistle, but if you have not pray read it through and when you read it pray to God to teach you the meaning of it by His Holy Spirit, for I assure you it is impossible to understand the Scriptures without, and when we do pray, we have good reason to think that we shall be heard, for Christ himself tells us " Whatsoever ye shall ask the Father in My name He will give it unto you." Perhaps you wonder at my saying that you are wicked, and that I and all men are very wicked, but Christ hath said so. Mark vii, 21. " Out of the heart of men proceed evil thoughts, adulteries, fornications, murders, thefts, covetousness, wickedness, deceit, lasciviousness, an evil eye, blasphemy, pride, foolishness, all these evil things come from within, and defile the man." Observe, not some few only of these sinful things dwell within us, but all of them. And I and many others can tell you that it is indeed true, and that it is impossible to describe all the wickedness of our hearts, but there is one comfort that Jesus Christ died to atone for our sins.

" There is a fountain filled with blood
　Drawn from Immanuel's veins,
And sinners plunged beneath that flood
　Lose all their guilty stains."

This is a verse of a hymn which I am very fond of. How delightful it is to think that if we believe in Christ and have an interest in His precious sacrifice of Himself to atone for our sins, we shall be for ever happy with Him in heaven long after this world will have passed away and be forgotten.   Our life here is very short and often a very sorrowful one, but we shall live for ever hereafter.   If we are Christ's disciples and servants we shall be with Him in glory, but if we are not, our lot will be indeed dreadful, for we must dwell in everlasting burnings.

You will think I am very conceited to try and teach you, but though I am very ignorant, and have need to be taught yet I feel so much concerned about you for I know that you have an immortal soul to be saved as well as I have that I cannot help begging you to examine these things for yourself, and above all to search the Scriptures, to pray over them when you are reading, and remember, my dear John, you are older than Henry and George, and you ought to take care to teach them something about religion for they are not too young to die, and if they died without knowing anything about Christ, who shed His blood for them and who is willing to save them, only think how very dreadful it would be.   Think that we must all either go to Heaven or Hell.

Give my love to both of them, and show them this letter.   Good bye, my dearest John.

Your affectionate Sister,

EMMA.

EMMA PARNELL AT CARNEW, CO. WEXFORD, TO
JOHN PARNELL AT EDINBURGH.

January 8th, 1823.

My dear John,

I cannot tell you how delighted I was with your letter which I received this morning.   When

I wrote to you from Tullymore, it was with the most perfect hopelessness that you would care at all about the subject of my letter, and I only talked about it because I felt it was my duty to tell you or any one who would listen to me what my views were.

If we had been living together I don't think we should ever have found out each other's sentiments for I should have been afraid to *say* any thing thinking you would not listen, but I thought to myself that you could not help reading a letter through, out of mere curiosity. But I have ever since I saw the necessity of salvation myself, felt very anxious that you and all of us should see it too. For observing many people I had known and loved dying around me, and having once been very near death myself when I was so ill last year, or rather the year before last, it has often occurred to me, well if I die, or any of us die, where shall we go and what will become of us? We are every moment liable to death, neither youth nor health is the least security, and it is an awful thought what will become of the spirits, the immortal spirits which animate these bodies, when the bodies themselves are mouldering in the dust? There is a great difference between *our* condition and that of many others in the world, many are richer and nobler and higher and thought more of than we are, many have the kindest parents and the most delightful homes, while we are separated from our parents and from each other, and there are many too who are not near so well off as we are who are exposed to all the miseries of sickness and poverty, but after all however different our circumstances as to this world may be, in one respect we are all alike, the whole world is guilty before God: "All have sinned, and come short of the glory of God," Romans iii, 23, and in that beautiful chapter of Isaiah (which so exactly describes our Blessed Saviour and His work of redemption that a great infidel, the famous Lord Rochester was converted by reading it) in the fifty-third it is said: "All we like sheep have gone astray, we have turned every one to his own way: and the Lord hath laid on him the iniquity of us all." And the description of the human heart in Jeremiah xvii, 9, applies to all of us alike. "The heart is deceitful above all things and desperately wicked, who can know it?" I am sure this is true, by what I know of my own heart, and can remember about my own thoughts and actions all my life long. Even in performing what may seem to others a very good action, one's motives are often deplorably *bad*. All the best and wisest of us who have examined themselves attentively have all agreed to this. We have all reason to say with Daniel in his 9th chapter "O Lord, to us belongeth confusion of face, to our kings, to our princes, and to our fathers, because we have sinned against thee: neither have we obeyed the voice of the Lord our God, to walk in his laws, which he set before us by his servants the prophets. We have sinned, we have done wickedly." And as it is said in many parts of the Scripture, particularly in Psalm 9,

34

verse 17, that the *wicked* and those that forget God shall be turned into Hell, it seems very incomprehensible at first how any of us are to be saved from Hell, for we are all wicked we have acknowledged.

We also read " Without *holiness* no man shall see the Lord," but the New Testament explains this, how God can be just and yet receive us to heaven. This you know of course namely that Christ was slain for us, that His death upon the cross was a full and sufficient sacrifice and atonement for our sins. He bore *our* punishment instead of us and justifies us by His precious blood, He is the Good Shepherd, He laid down His life for the sheep. In short He redeemed us. I cannot explain these things well, but I feel and believe that Christ is the propitiation for my sins, that He has borne God's just wrath instead of me. But now I am talking of understanding the Bible, I will tell you one of the best ways, which is to get a Bible with *references*, the best edition is printed at Edinburgh I suppose it would cost very little more than another Bible, and it is quite wonderful how much light is thrown on a passage by comparing it with the other texts referred to in the margin. It is not only of great use in making one understand the Scriptures but is very amusing.

Do try and get one if you can afford, for I suppose you are allowed more money than you were. I am very glad you read a portion of the Bible daily ; certainly we ought to be very thankful for having such a blessing as the Bible, for it is indeed a blessing. It shows us the way to glory, it tells us of that kind Saviour who willingly died to save us, it tells us what we all must feel that this world is not our home, that there is no happiness here for us, for sin and sorrow contaminate every enjoyment, but it also tells us that eternal happiness is prepared for the redeemed of Christ, that a time for them is fast approaching, when all tears shall be wiped from their eyes and sorrow and sighing shall flee away. Eternal life is offered to us. How then shall we be so mad and so blind to our own interests as to refuse it? Jesus told Martha when she was troubled about many things that but one thing is needful, "and" he added, "Mary hath chosen that good part which shall not be taken from her." Now this Mary was sitting at Jesus' feet, and hearing His word. She was doing what we may imitate her in. She was listening to His words, and the Bible is His word, and happy will it be for us if we spend much time in studying it. And though we cannot see Christ or literally sit at His feet, we can as often as we like draw near to Him by prayer. We can also frequent as much as possible the company of his people, and go as often as possible to hear His word faithfully preached. I say faithfully or truly, because perhaps as you have already remarked there are many clergymen who either do not read the Gospel or do not understand it. For instance, I have heard many of these clergymen say in their sermons that regeneration is the same as baptism. Now Christ says except a man be born of water and of the

Spirit he cannot enter into the kingdom of God. Read the third chapter of John and tell me if you do not think it means something besides baptism. In the third chapter of Matthew, John the Baptist says, "I indeed baptize you with water unto repentance, but He that cometh after me is worthier than I whose shoes I am not worthy to unloose, He shall baptize you with the Holy Ghost and with fire," and in Titus it is said in the third chapter, fifth verse, "Not by works of righteousness which we have done but according to his mercy he saved us, by the washing of regeneration and renewing of the Holy Ghost." It says in another part, "If any man be in Christ he is a new creature," and Galatians vi, 15, "In Christ Jesus neither circumcision availeth anything, nor uncircumcision, but a new creature." Now all these texts certainly mean, I think, being renewed by the Holy Spirit, having one's heart changed and renewed by the Spirit of God, in short, being made holy and good by His holy influence. Tell me whether you agree with me in this. If you do, I am sure you will also agree in thinking it highly necessary to pray for this valuable blessing. It is said in Luke, "if ye then being evil know how to give good gifts unto your children, how much more shall your Heavenly Father give the Holy Spirit to them that ask him." The more time we spend in prayer the better it will be for us. Besides praying at night and morning it is very useful to [have a quarter of an hour in the daytime to spend in prayer. Whenever we read the

Bible, we should pray to have our understandings enlightened that we may understand it. I think I must have tired you with my long sermon only as perhaps you know no one of your own age who thinks as you do you may like me to tell you a little what I think now and then. Don't enclose to me any more at Lord Roden's as I left them about ten days ago, and so it would not be correct, but enclose to Papa at Emo, for whether he is there or not the letters are always sent to him. In my next letter I mean to write you a long account of Lord and Lady Roden and the delightful time I spent there. Uncle Tom came down to fetch me, and brought me up to Lady Westmeath last Monday week. Mr. and Mrs. Henry More, great (friends) of Uncle Tom's, asked me to come and see them, and as Lady Westmeath was coming down she brought me with her, and so I am here at Carnew, in County Wexford, a very wild part of the country, but a very pleasant place to be in. I have got such a number of nice friends through Uncle Tom who is very much beloved and respected. Some years ago there was hardly one person in Ireland of good family, or either of the higher class who had any idea of religion. He was the first, but now great numbers of the higher class in Ireland are religious characters and many of them through Uncle Tom's means. When you come to Ireland you must be acquainted with them all. I am sure you will be delighted with the Rodens especially.

I have never been to a ball and never mean

to go (by) my own consent, because I could not go without feeling so much vanity and emulation, and hearing so much flattery and nonsense as would make me, I fear, grow indifferent to my spiritual welfare, but perhaps for a young man the case is different, though I dare say you will not find much pleasure in them. If you should however get fond of them, I would advise you to beware, for we are commanded not to love the world, I John iii. I long to see you all. I remember a book which I found very useful, Pilgrim's Progress with Scott's notes. I am sure Mr. Gray has got it, ask him to lend it you, and look out all the texts which are referred to, but remember without the Notes by Scott it is nothing.

Mary is at Abbeyleix with the Dawsons. Lady Westmeath will take me to Emo I believe. Of course I will not tell anyone what you say in your letters, not even Mary if you don't like, but if you meet with anybody who could give you good advice don't be ashamed of talking to them a little about the subject of religion, for it is very useful to hear the opinions of others. I saw your friend Kate Brown the other day. John Pug has been kept at Cambridge by a bad cold. Mary rides every day at Abbeyleix, she has become a great horsewoman. I· hope you will take care not to get drowned in the ice for skating is very dangerous. So pray take care. Give my best love to Henry and George.

. Your very affectionate sister,

EMMA PARNELL.

Sir Henry Parnell now arranged with

his brother-in-law, Lionel Dawson, that he and his wife, Lady Elizabeth, should take Emma and her sister Mary to live with them at Emo. This arrangement went on till the end of the year 1823, when Mr. Dawson, finding life at Emo beyond his means, determined to remove his family to Brussels and to take Emma with them. Mary Parnell went to stay with Lady Elizabeth Dawson's mother, Lady Westmeath, where she met her future husband, Lord Henry Moore. The Dawson family, including Emma, started from Ireland and got as far as Dover, when Tom Parnell, horrified at the idea of the dissipations of Brussels for his favourite niece, pursued the party and after a somewhat stormy interview with the Dawsons, persuaded Emma to leave them and return with him to Ireland, he undertaking the responsibility of providing for her.*

Here now was a bachelor uncle with a pretty and charming niece on his hands, not knowing the least how to dispose of her till he bethought him of his cousins Lord and Lady de Vesci, the kindest and most amiable of people. He took Emma to stay with them at Abbeyleix where she

* See letter from Hon. Lonel Dawson, June, 1825, p.

was kindly received and they, liking the girl, allowed their house to become her headquarters until her marriage in 1825. During this time she seems to have visited several friends and relations in the North of Ireland and according to letters of that time she was everywhere much admired and liked.

She thoroughly enjoyed herself in the cheerful, friendly atmosphere of Abbeyleix with cousins of her own age, Tom, William, and Catherine Vesey, John and Tom Nugent of Portaferry and many other young people. Emma often described the life at Abbeyleix to her children. Early hours were the rule there but after Lord de Vesci had partaken of his glass of beer at 10 o'clock and he and Lady de Vesci had gone to bed, the young people used to meet in another part of the house and held high jinks every night. Hot suppers were cooked by them and dancing and all sorts of games went on, which even the serious Emma, then full of life and high spirits, enjoyed as much as her cousins.

As Lord and Lady de Vesci were later on much concerned in arranging Emma Parnell's marriage with Lady de Vesci's nephew Edward, Lord Clifton, it will be well to point out the way in which they were both related to the young people they introduced to each other.

It will be remembered that Emma's grandfather Sir John Parnell married Letitia Charlotte, one of the two daughters and co-heirs of Sir Arthur Brooke, Bart. The other sister, Selina Elizabeth Brooke, married in 1769 Thomas, first Viscount de Vesci, so that Emma's father Sir Henry Parnell, and John, second Viscount de Vesci, were first cousins.

Edward, Lord Clifton, eldest son of the fourth Earl of Darnley, whose acquaintance we shall make in the next Chapter, was the nephew of Frances, Viscountess de Vesci, the youngest of the four beautiful and charming daughters of the Right Hon. William Brownlow of Lurgan by his second wife, Catherine Hall of Narrowwater. Elizabeth, Countess of Darnley, mother of Lord Clifton, was the third of these daughters; Catherine, the eldest, had married Mathew Forde of Seaforde and died in 1808; the second, Isabella, Viscountess Powerscourt was the widow of Richard, fourth Viscount Powerscourt. The three eldest daughters

"MODERN GRACES."
Portraits of
Isabella, Viscountess Powerscourt ; Catherine, Mrs. Forde of
Seaforde ; and Elizabeth, Countess of Darnley; daughters of the
Right Hon. William Brownlow, of Lurgan.
From a Coloured Engraving by E. Scot, after a drawing
by H. W. Bunbury.

were the subject of a charming drawing by
Henry Bunbury, engraved by E. Scot, under
the title "Modern Graces."

Poem by Emma Parnell [probably written 1821.]

St.. Helena.

Grave of the mighty, melancholy isle,
Whose sea-girt rocks, a high and gloomy pile
In lovely grandeur, on the Atlantic's maze
Look down with cold and stern repelling gaze,
When passion's meteor reign shall have expired
And other men with no resentment fired
Shall read the tale of Europe's wayward strife,
Shall feel with hurried throb the pulse of life
Beating within them, while the glowing page
Unfolds the records of this warlike age,
Shall they not often turn with wondering eye
And gaze where low Napoleon's ashes lie,
Conqueror of Europe, when in youth's bright hour
Italia owned thy stern resistless power
When awe-struck France before thee kneeling low,
Beheld thee place her diadem on thy brow,
When the proud eagle fluttered in thy sky
And waved his golden wings in triumph high,
O mighty Emperor did thine eye of pride
Ere seek to draw the veil of fate aside.

CHAPTER II.

Lord Clifton.

LADY de Vesci had taken a great fancy to Emma Parnell and the more she knew her the more she liked her. She now took into her head that Emma would make an admirable wife for her nephew, Lord Clifton, eldest son of the Earl of Darnley and her sister Elizabeth.

Lord Clifton was born February 25th, 1795, he went to Eton at the early age of eight and passed through the school with distinction, proceeding to Christ Church, Oxford, in October, 1812. Here also he distinguished himself and was chosen to recite some Greek verses of his own composition on the occasion of the visit of the Allied Sovereigns to the University in August, 1814. He finished a brilliant and successful University career by taking a first class in classics, at that time a most unusual distinction for a young nobleman. He came of age in February, 1816, and the

EDWARD, LORD CLIFTON.
Fron the painting by John Hoppner, R.A.
at Cobhan Hall.

following letter gives an account of the festivities at Cobham.

REV. JOHN STOKES, VICAR OF COBHAM, TO ISABELLA, VISCOUNTESS POWERSCOURT.

Cobham, February 29th, 1816.

Dear Lady Powerscourt,

Knowing how sincerely you and your amiable daughters participate in all the feelings of your excellent relatives at Cobham Hall, I am persuaded that a detailed account of the proceedings on the late joyous occasion will not be unacceptable to you. And altho' I have no doubt you will have an account of the whole, either by Letter, or when you see them, from the young Ladies, yet I am willing to seize this opportunity of showing your Ladyship that I am desirous at least of making all the return I can for the uninterrupted series of kindness and condescension I have experienced from you, ever since I have had the honour of knowing you. And however unnecessary this account may be render'd by those you will receive thro' better channels, I know I may trust to your Ladyship's tried goodness to excuse the liberty I take. The whole thing has gone off with so much satisfaction to everyone at all concerned it, and there has been such a natural and unaffected display of the best feelings of the human heart, that I could have wished (had it been possible) that it had been witness'd by every friend of the family.

On Saturday last, bread, beef and beer were distributed, in proportion to their families, to all the poor of Cobham and the other villages, in which Lord Darnley's estate lies, viz.: Shorne, Chalk, Luddesdowne, Cuxton, and Cliffe; and in the Towns of Gravesend and Strood there was also a distribution of the same articles, or of firing. And neither Bounds nor Sandgate were forgotten. So that, altogether, I suppose upwards of 2000 hearts were gladden'd by a *real* benefit on the *very* day; for they were all provided with a good Sunday's dinner at their own cottages. And this was done, in lieu of that injudicious and often mischievous plan of giving roasted oxen and beer to the populace. On Sunday, Lord and Lady D. enjoyed in quiet the sincere congratulations of a few friends, most of them indeed of their own families, on an occasion render'd by the uncommon (I will say) though unobtrusive virtues of their excellent son, most truly joyful. And never, I will venture to say, did any parents on the like occasion, feel a more complete and heart-affecting joy. But why do I say all this, to one who knows them all so well? One circumstance I cannot omit to your Ladyship; for to me it appeared a delightful one. It happen'd to be a Sacrament Sunday at Cobham, and the happy parents had the satisfaction of seeing the dear youth (with that unaffected piety which he always shows on that solemn occasion), sealing as it were, by that sacred act, the promise which his early youth has always given of a virtuous and pious manhood. I know not whether this circumstance struck any other person as did me. But, I confess, my heart was full when I saw the whole family (except our dear amiable Johnny, whom indisposition prevented) joining in that holy rite, on that particular day.

On Monday, notwithstanding it had been declared that there would be no public rejoicings in the Park, a great concourse of people of all descriptions were drawn from their homes, some in expectation of fireworks, others of beef and ale. Several came from Northfleet and Dartford, and, I am told, some even from London ; so that the village of Cobham had all the appearance of a Fair. The people, however, notwithstanding their disappointment, were in perfect good humour, so that no bad consequences ensued from their having assembled. A magnificent Dinner was prepared for upwards of 100 persons in the great Dining Room, and the company assembled in the Gilt Hall. It consisted of the Mayor and Corporation of Gravesend (of which your Ladyship knows Lord D. is the hereditary High Steward) and all his Lordship's Tenants, and some of his most respectable neighbours, and a few select friends. About 5 o'clock the Mayor and Corporation arrived in all their Paraphernalia, and were received by Lord D. and Clifton, surrounded by their family and friends, in the Gilt Hall, upon which a very appropriate speech was deliver'd in a very feeling manner by Mr. Evans, the Town Clerk. Lord D. and C. both answer'd him in very neat and proper speeches ; and soon after this ceremony, the company went to dinner. The entertainment was truly sumptuous, and it was enliven'd by the attendance of the Local Band, and of four

Professional Singers from London, who commenced their operations by relieving me with the "Non nobis" for grace after dinner, which they sung most delightfully. After three Toasts (the King, the Regent and the Queen and Family) each followed by an appropriate song, Lord D. gave the Toast for the day, first expressing his happiness in such a son. After this was drank, with three times three (and never I believe was a Toast drank with more expression of feeling) the dear youth arose, and in a most animated and a most feeling speech, which came evidently from his heart, first thanked the company, and then proposed his Father's health, saying that he hoped he should for many years have the happiness of meeting his friends in that room holding exactly the situation he now does. Several other speeches were made, and amongst them two good ones, from Mr. Moore and Mr. Twopenny. But I must not omit one thing which was heard with rapturous applause, and seemed to be felt like an electrical shock by all the company (tho' a *shock* of an agreeable nature). It was a charming and richly deserved compliment to Lady D. When Mr. Twopenny spoke, her Ladyship had left the room, and he having in the course of his speech spoken of Ld. Clifton's virtues as derived from his ancestors and from his noble Father, Lord D. arose to disclaim in the most unaffected terms the compliment paid to himself, and then with his usual warmth declared that whatever there was of good in his son was derived, he firmly believed, from the other excellent author of his being, from his incomparable Mother. Some people object to these sort of compliments on such occasions; but for my own part, when they come from the heart, and are merely honest expressions of feeling, I think they deserve a better name than compliments and are very delightful. The company sat till past 12 o'clock, and altho' all were perfectly jovial and happy, there was not, I believe, one instance of intoxication or impropriety of conduct. When they left the Dining Room there was coffee and tea in the Gilt Hall; and the singers again entertained the company, being accompanied sometimes by the Piano and sometimes by the Organ. The whole party had not left the house before two o'clock; and if you may judge by the appearance of joy and satisfaction which shone in all countenances every creature departed highly pleased and gratified. On the Tuesday there was a Feast of another kind. All the Labourers who work for Lord D. with their wives (to the amount of 90 or 100) partook of a plentiful Dinner in the Gothic Passage at the entrance. I reckon'd the Dishes. There were 17 Joints of Roast and Boiled, 6 large Mutton Pies, 4 brace of Hares, and between 20 and 30 Rice and Plum Puddings. They had plenty of ale, and seem'd to enjoy themselves very much. And the whole Festival was closed on Tuesday night, or rather Wednesday morning by a Ball for the Servants in the great Dining Room. Lord and Lady Darnley and all the family joined in the Dance, and this part of the Fete also appeared to give high satisfaction to those for whom it was intended. All the female servants appeared in blue, having received each a new gown of that colour, the upper servants one of sarsnet and the under servants of poplin.

I believe I have given your Ladyship now all the particulars, and I hope they will not be unacceptable. Allow me to present to your Ladyship, and the dear young Ladies, my own and my Mother's most respectful compliments.

I have the honour to be, with the greatest esteem and regard, your Ladyship's faithful and obliged Servant,

J. STOKES.

Sonnet by John, Fourth Earl of Darnley.

To my Son Twenty-one Years of Age. (1816.)

Hope of my youth and comfort of my age
Now time begins to steal my strength away
And marks my temples with increasing grey,
The thought of thee can mortal ills assuage
And I might set at nought the tyrant's rage
To whom I soon must nature's tribute pay,
And I should bend with joy beneath his sway
If he to spare thee, only could engage.
But thou alas! art but a fading flower,
Exposed like me to life's uncertainty,
Like me a perishable thing of Earth;
Else I should look beyond the fatal hour
And fancy I might live again in thee
Too proud of this blest day that gave thee birth.

D.

Lord Darnley might indeed be proud of his son, and all the family were fondly

EDWARD, LORD CLIFTON.
Fron the painting by Thonas Phillips,
at Eton College.

attached to him. A more dutiful and loving son or a kindlier brother never lived, and he was a great favourite with his aunts and cousins, with many of whom he kept up an affectionate correspondence. He was well read and well informed, and his father who took the deepest interest in the welfare of both his sons, thinking it bad for a young man to remain too much at home, had encouraged him to travel, especially in Italy. He had entered the House of Commons at an early age, and was M.P. for Canterbury from 1818 to 1830, supporting the Whig party, then almost continuously in Opposition. He was not considered very good looking, but he had fine eyes, a pleasant expression, and a tall manly figure. A letter to his brother John at Paris, on September 17th. gives an idea of his life and disposition at this time.

LORD CLIFTON AT 46, BERKELEY SQUARE TO HON. J. D. BLIGH, AT PARIS.

17th September, 1824.

My dearest Johnny,

Although I wrote to you on Monday, I must again take up my pen to thank you for the letter I found here on my arrival last night. My Father went on Wednesday to Sandgate by Canterbury, and I came yesterday to Town by steam. I had intended to come by the regular Gravesend boat, but was too late for it in consequence of its starting at three instead of four o'clock, as I supposed, and accordingly I went on board another which I saw coming up the river, in which I was much amused. I had plenty for my money as I only paid three shillings the ordinary fare from Gravesend. I found on board a motley group (not of fashionables), several of whom in masquerade characters, with a clown, etc., and an affiche against the chimney, with "Dresses to hire for 2s. 6d. each in the fore cabin," of which however I did not avail myself, and after a while sat down to read a book I had in my pocket. I had not got through many pages, for there was a band on board, and a sprightly country dance (Anglaise) was set on foot by the man who I discovered had hired the boat on speculation, and a portly dame, which was followed up by many other gay couples, and continued during the greater part of our voyage, which with a flood tide was short, and in two hours-and-half I found myself at the Custom House about 7 o'clock. But our fun was by no means over, for a French conjuror who had been endeavouring to perform his tricks in the cabin which was described like the Black Hole at Calcutta, came on deck, and a circle being formed, did some tolerable tricks with cards, balls and boxes, and made some puppets dance prettily enough. Many were the boats alongside and numerous the bystanders at the Custom House Quay, but no one stirred. The steam had evaporated, and we were quietly lashed to other similar boats, where I certainly never expected to pass an hour or more; but so it happened, for when the conjuror had finished, there was a grand display of fireworks, blue-lights, etc., on board. I should tell you that Monsieur, understanding no tongue but his own, performed his tricks in French, which was as speedily interpreted by a lady at his side, or it would have been sadly thrown away upon the far greater part of his audience. On the whole I was much amused, and well enough pleased to have come across such entertainment which I never could otherwise but accidentally have enjoyed. I hope the account of it may amuse you. On Tuesday we shot at Cuxton, and I had very good sport killing eleven brace. My father went home early and killed four brace. The birds were strong, and we met with several fair coveys.

I went on Wednesday, after seeing my father as far as Strood, to Chattenden, where, and at Cliffe, "Zargents" account of the *pats is very bad indeed, as also throughout the hundred, and all the lands towards the Thames; among the hills, Luddesdowne, Meopham, etc., the birds have fared better. Squire Jaquier has the manor of Luddesdowne this year, and with two friends had good sport, killing thirteen brace. Mr. Hickman has Meopham Manor, and killed with another gun or two eleven or twelve brace. At Cliffe, etc. there are no young birds of any size. I think Roberts will not do for the Mausoleum House

*Partridges.

53

as he does not appear capable of rearing game. I have some thoughts of putting him in Ellison's Bottom, and Clayton with Wells. Huggings exclusively to catch rabbits and to remove "Zargent" from Chattenden to the Park as he is certainly expert at rearing young game, and a good hand at trapping. I throw this out for your opinion as I have not mentioned the idea to anyone. Z. is certainly clever at his business and understands it well.

And now, my dearest Johnny, I must refer to your letter, from which I am sorry to see that you are not quite comfortable in your situation in Paris, although I suspect from accounts from other quarters that you are more in favour with your master than you seem to suppose. When you come home I shall be glad to talk to you about your affairs, by the way I must beg that you take leave to come towards the middle of next month, the family is to be at Cobham Tuesday three weeks at latest! Now really, you must not defer your return, and I think you cannot entertain any scruple on the subject, and may stay a good while when you come! I suppose poor old Louis* must be dead by this time though we have as yet no account later than the 14th and no account of him to half past three p.m. on that day. I hope you will like your new servant, mine is a good natured attentive, assiduous, stupid fellow. I ave done nothing about horses yet.

* King Louis XVIII.

Pray, let me hear that you are coming now my dearest Johnny.

Ever your affectionate brother,

CLIFTON.

Uncle W. and Sophy at Sandgate. Mean to go there Monday or Tuesday.

Lord Clifton had hitherto not been lucky in his love affairs ; when quite young he had suffered, he told his wife later, great agony of mind at giving up, at the wish of his parents, an attachment to a girl not his equal in rank. It would seem that another young lady had refused him, for his father wrote to his son John in November, 1822, " Fanny ——— refused Clifton who was desperately in love with her, but so jealous that she thought it better not to marry him ! ! !"

In 1823 he spent four months in Paris with his brother John, lately become an attaché at the British Embassy. Their aunt, Lady Powerscourt and her daughters, Catherine and Emily Wingfield, were living in Paris at the time and it appears from John Bligh's Journal that the Wingfield girls did not go out much, but Lady Powerscourt enjoyed a very gay time with her two nephews and Lady Charlotte Osborne, only daughter of George, 8th Duke of Leeds. The Journal is very discreet and does not tell us how far either or both of the young men were interested in the young lady, but John met her constantly during July and August and after the arrival of Clifton on August 24th, scarcely a day passed without their all meeting at least once and often twice. The little *partie carrée* made expeditions to St. Cloud, St. Denis, and other sights and places of interest besides meeting constantly at china and curiosity shops, the Tuileries Gardens, the Opera and parties. Lady Darnley was very fond of Sèvres china and Paris clothes, and her sons executed many commissions for her apparently assisted by Lady Powerscourt and Lady Charlotte. The Duke and Duchess of Leeds and their sons, Lord Carmarthen and Lord Conyers Osborne, were also in Paris, but Lady Charlotte seems to have spent most of her time with Lady Powerscourt.

On October 28th John Bligh went to England for a month, and he never mentions Lady Charlotte again in his Journal. What happened exactly we cannot tell but Lord Darnley accompanied John to Paris on his return on November 27th and apparently inspected the young lady, for Lady Darnley writes to John in December, "Your Papa was evidently taken with the short sight he had of Lady C.," and speaking of Clifton says "poor dear fellow, he has had more trials than many of his age and condition, but I trust it will even in this world be *made up to him*." Writing again on Christmas Day, 1823, she says that Clifton often talks about Lady Charlotte and that " he never saw her so much dressed as to receive Lord D." On January 19th, 1824, Lady Darnley writes : " Poor dear Clifton who with J. Brownlow and two Navy Lieutenants have been all day shooting at Chattenden, has not, I am sorry to say, by absence got the Charmer out of his head ; Beppy* and I do not encourage, but to our annoyance, he talks to the Dr. (Mr. Stokes) and still more to his wife continually about Lady Charlotte's charms, so as to have made her remark to Beppy that he showed how much he was interested on the subject. She had heard reports at Rochester, some I believe through the Laffans. I assure you it makes me very uneasy, as I fear if really disappointed by her managing mother, it will have a deep effect ; I cannot think on the subject without great fears. But we will trust in Him who alone can direct right."

Probably the match was not sufficiently good to satisfy the ambitions of the Duke and Duchess for their only daughter: Lord

* Lady Elizabeth Bligh.

E.

Darnley's financial position was not very good just then, and he could not have made his son a very large allowance. In any case, the affair seems to have gone no further and Lord Clifton met his fate, as we shall see, in the following year, while Lady Charlotte made a runaway match with Mr. Sackville Lane Fox in 1826. Her son inherited through her the Barony of Conyers and her granddaughter, Marcia, Countess of Yarborough, is now (1913) Baroness Conyers in her own right. There are several allusions to Lady Charlotte in the latter letters of Lord Clifton and his wife.

We must now return to Lady de Vesci and her matchmaking. Her first attempt to arrange a meeting between Emma Parnell and her nephew Clifton seems to have been in November, 1824, but at that time he could not come to Abbeyleix. In the following March, hearing that he was again in Ireland, she renewed her invitation, he came to Abbeyleix and met his aunt's protégée. The letters which follow show the course of events.

VISCOUNTESS DE VESCI AT ABBEYLEIX TO LORD
CLIFTON.

November, 1824.

My dearest Clif,

Will you frank the enclosed to your Aunt P.,

and don't lose it as there is money in it.

I wish you would come and see a wife I have here for you. She is quite handsome enough on a *large* scale, very pleasant and agreeable, perfection in temper, lively and very good, but no fortune, very well connected. If I have any chance of success I will describe her more accurately, and I think I am very disinterested.

Yr. very affecte.,

F. L. De Vesci.

Viscountess de Vesci at Abbeyleix to Lord
Clifton.

March 5th, 1825.

My dear Clifton,

I have heard an " on dit " that you are to be in Ireland this day and hope you have not made a party to go to the North *this time*, remember you promised me a visit whenever you came to Ireland, and I shall expect you when your Assizes will not interfere.

You must come with your heart disengaged, as I have two young ladies for you to chuse from tho' they have neither of them *blue* eyes. I don't know where to direct to you but Francis will of course find you out.

Ever, dear Clifton,

Yr. very affecte.,

F. L. de Vesci.

We know the exact date of Lord Clifton's arrival at Abbeyleix from a letter written to his wife six years later, March 15th, 1831, and though out of place, an extract from it must be inserted here.

LORD CLIFTON TO LADY CLIFTON.

March 15th, 1831.

"My dearest Love,

Look at the date of this and consider whether you made an acquaintance six years ago of which you have never repented—I have not—and the sound of Aunt de Vesci's voice still rings in my ears pronouncing the fatal words of introduction, "Miss Parnell, Miss Emma Parnell, Mr. Ross of Bladensburg and Mr. Thomas Nugent." No dearest wife, I do not repent but on the contrary, every revolving year contributes to assure me, how inestimable the treasure is, of which that introduction led me to the possession."

A scrap of a letter from Lord Clifton, probably to his father, was amongst Emma, Lady Darnley's papers, and records his first impressions of his future wife.

"I have seen of course Aunt de V's *Belle*, and what I have seen I like very well. She is quite handsome enough to be admired for her personal attractions, has a very good countenance, and bears an excellent character for temper etc. In short she is a person with whom I am sure I could fall sufficiently in love to make me wish to marry her, but I know not how I can pass time enough in her society to make me judge whether I could safely do so, or whether she *would* if I would; particularly

ABBEYLEIX, QUEEN'S COUNTY,
in 1825.

From a painting at Abbeyleix.

after the experience I have had : experience, they say, makes men wise, and I hope that contrary to general practice, I may become wise in the affairs of love. I really am very anxious to be settled, as you, I know, are to have me married : nothing damps my anxiety to cease to be an old bachelor, but my wretched skin complaint, by which I wish no one to be a sufferer more than necessary, besides myself.

I found all here quite well with the exception of Aunt de V's rheumatism. She however is looking remarkably well. Catherine looks rather delicate and is not improved in beauty. There are here, Mr. Frederic Trench (not of Ballynakill) and his lady, and two sons—Thomas Forde and his wife and three children, the Miss Parnells and Tom Nugent, A.N's 2nd son. I believe Charles Vesey comes to-day and Arthur dines here."

Very soon, the young people found that they were all in all to each other, but Lord Clifton was a dutiful son, and did not like to propose to the fair Emma till he had consulted his parents. He took Lady de Vesci into his full confidence, and arranging to meet her and his uncle at Buxton early in May, went off to Cobham. His aunt wrote from time to time to give him news of the young lady.

Saturday, April 2nd.

Dearest Clif,

We were all very melancholy after your
departure on Thursday, tho' to all appearance a
certain person kept up wonderfully, which was
evidently to me put on for the company, and she
said to Kits, "are you not surprised to see me
in such good spirits?" She would not act words
in the evening, but played Backgammon with
B. Johnston.* I had no opportunity of saying
anything of Buxton until yesterday evening, when
I said exactly what you desired, that I expected
you to come to see *me* and asked would she like
to be me. She said, y-e-s, and blushed, I read
your "kindest love and remembrance to any who
loved or remember'd you," and asked if she would
take any part of it herself, and she said y-e-s the
latter. And you do not wish to have any of the
former, again I asked, when she laughed and hid
her face and said "O yes." I have not had an
opportunity to ask for the drawing, but hope I
shall before I close this tomorrow. I wish you
could have staid longer, dearest Clif, but I am sure
you have done what was right and trust you will be
rewarded in the way you wish most, and that
I shall shortly see you a happy man. I expect we
shall have a most interesting meeting at Buxton.
We shall probably go there early in May if the
weather is fine and that I do not get quite well

*Probably John Brett Johnston, of Ballykilbeg, Co. Down,
who was refused by Emma Parnell about this time ; see Lady
de Vesci's letter of April 21st.

without it, which I fear I shall not now have your good prayers for. However, I will excuse you. Adieu pour le présent. I fear I have written a great heap of nonsense, but perhaps you will not consider it such, and pray don't shew it to anyone.

Sunday. Qr. past four.

We have been so long in Church I have but little time to finish this. I have had a good deal of conversation with E. She is delighted with the idea of going to Buxton, but fears it will appear odd to Lord Clifton, "but maybe he will excuse it if he knows it is from anxiety to see him again." I stole the within head as I thought it like, and have asked for the drawing, which will be done, but she fears it cannot be an original.

She is sure Uncle Tom would like you very much, you are so good. By the bye he came yesterday and expected to find you here. I shall long to hear from you again and how all appear to like what is likely to happen. Pray do not let all this nonsense be seen, I have half a mind to burn it, only that I have not time to write another.

Adieu, dearest Clif.

Ever yr. very affecte. Aunt,

F. L. De V.

"Kits" *sends her love.

VISCOUNTESS DE VESCI AT ABBEYLEIX TO LORD
CLIFTON, AT COBHAM.

Monday, 11th April.

Dearest Clif,

I am now glad that I had not time to write

*Hon. Catherine Vesey, who married, 1883, John Nugent, of Portaferry.

63

to you yesterday, caused by visitors after Church, and I have this day received your letter and two enclosures; the Violets I do not intend to keep to myself, as I am sure they were intended as "sweets to the *sweet*," and there they shall be embosomed. The end of the month we shall, please God leave this and the first week in May we shall most likely be in Buxton, so arrange your plans accordingly. I think we shall all be delighted to see you. Em. asked me the other day, "was it quite certain that she was to go to Buxton?" (as I had only asked her before if she would like it). I said not (as I really did not wish to give her false hopes, and I waited to hear from you again to be myself certain. I am sure you will be very angry with me for saying this, but it was not that I mistrusted your constancy, but from not knowing how it might be received by Pip and Mim, you might not wish to go on with it if they did not approve). Em. looked very doleful when I made my reply. We had then a great deal of chat about you, and you would not have been a little happy had you overheard us. I was wishing for you to be invisible, as my memory is so bad at remembering conversations. In answer to my queries, she said she liked you very much, and had you stayed longer she thought she——"would have been in love" says I, as I could not get her to finish the sentence. The first of the tender feeling was from a long conversation you had on the couch (and which I set you upon, by the bye), about religion, etc. She says Car liked you much better than she did at first, but from not

64

thinking you well looking when you came you were quite handsome before you left the house, your smile is the sweetest she ever saw. She was very melancholy after you went, she missed your conversation so much—you are so good and so unlike other young men.

I wish I could remember more, tho' I feel I am acting unfairly in repeating what was said in confidence—but I cannot help myself as I know it will give you pleasure to hear her sentiments about you. I really think, dear Clif, that she will make you a happy man, she is such a sensible, good girl. She is now busily engaged in your service making a little drawing, which she prefers to driving or walking with the rest of the party.

I wish you had told me what your Father and Mother say about it. Make Beppy write to Catherine. What does Uncle James say to you? I expect he will be jealous, as I told you he was a great admirer of hers, but don't for the world say so to him or I shall be in a horrible scrape.

E. was quizzed about you before you left the house, but never before me. However, you need not fear her being a second Miss F. I hope you found Baby* quite well.

Dearest Clif, yr. most affecte. Aunt,

F. L. De V.

* Mary Brownlow, whose mother, Lady Mary Bligh, sister of Lord Clifton and wife of Charles Brownlow (afterwards Lord Lurgan), had died in 1823, at the birth of her only child. Mary lived at Cobham with her grandparents until 1831; she was the pet of the whole family, and often affectionately alluded to in their letters as Baby and Baboo. She married in 1848, Robert Peel Dawson of Castle Dawson, and died 1888.

I will write again before we leave this or Dublin if I have anything interesting to tell you. Write soon again. Will you frank the enclosed to Aunt P., Sandgate?

It is interesting to know that the violets mentioned in this letter were treasured all her life by Emma Parnell. After her death in 1884 these same faded violets were found carefully put away in her desk, wrapped up in a sheet of paper with the date in her handwriting, April 11th, 1825, and outside the little parcel these lines in Lord Clifton's writing (written, of course, after their marriage).

Sweets to the Sweet! before the day
That follows the nineteenth of May
Which my dear love intends to keep
Till in the grave she falls asleep.

VISCOUNTESS DE VESCI AT ABBEYLEIX TO LORD CLIFTON, AT 46, BERKELEY SQUARE.

Thursday, 21st April.

My dearest Clif,

I have two letters to thank you for. I am happy to see your ardour has not cooled by absence, nor has that of your fair one. She was in high delight the other day when I told her that I had got her Father's consent for her coming with us, as she was not sure of it till then. She asks me if I think Lord C. will come very soon after we go, but

I leave that in great doubt, as I don't wish to give her too great hopes. I have written this day to enquire about apartments for the end of the first week in May. We talk of sailing the 3rd. I believe we shall go by Shrewsbury to consult Dr. Darwin, (what will you do if he sends us back to Ireland?) as I hear he is very good for rheumatism. Our stay will depend upon my infirmities, but I trust five or six weeks will set me up, as we shall be anxious to have as much of "home sweet home" as we can before August. Your rival, Mr. J.,* is in the depth of despair. I must transcribe an extract from his letter in answer to his positive refusal through me. "I now see my presumption in aspiring to the hand of one of the best, most amiable, and (in my opinion) highly gifted lady I ever met. I grieve much that we did meet. I only wish that whatever nobleman she is united to may estimate her as I do, and hope she may gain such a one as the Baron of Knapton," meaning Tommy, I conclude. She has certainly the good opinion of every one who knows her and must be a great hypocrite if her character is different from what I take it to be. Your Violets were duly received and honored. I find you had promised them and that they were expected. I don't think I have had much converse about you since my last, it is difficult sometimes to get an opportunity, so this letter must be dull and uninteresting, but I am certain she has not changed her opinion and longs to see you again. We shall be very triste at Buxton until you come, as (I forgot whether I mentioned before) that

*J. Brett Johnston, see letter of April 2nd.

dear Bill* does not come with us, he must remain to read for July Examinations. So till you or Tommy join us we shall have no Beau ! Billy and Tom Nugent leave us on Saturday, and their ordeal comes on the following Monday.

Ever, dearest Clif,

Yr. affecte. Aunt,

F. L. De V.

Why don't Beppy write to Kits ?

I am glad the little profile is approved (she has been reckoned like Lady Downshire). It was done rather in agitation just before you went away. I do not shew your letters to anyone, so you need not mind what you say.

I will write soon if I have anything interesting to tell.

Caroline† is to be one of our party.

VISCOUNTESS DE VESCI AT DUBLIN TO LORD CLIFTON, AT 46, BERKELEY SQUARE.

Monday, May 2nd.

Dearest Clif,

I hope this will sail with me to-morrow, I shall write a line from Shrewsbury as you desire. We are all well and *some* of us very uneasy lest the Catholic Question may detain you longer than we expected.

I am surprised to find how much this intended event is talked of here. Anna Close says, "when she heard Clifton was going to Abbey Leix she was certain he would fall in love with Emma," and will not believe that it is not all arranged. Several

*Hon. William Vesey.   †Caroline Parnell.

people have also been enquiring about it. I hope their curiosity will soon be gratified. I suppose I am not in favour in B. Square, as I never hear from that quarter. I shall be very nervous when Ld. D. comes to inspect. I hope you will find an improvement in E's carriage. She is certainly taking great pains to improve it, I don't know for whose sake— as some time ago she did not much mind it. The young Ladies are going to a Ball this evening, which will not agree with getting up at five tomorrow morning.

When you write again mention Baby, and you must tell me when I am to engage an Apartment. I find Buxton is fuller than we thought it would be at this time of the year, and we cannot get the rooms we wished for.

In haste, good-bye, dearest C.

Ever yr. affecte. Aunt,

F. L. De V.

VISCOUNTESS DE VESCI AT SHREWSBURY TO LORD CLIFTON, AT 46, BERKELEY SQUARE.

May 5th.

Here we are, dearest Clif, waiting for my Doctor, who we shall not see till this evening. In the meantime my pen shall be at your service.

I wish you were here also as I would like you to have his advice. You must not make use of either Baths or Water at Buxton without advice as they are not to be trifled with. I am vexed at your being so plagued, dearest C. and partienlarly just now; if you will put the least bit of shoemaker's wax on leather and apply it to the boils you will find it have a much better effect than a poultice, which always brings more I have often seen it used so you need not be afraid of it. It ought to be left on until it is quite drawn enough. I will do as you desire in regard of E. but have had no opportunity as yet. You need not fret yourself on that account as I will answer for its making no change in her sentiments for you, she is very anxious to see you. The two C.'s say they heard of nóthing but the odious Canterbury Committee when I announced what was to detain you, and that she supposed after that there would be another Catholick question debate; in short I think she is very much in love. I fear you will not think her looking well. I think she is grown pale and thin, or at least thinner than she was. When do you think Lord D. will come, you ought to be some time before, to put her in good looks. We hope to proceed to Buxton tomorrow, but more of that anon.

We had a quick passage of little more than six hours, but a very rough one and a great gale. The waves beat over the carriages where we were sitting. I felt very melancholy leaving dear Bill, the first time we have been parted for so long, he was to go as the King's Page to a fancy ball the night we left him. I am sorry Pilcher has proved ungrateful.

Thursday evening. Dr. D. allows of our going to Buxton tho' too early in the year, so off we shall be off, please God, at seven, always our hour of starting. I believe he don't think mine a hopeless case, and has ordered me nothing but chalk.

I received your last in Dublin, not an hour after mine was gone to the post. Ld. de V. has desired a book to be sent from Ridgway to B. Square which he begs you will bring him. All send love to you.

Always yr. affecte. Aunt,
F. L. De V.

The enclosed is for Aunt P.

VISCOUNTESS DE VESCI AT BUXTON TO LORD CLIFTON AT 46, BERKELEY SQUARE.

Tuesday Eveng, 10th May.

Dearest Clif,

I am delighted to find you are able to fix a day for coming here. We shall all be ready to receive you with open arms, at least if I am not justified in saying so I have been very much deceived myself, but of that I have not any fear. I flatter myself you will find in a certain person everything you can wish to make you happy, the more I see of her (and I have certainly watched her more narrowly lately) the more reason I have for thinking so.

Lord de Vesci advises your coming in the mail no further than Ashbourne, about 20 miles from this (the mail does not come on here) and to post from that. Leek is the nearest place to this that the mail goes to, but it is a very hilly unpleasant stage from that here. You will come to the Great Hotel where we are, and I shall take care to have your apartment ready. I suppose you will not desire a sitting-room as you probably will not occupy it much. But let me know if you do.

I hope from what you said in your last that you have got quite well. I said something to E. as you desired, but she laughed and said she had got a rash to keep you in countenance. I must have done or shall be late for the post, and I scarcely know what I am writing, listening to very pretty music from my next room neighbours the Curzons. So good night, dearest Clif. If anything occurs worth mentioning I will write again.

> Ever yr. most affecte.
>
> F. L. De V.

Viscountess De Vesci at Buxton to Lord Clifton at 46, Berkeley Square.

Wed. 11th.

Dearest Clif,

Tho' I wrote to you yesterday even, I must not defer answering your questions, imprimus we have not brought our Horses this year as it was thought the water here disagreed with them, Catherine is the only one habited for riding, but I think Emma, tho' a bad horsewoman, would like it on a quiet pony if we can get a Habit made for her.

She has not got a watch and I could scarcely keep from laughing when I heard her complain of the very thing not many minutes after I received your letter this morning. I suppose I am to give out that your Lordship has got the rheumatism in your *Heart*, it is a dangerous complaint but I trust in your case there is a remedy at hand which will have the desired effect. There is a great lack of books here, nothing but Novels, so if you think you will have time to read, bring some I advise you.

Unless you can get here early in the day I advise you not to hurry to dinner, the dinner hour being half-past five. Some of us will be sadly disappointed if there is a put off for Monday. I am not deceiving you if not deceived.

Always yr. affecte.

F. L. De V.

Emma Parnell was considered remarkably good looking, with laughing black eyes and still darker hair dressed in ringlets, a small straight nose, full red lips and a lovely pink and white complexion. Her unfinished portrait by Sir Thomas Lawrence (now in the Liverpool Art Gallery) was not considered to do her justice, but gives a good idea of her appearance. She had received a good education, was fond of reading, especially history, and could draw fairly well. We shall soon see that "Pip" and "Mim" (Lord and Lady Darnley) were only too delighted to consent to their son's wishes as it was the desire of their hearts to see him happily married.

CHAPTER III.

𝕷ove-𝕷etters.

LORD CLIFTON'S arrival at Buxton must
have been very welcome to the fair
Emma, and she had not long to wait for
the declaration of love which he felt for her.
He seems to have arrived on Monday, May 16th,
and an expedition having been arranged that
week to explore the beauties of the Peak
country, he found an opportunity to make his
formal proposal at Matlock on May 20th.
Lord De Vesci's party slept at Bakewell that
night, which we know from the prayer which
follows, written by Lord Clifton on the evening of that eventful day. It shows in what a
sober, serious spirit he entered on this new
phase of his existence, and how amply his
prayer for a blessing on their union was
granted will be seen in the record of their
happy though too short married life.

Only a few delightful days could be
spent by the lovers together as Lord Clifton
was summoned back to London on May 30th,

having to appear in the Court of King's Bench against an elderly, half-mad cousin, Captain Robert Bligh, nephew of the 1st Earl of Darnley, who for some fancied grievance had assaulted both Lord Clifton and his father more than once. Other duties detained him in London, and it will be seen in the following letters that his father, Lord Darnley, and Emma's father, Sir Henry Parnell suggested that the young couple should be married at once at Cobham. Emma had however, promised Lady De Vesci to stay with her till she was married, and Lord Clifton finding that his aunt would be much hurt if the marriage should take place anywhere excepting at Abbeyleix, gave up the plan, "the little expeditious plan" as it is jokingly called in the letters.

Our engaged couple were obliged to take refuge in writing to each other, and we must let their charming correspondence, which throws so much light on the characters of both the writers, give the history of the next month. These letters were found in Emma's desk after her death in 1884, carefully done up in separate packets and endorsed and numbered in his handwriting. There seems to have been a little contest between them about the number each had written. The packets are marked "16 a PIECE," the latter word being a sort of anagram of their joint initials read backwards. Lord Clifton having apparently found a seventeenth, adds this verse :

"Another found
upon the ground
gives Em a qualm
but me the Palm."

C.

PRAYER WRITTEN BY LORD CLIFTON ON DAY OF HIS ENGAGEMENT.

O Almighty God, Father of all mankind, trusting in the multitude of Thy mercies, I prostrate myself before the throne of Thy grace to return my thanks for the manifold blessings which Thou hast showered upon me, and more especially for that Thou hast opened unto me a happy prospect for my future life, by the event which has this day occurred. Grant, heavenly Father, that my fondest wishes may be fulfilled only as appears most expedient to Thine infinite wisdom. Let me not be led away by passion to forget Thee, and let me ever remember that I owe all happiness to Thee ; further me with Thy continual grace, that in the pursuit of pleasure in this world, I may ever keep in view the blessed end of all happiness in the world to come, where through the merits of my Saviour, I confidently hope for the blessings of Thy Kingdom.

Bless, O God, her whom I have asked and who

has consented to share with me this world's cares and goods. Suffer me, if in Thy mercy Thou shalt permit our union, to prove myself a kind loving and affectionate husband ; grant her the happiness, I beseech Thee, of contributing by her example and conduct to my observance of Thy holy ordinances ; and so far bless Thine unworthy servant with the grace of Thy Spirit, that he may guide both her and himself through life, in the peaceful ways of religion and truth. All this I ask through the merits of our Saviour Jesus Christ. Amen !

BAKEWELL, May 20th, 1825.

MISS EMMA PARNELL AT BUXTON TO LORD CLIFTON AT 46, BERKELEY SQUARE.

May 30th, 1825.

My dearest love,

Does that expression give you as much pleasure in reading as it gives me to write it ? I feel sure it does.

The time goes very slowly without you and yet I have been very busy all the morning.

I got a congratulatory letter and have been answering it, but I missed a certain person who has lately had all such letters shown to him. They have found out that I am writing to you and are all laughing at me for it but I do not care, for it is my greatest pleasure now and I will not be laughed out of it. Do write and tell me how your cold is and all about your journey and everything about your self, and if you think I am very foolish for scribbling the first day of our separation, you must think too that I am fond as well as foolish and am willing not to be thought very wise if I can succed in convineing you that I am very affectionate. I remember you told me not to say anything foolish in my letters, so you must tell me what kind of letter you like me to write and whether this is too foolish. I had, or rather Car. had, a very affectionate nice long letter from dear Mary. She is a dear little creature, and I am sure you will love her. I feel as if I should love all those who are dear to you for your dear sake, and I am sure you will do the same for me.

How confident I feel that you love me as much as ever I could wish and a great deal more than I deserve, but not more than I love you— so do not think you excel me in that respect though you may in every other. If I were not a little afraid of your thinking me too unreserved I should say a great deal more, but I think you will not have time to read more, so I will end my first letter to my dearest friend of all friends, and sign myself my dearest Clifton's most truly and affectionately,

EMMA PARNELL.

I hope you will not forget to write to your own Gypsey girl. The young ladies are going out riding and I shall be all alone in the shrubbery where we were walking together yesterday. But after all do not think that I am melancholy for I am quite happy with the thought of our meeting before very long. I shall not expect so long a letter as this but I shall like it very much whether long or short.

House of Commons,
May 31st, 1825.
Half-past one p.m.

My dearest Love,

I have repaired hither from the Court of King's Bench, where I have been waiting all the morning in expectation of the unpleasant business I mentioned to you; it is still uncertain whether it will be tried to-day or to-morrow, but I must be in attendance till 4 o'clock.

The Regulator deposited me in due time at Islington, from whence I hastened home to receive the hearty congratulations of my dear parents and sister; they indeed feel happy in the prospect of my happiness.

You will be I am sure glad to hear that I have cured my cold tho' by the oddest of all remedies, passing the whole day and night on the top of the coach, which I preferred as less heating.

You cannot expect much interesting matter· from so short a journey, but I will tell you all that happened. In the first place I could not but feel as it were benumbed in my feelings; I could hardly believe my real situation, and it seemed as it were a waking dream. The first object that interested me was Derby, which I looked at with more than ordinary pleasure, as the somewhile residence of her whom I love most dearly, and as we passed the Infirmary I looked about for a house that was likely to have contained her, and enquired of my fellow passengers, but in vain, if they knew where Mr. Fowler had resided. I thought moreover, that it would not be altogether uninteresting to you to hear some account of a person for whom you had once felt a regard, now on a sick bed, and I asked without giving any name, at a house on the bridge and whose owner is at present in Wales, and better. This I thought you would be glad to hear, and I hope you will excuse my anxiety to find out the means of gratifying you. In the course of the evening we were amused by a drunken man who was in a gig and chose to keep in company with the Coach to the great danger of his own neck ; but thanks to the very quiet horse which he whipped unmercifully, after being with or near us for 16 or 17 miles he was safely landed at Northampton, where we drank tea just after 10, which led me to think of John and the candles and Lord de V's beer. I will not speak or write of other more interesting objects with which my thoughts might have been occupied. We dined at five precisely at Leicester which made me look back upon the Welby party &c. at the table d'hôte. Let me hear how you sit now. By the bye I narrowly escaped an accident in the night for which I ought to be most grateful. Near Woburn they have dug through the sand hill to a considerable depth to improve (eventually) the road, in the meanwhile however it is in a dangerous state. At the bottom of the Hill the coachman asked the "Gemmen" to get down and walk, but whereas I was warmly enveloped in a ponderous great coat &c., and moreover rather sleepy, I declined doing so. There was a doubt whether he would be able to get through a very narrow place, where two carriages could not pass before the down Mail should be in it, and to effect this purpose he whipped on his horses and galloped up the hill : before however we got out of the pass, we saw an opaque body before us, and thinking that it was the Mail coming down the hill, called to them to stop, which was however needless as we found that they were already brought to a standstill, by an upset. A considerable quantity of sand had slipped down from the bank, and formed a mound which had overthrown them : in all probability had that not occurred it might have been our fate to have lain prostrate. Providentially no person was hurt, and only one old woman frightened. Such, love, is the amount of interesting occurrence, as far as I can recollect, except you can laugh at an expression of one of our numerous Jehus, "This is the most unriglerest set of horses I ever seed." So much for my journey, and I almost fear the recital will have tired even my own dear.

On my arrival I found all well, and on my way here, called on your papa, who was also blooming. I must tell you that he and mine have laid a scheme for marrying us at Cobham, for which purpose Sir H. talked of going to fetch you from Buxton. It immediately occurred to me that, altho' I could for my own sake desire nothing better, we should both of us be most unwilling to do anything that could possibly hurt the feelings of our dear dear relations with whom you are staying, and I required at least that Aunt de V. should be sounded on the subject before it was seriously proposed, and believe this will be done. It certainly would be very agreeable (and probably more expeditious) but I am sure that you will agree with me that we should each and both of us be peculiarly cautious of the possibility of doing outrage to the feelings of the parties I mentioned.

God bless you, my sweetest girl ; born to delight and better your most affectionately and dearly attached

C.

All are most anxious to see you and send their love. Give mine to all with you.

Have not time to read my scribble and fear you will not be able to do so.

MISS EMMA PARNELL TO LORD CLIFTON.

June 2nd, 1825.

My dearest love,

I am delighted to hear that you have got rid of your cold. I was rather afraid the journey might have increased it. I had no expectation of receiving a letter to day from you, so it was quite a joyful surprise to me, and then such a nice long one and such a circumstantial account was exactly what I like and as I did not expect more than a few hurried lines, it was so much the more acceptable. My dearest Clifton you must not be angry with me if I ask you not to say any more about the plan mentioned in the last part of your letter. It is quite impossible, and I have promised dear Lady de Vesci not to leave her till we are married, and I own I should be very much annoyed and grieved if Papa was to take me away from my dear Welsh Aunt and

Uncle. In short it would make me quite unhappy to leave them, and I know they would be quite hurt and think me very unkind and ungrateful if I did. I like you the better for thinking directly of our dear relations and for being as anxious as I am to avoid hurting their feelings. I have sounded them on the subject and they seem annoyed at such a plan having been proposed, although not seriously. Do not be uneasy about it, though, my dearest love, for they have been laughing very heartily at what they term your expeditious little plan, and I fancy they are sending you some message. Yesterday we were all a little annoyed by a letter from my aunt Mrs. Evans,* in reply to one of mine, telling her I had promised to remain with your dear Aunt. My Aunt seemed vexed about its being so arranged, but as it is settled so, I hope she will soon make up her mind to it. I don't know why I should tell you this however, but only that I could not help seeing that Ld. and Lady de Vesci seemed both quite hurt at my aunt's letter, and seemed to wish very much that I should remain where I am. Perhaps I have said a great deal too much about this, and I hope you will forgive me, my dearest Clifton, if I have. But you know you have often told me, you liked to know all my thoughts, however far from being wise ones. I cannot tell you how much I love our dear relations Lord and Lady de V. Long before the beginning of our friendship I had been accustomed to look upon them as my dearest and best friends, and

* Sophia, sister of Sir Henry Parnell.

I think the last two months have rendered them still dearer to me. I am so much obliged to you for your enquiries at Derby, and I will not deny that your favourable account gave me pleasure—though perhaps not quite so great as that which I felt on thinking how dear I must be to you if you can thus feel for my feelings, and think so kindly how to gratify them. Every such little instance of love and kindness makes a deep impression on me, and I feel as if I were hardly worthy of such affection. Dearest Clifton, how I wish you were here and that we were whispering to each other according to our pleasant (though somewhat rude) custom. What a foolish creature I am, but I like to write all that comes from my heart when I write to you, for I know you will make allowances for my folly. I was very much amused with the account of your journey, and I am delighted with you for writing to me so soon. Caroline and Catherine have been out riding twice C.V. on one of your poneys, and C.P. on a Buxton poney, and both of them were delighted with their ride. Car. and I have changed places at dinner, so I am between her and Lord de V. and she has Mr. Sitwell by her, and they talk away and amuse us all. There have been two arrivals which you know are matters of importance at Buxton. They are to appear at dinner to-day. Lady de V. and I are now companions in our walks. I received a letter from dear Henry, he sails almost directly and says he has not time to come and see me, which I am very sorry for. He desires me to thank you for your lines to him in my letter, and longs to make your acquaintance. I get a great many congratulatory letters and mean to keep them all till we can read them together. Dear Mary is very busy on my account at Bath. She says Lord Henry improves in health though slowly, she says the east winds are against him. Dearest Clifton, write to me soon, and in the mean time believe me to be ever yours most affectionately and sincerely,

EMMA PARNELL.

You must have got my first letter yesterday.

LORD CLIFTON TO MISS EMMA PARNELL.

London,

June 2nd, 1825.

Altho' I have only time to scribble one line, I must thank my dearest love for her dear letter received yesterday in the Court of King's Bench, where I was engaged till past Post time or I would have written yesterday. I have been to-day talking over law matters, and am happy to inform you that I hope they will be very easily and speedily arranged. The bell is now ringing, so God bless you. I will write to-morrow. I shall be delighted if it can be arranged as I told you it had been suggested.

Adieu my dearest,

Yrs. most affecy,

CLIFTON.

MISS EMMA PARNELL TO LORD CLIFTON.

Saturday. Buxton.

My dearest Love,

Many thanks for your dear little letter of the 2nd which I received this morning. You do not say whether that disagreeable business you mentioned to me is likely to be soon over. I hope it is over by this time for your sake, my dearest love.

You have just got my second letter, I think, and now you know what we think of the plan in this part of the world. I cannot, Love, be angry with you because I know that your love to me is the only motive of your plans, but I wish you had been a little more considerate, and had not suffered it to be mentioned to your dear Aunt, as I fear she is a little hurt at such an arrangement having been suggested. She says that it would be the most unpleasant arrangement for me that could have been thought of, and she adds, far from being the most proper according to the established customs on such occasions, and as you know, love, that reserve with you is not one of my ways, either in speaking or writing, I will say that I quite agree with her in both points, and am quite determined to stay with her. Is not that a very positive little speech? But you know if my naughty Papa chooses to forget that his fair daughter ought to be consulted on such points she must be a little saucy and speak for herself. So this morning I wrote to him to ask him to let me stay with dear Lady de Vesci. I should like to know whether you are in the least degree affronted with me for so openly avowing that your plan does not please me—if it does, dearest Clifton, you must forgive me, and believe me when I say I shall not be the least happy when we meet again. At Abbeyleix, I hope we shall all meet, and then I shall be able to get acquainted with your relations. I cannot tell you how anxious I am that they should like me. If they think me amiable, and that I am likely to make you happy, I shall not care much if they should not think me at all pretty. I shall be quite content if for the future one dear person should be satisfied with whatever share of good looks I have. You see I want to pass myself off for better than I am by pretending to be so free from vanity, but you know me too well to think so well of me, I believe. Dearest Clifton, do not think me in the least unaffectionate or cold if in one instance we have not been "*toujours d'accord*." If you do, love, you will be very naughty, for none could love another more than your own (I will not say who) loves you. I think I shall have another letter from you to-morrow. It is very good natured of you to write so often, for I am sure you must have a great many other claims on your time. I conld willingly write a great deal more than you would have time to read but have not time as it is near two o'clock. Dearest love, adieu, ever yours most affectionately,

EMMA PARNBLL.

Remember, you are not to let Papa take me away from Lady de V. He never minds anything that I say, so I must depend upon you dearest. Once more, adieu.

Send Lady de V's Italian Grammar by Uncle James.

LORD CLIFTON TO MISS EMMA PARNELL.
Berkeley Square,
June 3rd, 1825.

I look forward with the greatest eagerness for tomorrow's Post, as I feel assured that it will bring me a letter from my dearest love ; and also because I think it possible that some light may be thrown upon our future proceedings by it, and by the answer to a letter from my mother to Aunt de V. My hurried scrawl of yesterday's date was written after my return from the City, where I had been consulting with my Father's Solicitor on necessary arrangements, and I am happy to say that by the great kindness of the best of Parents, matters are likely to be more expeditiously settled in that quarter than I expected. I have this morning been with the Coachmaker who will not cause any delay. Under these circumstances you will not be surprised if I am somewhat anxious that the plan suggested by our fathers before I arrived in Town may be acceded to. The only difficulty is in the fear of possibly hurting the feelings of our dear friends at Buxton, but I do feel somewhat sanguine that the Post will bring intelligence which will gladden my heart, and that you will not, if it is so arranged, object to the anomaly of coming to your *caro* to be married, instead of his going to you. Remember, sweetest, that this would be the speediest, and I think the pleasantest mode of finishing my court-ship—what the sweets of matrimony may prove, I think we are both willing to try, and *selon mon idee* the sooner the better. I am moreover, particularly anxious that you should become acquainted with your new relations who are most desirous of seeing my best beloved : furthermore, your being in Town would be in favour of the well-fitting of certain articles of dress which it is needless to name. Notwithstanding all this I hope you will not even hint at such a thing, if you think it will not be perfectly agreeable to those under whose care and by whose means our delightful acquaintance has been commenced and carried on, but in this as in all other matters I know that your own good sense will be your best guide.

How delighted am I by your dear letter which breathes love and affection and comfort to my heart, under the restraint of absence which I trust will be but short. I feel certain that you would have written to me again 'ere this, had you not been restrained by the apprehension of being thought forward. Now, my dearest Emma, write as often and as much as your inclination leads you to take up your pen and address me, and the oftener and the more you write, the more will it please me. At the same time, I only wish you to write when you are not better employed, and I am aware that you have plenty to do. My pen runs on at such a rate that I finish a sheet of paper before I know what I am doing : I hope you may be able to decypher my writing which is unusually bad to-day. Tell me . every particular of your dear self; every little incident however trifling will interest me more than all the other letters I can receive. All here seem to agree that after a match is settled the sooner a pair are united the better : let not us, my dear, dissent from the general opinion, as I long for the moment when I shall be able to call you my own sweet gypsy girl : my wife! How I long for to morrow's Post. How anxiously shall I open my letter.

I am sorry to tell you that my poor skin has

been unusually bad since I arrived in Town, and my forehead &c. less good looking than ever, which I cannot but lament, but principally on your account. I hope however it will be soon better, and I am sure that seeing you again will do me good in every respect. If I find that it is determined that you should stay at Buxton and return thence direct to Ireland it shall not be long ere I *make* it convenient to be with you somewhere or other. I have a mind to send to Paris for some shoes for you. We are going about them directly. I have been so entirely taken up by graver matters for these three days that I have not yet been able to attend to any minor concerns. Do write sweetest, at length and as often as you can. God bless and preserve you, for your constant and most affectionately attached

C.

I have desired Beppy to write you a line and I hope she will.

Lord Clifton to Miss Emma Parnell.

Berkeley Square,
June 4th, 1825.

Thanks dearest love for your nice dear long letter which I prize most highly : I regret that I have not time (as I have promised to attend my father on business to the City), to write at length as I could wish. Indeed you're a dear good girl to write so delightful a letter, pray continue them as often as you can, as the oftener, the better for me. I am vexed, much vexed, that I should have written yesterday in the strain which I then adopted as I find, as I might have expected, that there is no chance of arranging as I ventured to wish : however time will soon pass away, and I do hope that it will be not long ere I can call you my own. I hope to see you soon again but cannot fix a time as yet. Let me hear exactly how long you are likely to stay at Buxton. Uncle James talks of going down about Thursday next. You do not mention your own cold, my sweet love ; how is it? Write every little particular of your dear self, to satisfy the anxiety of your poor Clif. I hope my scribble to Aunt de V. may make you laugh. I am glad the ponies are of some use, perhaps they had better remain, and will you ask Lord de V. to give my groom some money, if he wants any, for me. I have been reading over again your dear dear letter, and you cannot conceive what pleasure it gives me to see the workings of your affectionate heart in a variety of ways. It makes me shed tears of joy and gratitude. I have not time to remark upon it in detail, but must generally observe how I love you if possible more than ever on account of the really good feeling therein displayed. I am glad to hear Lord H.* is better. Do write, my sweet, all that comes from *your* heart, it delights mine. I am sorry dear Henry cannot partake of our happiness by being present. I begin to be quite reconciled to your Christian name. I care not how soon you change the other, and would not exchange Emma

* Lord Henry Moore, the husband of Emma's sister Mary.

for all the world, nor twenty worlds. Continue to
write, and to love as much as you can.

Yours most truly and most devotedly,
CLIFTON.

O cari accenti
O soavi momenti.

Berkeley Square,
June 4th, 1825.

" *My little expeditious plan* "
Upon my word, my dearest An-
-ny Fanny, it was none of mine,
However I must not repine,
If 'tis decreed as 'twas before
That we must wait for six weeks more
Ere I can cease to live alone,
And dearest Emma call my own.
When first I jump'd from off the coach
Our glad Papas began to broach
The scheme which you have laid to me.
I answer'd that it must not be
Till we had sounded Aunt de V.,
To whom both I and Emma owe
Much of the bliss that here below
We may expect; without her aid
I ne'er had seen the lovely maid,
Nor had she known that constant hearts
Sometimes withstand the noxious arts
Of London's fashionable sphere,
And that, there may be station'd here
A person she might wish to love,
Who by his simple ways might prove
That fashion, raking, concerts, balls
And all the mischief that befalls

Fine gentlemen, could not impart
Deception to a faithful heart. –
Too much of this—I cannot say
That I rejoice in the delay
Of what my happiness I deem ;
But still I see I did but dream,
When possible the plan I thought
That you to Cobham would have brought,
And sent us off to Sandgate soon
To pass the joyful honey-moon.
As 'tis arranged, at Abbeyleix
I hope to take a lasting lease
For our joint lives of sweetest Emma,
And to get out of the dilemma
Of single wretchedness, to guide
In trav'lling chariot side by side
To Clifton Lodge my lovely bride.
I hope that sister Car. and you so
Completely will arrange the trousseau
That ere the happy hour we greet
As man and wife when we shall meet
And may be ready without flaw,
As in ten days will be the law
Proceedings, by my father's care
Who bade his lawyer quick prepare
The settlements with least delay
And to be ready any day.
Pray tell me how your health has been
Since last I saw you : do you mean
So long at Buxton to remain
That I may visit you again
Ere you shall leave it ? in a week
Or at the most ten days the Peak

Might see my face again, if there
You think of staying : so beware.
But if I come methinks the waiter
If to arrive there is none later
Vice-President will me decree
And separate my love and me,
Which I no longer can endure.
My happiness then to ensure
Pray dearest Aunt no longer tarry
But suffer Em and me to marry.

MISS EMMA PARNELL TO LORD CLIFTON.

Buxton, June 6th.

I wish so much I had not written my last letter,
because I am afraid it may annoy you, as there was
more in it about the discarded *little expeditious plan*
—indeed dearest Clifton your poetical letter amused
us all very much, and it seemed to be very satisfactory to your dear Aunt. Mr. Spencer has lent
me the Sybil to copy and I am drawing it for her
and hope I shall do it well. I would have written
to you yesterday to thank you for your letter which
I got then, but I knew that this morning's post
would bring me another, and thought I would wait
till then. I am so glad you say you were pleased
with my letters ; I suppose it is for the same reason
that I like yours, because they are so affectionate.
As you really like long letters I will write another
to-morrow for I have not much time left, and I must
write a few lines to thank her for her kind note. I
am sure she will think it very stiff, but do tell her,
dearest love, that I am longing to know her better,
for Catherine Vesey has for these two years past

been giving me the most delightful account of her. So make my apologies to her, if she thinks my note very disagreeable. You cannot think how eagerly I watch for the letters now at breakfast time. If you have time pray continue to write very often. Lord de V. says we shall leave this the end of this month. I am very much amused at your fancying I have a cold, on the contrary I am in rude health. Catherine and Car. are going to ride to-day. I gave Lord de V. your message. Your letter made Ly. de V. very happy I think, for she had previously *suspected* you of having formed the plan of my leaving her—which I would not do for the whole world. Dearest love do tell me that you are not annoyed with my last letter, for I cannot recollect what there was in it, but I know at that time I felt vexed at seeing dear Lady de V. was annoyed about it.

I must stop for it is just *post-time*. Adieu, my dearest love, ever yours most affectionately

EMMA PARNELL.

I am very glad you are reconciled to my *Christian* name.

Excuse this being so shockingly folded up.

LORD CLIFTON TO MISS EMMA PARNELL.

Berkeley Square,
June 6th, 1825.

Thanks for your letter, dearest love, and pray continue to write as often and as much as you like, in the same free, familiar, confidential style. I believe I shall forgive this once what you call sauciness, in consideration of the warmth of

generous feeling which you evince towards my dear
Aunt : as to etiquette, which is the second point in
which you agree with her, I do not set a paramount
value upon it.   In fact, my sweet girl, so far from
its being my plan I must inform *you* (but I do not
wish you to say anything about it), that instead of
being the proposer, I was the person who instantly
upon hearing that it was in contemplation, said
that I was sure that neither you nor I could agree
to anything that could be calculated to hurt the
feelings of those kind friends and dear relations to
whom we owe so much.   I believe it was originally
an idea of my father's, in his anxiety to promote my
wishes ; which was without consideration acceded
to by yours, who when I arrived was ready to start
for you, had I not made objections as stated before.
Now think not, my love, that I state this, and
inculpate our Papas, by way of exculpating myself,
for really I think that the suggestion was merely
made to accommodate us, and without reflection as
to the effect in other quarters : I must say that the
moment I objected, which I did at once, and as
peremptorily as is decent with one's parents, they
both saw the justice of the objection, and
acquiesced in my proposal.   I am sorry that the
subject should have been mentioned to Aunt de V.
for to this part of the proceedings I confess that I
was privy, but there I think I may calculate on
your forgiveness, as my sole motive was that of
indissolubly uniting our hands as well as our
hearts. I never dreamed of having taken you away
from Aunt de V.; the only possible alternative was
the chance of their coming here in their way from
Buxton, which after all would only have made you

my own dearest wife two or three weeks sooner. But I was very selfish even to accede to the idea of giving them that trouble, and I must beg you to forgive me. At the same time pray make it clear to them that I was by no means the contriver of the plot, but on the contrary frustrated it ; for at all events I do not wish to be thought ungrateful to your Welsh Aunt and Uncle for the manifold favors they have done me, and above all for the last and greatest that they can possibly grant me. The idea was given up by all parties the moment your letters arrived on Saturday, so that you have not to apprehend Sir H's arrival to take you off. I believe Uncle J. means to cut me out by taking you to Gretna Green ! ! By the way he is going into Berkshire to fish for this week, so that it is doubtful whether he will go to you at all at Buxton. I am anxious to know what your probable stay there will be, as if you prolonged it, I would try to get down again. If you go as intended at the expiration of six weeks it would be hardly worth while, as I must leave some things undone here and have to return. The plan now talked of is this. My father and mother intend going to Cobham about the 20th for ten days or a fortnight, and then to set out for Ireland, so that the earliest time for the completion of my happiness by calling you my own would be the middle of July. This being the case, (according I believe to etiquette) may I request of you to take the matter into consideration, and fix a time founded on these premises, for a conclusion. Your Papa says he can be at Abbey Leix at any time.

Fix then the day, my dearest dove
When I may marry my sweet Love.

I hope and think you will not propose any
unnecessary delay; and be it when it may it will
seem an age till then. How slowly has this last
week passed. How dull when compared with the
last. I do not suppose that many young men
would draw such a comparison between London
and Buxton. Uncle Tom has just been here, and
been kind enough to stop a long while, talking
upon a subject most interesting to me. I see that
my estimate of a certain Lady about to marry the
man she loves, and his agree very well. By the bye
I forgot to tell him of the stone ban-box, and
butterflies and maggots, &c. How I do run on,
writing to my dearest Emma! She will be doubtless weary of decyphering or trying to decypher my
scrawl: at all events I am too selfish to forego the
pleasure. You must know that you will be disappointed in me; at least I am disappointed in
myself, seeing that when occasion comes I am
exceedingly impatient,—I am not going to say of
seeing you, which is natural and excusable, but on
account of myself; my own unworthy self. The
reason is that now when I wish to be clearest, and
at my best, I am more than usually plagued with
my skin torment, and I find that far from taking it
with philosophy, now that I have an end in view, I
am impatient, and wicked in not submitting with
resignation to this what must be considered after
all, a very slight infliction. You must forgive me,
love, for it is for your sweet sake. God make me
thankful for all his mercies, of which I must rank

the first worldly advantage, the having known and gained, and I hope of soon possessing *you*. Write, dearest Emma, all that your fond good heart suggests, as your letters give me the greatest pleasure that I am susceptible of in your absence. Forgive me for being too fond. It is a venial offence. Say everything that is kind to our dear relations on my behalf—remember too that M.P.'s expect an envelope, and if the fourth side is scribbled on it will add to my pleasure. I delight in your letters, so fear not to tire me. May it be ere long that we meet again, never to part for many days together while we live. Shall I send the Italian Grammars by the Coach if Uncle J. does not go? I have got your writing box, and ordered the work box. The watch not yet. Addio, my dearest love, your most devotedly attached

C.

Give my love at the Great Hotel. *Beignet* has given a flourishing account of you.

It is impossible that a certain article of a lady's dress just returned can fit you exactly. They are Beppy's and not Emily's, and I suspect that you have thought it necessary to fancy yourself no larger than Emily, I mean about the waist and chest. However a pair will be ordered. Do not attempt to screw yourself up into too tight clothes, as I shall not like you to be so. We are going down about a gown for you directly.

The disagreeable business you spoke of is over to our satisfaction. I have some thoughts of going to the sea side for a few days, as I think it would be of use to me, and I could so see dear Aunt P. and

Catty Wingfield. It depends however in some measure on what I hear of your intended motions.

I think you will be properly tired by all this nonsense. Once more God bless my sweetest love.

Buxton, June 7th.

I do not expect another letter to-day from my dearest Clifton, so I will solace myself by writing to him. How kind you are to say you like my long letters, I was afraid you would not have time to read them. I generally read yours about three or four times over, the day I get them, and sometimes oftener. But then in this out-of-the-world place, my reading your letters four times, does not prove so much affection as the reading of mine once by you who are in the world. We expect John Nugent here, and I hope he will come as there is to be a ball on Wednesday and there is a great scarcity of partners for the young ladies. Catherine is very happy in the anticipation of this ball, but I am afraid she will be disappointed, for at present there is nobody to dance with but Mr. Sitwell, who by the bye is extremely amusing, now that we know him better. The Welby party go on Saturday. We all think they will be a loss, for Miss Welby amuses us excessively. She buys false diamonds for real ones, at Mr. Bright's shop, and then she is so proud of them and appears at dinner with a large ornament in the shape of an anchor pinned on her gown, which is made of glass or paste, and for which she paid 38 guineas. Did you ever hear of a Prince *Scimitelli*; she pronounces it so, and she is always talking of him. Mr. Sitwell is a very great gossip, and he brings new anecdotes every day of some of the inhabitants of Buxton. George sent me back my picture, which he says astonished him very much, as he thought I had quite different features, and besides that I was very dark. So I wrote him back word that he thought right, and that the portrait was much more like the pretty Miss Maria Webster, my cousin, than like myself. I am in great delight at getting the Sybil to copy, and am very anxious to succeed in copying it for dear Lady de Vesci. I am so ashamed of the horrid little note I wrote to your sister, in return for her very pretty one, but she must make allowance for the awkwardness of a rustic young lady. I am sure she is very good-natured, unless she is very unlike a brother of hers; and I think she resembles him in that point, from Catherine's description. Isabella Bayley* wrote to me, and she ends her letter by saying, "how I envy you, having Uncle James to quiz you." I suppose we shall see him on Thursday. He will be a great acquisition to most of our party, so I hope he will come. Tommy writes word to Lady de V. to tell him something of you. He does not mention me, but he says he has not heard any particulars, and is very anxious to know more. Poor boy, he has been disappointed and has only got a second class. I suppose I shall hear from you to morrow. I wish letters could go and come more speedily. But I think from what you say it will not be very long before you pay us another visit, and then you must

*Daughter of Lord Clifton's aunt, Mrs. Forde, of Seaforde.

stay here, and we can all go back to dear Abbeyleix together. I am fonder of that place than any other, for you know I have been there so much, and we ought both to like it very much, on account of that pleasant fortnight passed together there. How odd it seems that I should know you so well now, and not be the least ashamed to write to you as if I had known you all my life. If you were not the most good-natured person in the world, I never should have courage to write in this way—certainly I never had so much confidence in anyone as I have in you, and now I must leave off writing to you, so dearest love adieu, and believe me yours affecly.

EMMA PARNELL.

LORD CLIFTON TO MISS EMMA PARNELL.

Berkeley Square, June 8th, 1825.

As you will have reckoned rather without your host, dearest Emma, as to receiving a letter from me on Tuesday (when there is no London post at Buxton) I will not defer my answer for a day to your dear letter of Monday, altho' I shall not be able to write as much at length as I did on that day; so much the better perhaps you will think, for I am aware that some of my letters are unreasonably long. Beppy thinks your beginning "dear Lady Elizabeth" very formal, but likes your note much. I am rather pleased at seeing a marked difference in that and the one to "the person who was to give it to her." Specimens of a stiff and easy style. By the way I see that you follow my bad example of not reading over your letters after you have written them.

I do not mention this to complain, as well I cannot, seeing that I am the example, but to express a hope that you will not copy my many faults, inaccuracies and acts of carelessness. I am glad you are to prolong your stay at Buxton as I will endeavour to get down there. As it is I am prevented by an aggravated attack of the malady which I mentioned to you, and of which I shewed a specimen. I think I shall probably have to go to the sea coast to get a week's bathing. Indeed, my dearest girl, I am sometimes troubled and vexed with myself for having led you into a contract with an afflicted old fellow like myself, to make you share in his troubles altho' they be only skin deep: also because I find that I, who considered myself rather patient before, (now that I have so great an object in view, for which I wish for a sound skin) find myself impatient to a degree, I fear very improperly so. But God's will be done, and I hope he will of his mercy make me sensible of the innumerable blessings I enjoy, and teach me to value as I ought the blessing of having nothing but this to repine at. O, dearest Emma, if you knew how much I think myself a favored being, especially *now*, I am sure it would give you pleasure. There is no essential wanting to my temporal happiness, and yet I am wicked enough to complain about this little *malheur*— fie dear Clif!! It is chiefly on your dear account, and I cannot help lamenting that I should be worse at this moment, than I have ever been before. It is lucky I was not so a little sooner or I could not have been so bold as to have proposed, but perhaps it is more cruel to have led you into the scrape. I would however let you out if you wished it. But no, I feel that I cannot enjoy life without you, and I hope we shall not long be separated. Your letters give the greatest pleasure of all pleasures now you are absent; would that the time were come when letters were not necessary.

Forgive all this incoherent stuff, dearest love; look upon me with the eyes of compassion and affection, and believe me unalterably and devotedly yours,

CLIFTON.

Why do you never mention dear Aunt de V's health? I hope that no news is good news, and that she is better. I am glad the ponies are of use. Why do not you ride? I hope at least that you take long walks. Pray do take exercise, and let me see the roses in bloom when I go to you. Adieu! dearest.

MISS EMMA PARNELL TO LORD CLIFTON.

Buxton. June 9th.

My dearest Clifton,

I am so glad you ask me to write often, for it is pleasant to think that one is not reckoned *too* affectionate. I mean that my fond epistles do not tire you. Your long letter of the 6th was the greatest treat to me, I like such a one much better than a note, though I like a note very much when you have not time to write more. I am afraid Uncle Tom will give you too partial and favourable an account of his favourite Niece, so you must not listen to him. He is very fond of me partly because I am the only one of us who have shown him much affection, and partly because I am rather an *eleve* of his. I have always considered him more as a father than an Uncle, because he has always been like one in affection and kindness to me. He wrote me a most pathetic account of his miseries in London ; he says nobody seems interested in his Institutions, and that he is toiling away with stones for his food and dust for his sauce, and he ended by saying that if he thought I pitied him, it would be some consolation. He amuses me so excessively with his odd stories, and his droll face which he is always trying to screw up into a grave, solemn look, while he is longing to laugh all the time.

Lord de V. has just shewn me part of a letter from Mr. J. Brownlow. He says "give my love to my niece that is to be," so I suppose I am in favour with him—and in another part of the letter he says "I caught Emily tête à tête with Clifton in his room, she said she was helping him to settle his papers, but don't tell Beatrice."

Beatrice however was not jealous ; though indeed this morning she began to feel a fit of the above-mentioned disorder coming on, on seeing C. Vesey reading a letter from her cousin Clifton.

The party all went to the Races yesterday. It was such an uncommonly beautiful warm day, that I thought it would be very ill employed in going to the Races, so I spent my time in walking on the terrace reading, and as everybody was gone to the Races except two or three ladies, they and I had the terrace to ourselves. My own plan was to have

H.

gone to the shrubbery as being the most shady, but Lord de V. pretended I should be run away with, and so I contented myself with the terrace. The book I am reading is Capt. Hall on South America, and I think it is more interesting than the most interesting novel I ever read. However I believe I shall not be so unsociable to-day, but go with the rest to the Races. Mr. and Mrs. Spencer have had our engagement announced to them, and they say that Lady Boothby found it out long ago. Mrs. Spencer is a very pleasing person. I believe you said you should like to know when we leave Buxton, and I think from what Lord de Vesci says that we shall leave it the last week in June. So I suppose we shall not be at Abbeyleix till the beginning of July. At present the exact time for leaving this is not settled, it depends very much upon Lady de V's recovery. I think this fine weather does her good. Lord de V. has just said he thinks of leaving this next Monday fortnight, which will be I think the 27th. I am afraid I shall hardly have time to finish my Sybil. I suppose we shall as usual stay some days in Dublin. I have just sent my love to my future Uncle. Are you jealous, dearest Clif ? or do you feel too confident of my loving you better than all the rest of the world to care to whom I send such idle messages ? I believe there is no use in pretending to disguise that such is the case with me. I hope you will go to Sandgate, for I should think your presence would be a great acquisition to your Aunt and Catherine Wingfield.

I almost envy you going to the sea-side, for I am quite foolish about the sea. It actually makes me quite wild to stand and look at the sea, and watch the waves dashing in till I am quite tired. You see you will find out the hidden bad parts of my character by degrees, and here I have already acknowledged myself guilty of being a little romantic—that is in private, for I hate making a parade of such feelings. Do not forget to write soon, my own dearest love, and scold me if you like for writing such a stupid letter. Ever yours most affectionately and truly,

EMMA PARNELL.

Lady de V. wonders that you never mentioned Mrs. Forde's illness.

LORD CLIFTON TO MISS EMMA PARNELL.

Berkeley Square,
June 9th, 1825.

My dearest Love,

I must be very short to-day, but as my yesterday's letter was long enough to tire the dear girl who could read it three or four times I do not repent the brevity of this one. Thanks for your dear letter : continue the delightful correspondence we have commenced. A letter from Aunt de V. has released me from apprehension that she still was under the idea that I had tried to rob her of you before the time. No, my dear, 1 have too strict a regard for what is due to others, particularly when they are so kind and dear to us, to allow of my thinking of such a thing for my own gratification. Poor Tommy ! I feel for him from my heart, and will write him a line to-day. I had not seen the Class paper, and yours was the first intelligence I received of his failure. I the less expected it, as I had a good account of his performances from his tutor Mr. Longley. I have from him and many others the kindest congratulations, which I reserve for a quiet hour with you, when we may look them over together. You fancy me in the world, my love. I assure you that I am as much out of it as you are, having seen hardly any one, and not having been out except to one Opera and one Concert when I first arrived in Town. Do not flatter yourself that this is because I can relish nothing away from you, or degrade yourself so far as to suppose that I do not go out for fear of meeting with something I like better, which the Girls attribute as the cause of my secession from gaiety. The fact is that I have not been presentable on account of my malady, which was I believe brought to this pass by the long outside passage (at night) by the coach. I must not do this again, and when I go to Buxton again it must be in my own carriage. By the bye I have been, and am still, very busy about imperials, &c. Shall you require a great deal of room? I have ordered a summer lining of blue stripe on white ground. Do you like this? Is it becoming? etc.

I have just been looking over a draft for a contract between E. Bligh commonly called Ld. C. and —— Parnell, spinster, just now. So you see our lawyers get on better than your sempstresses.

Let me hear how the ball went off.

I have a letter from Elcho this morning, who says he was a little doubtful as to rheumatism, but had no suspicion whatever, and that I was intended by nature for a diplomatist (poor Johnny) so secret, and so successful.

I send you a broach which I hope you will like for the sake of your devotedly attached.

C.

I not only have heard of, but know Prince *Cimitile* to be one of the greatest of Bores. He is a Neapolitan proscribed by the authorities there. Send me Miss Maria Webster's portrait *s'il vous plait.*

I am better and in better spirits about myself to-day.

MISS EMMA PARNELL TO LORD CLIFTON.

Buxton, June 10th.

I am so much obliged to you, my dear Clifton, for writing directly you received my letter of Monday. I cannot resist beginning a letter to you to-day, although it cannot go till to-morrow, and this delay will probably tempt me to write about twice as much as usual. I am not sure whether you will be at all obliged to me for being so good-natured as to wish to take up so much of your time with my stupid letters, so you must really tell me if I tire you with them. I must thank you for your remark on the inaccuracy and carelessness of my letters, because I always wish you to tell me anything you observe in me, that you would wish altered ; I am afraid you will find when you know me better, that I have a great many different ways of being careless and awkward. I have often wondered how you could ever like me so much, for I feel I am so different from what I should wish to be in many respects. But then you know I *can* improve, and I will try to do so for your sake. I sent you a letter yesterday sealed most awkwardly, I was in a great hurry because I thought the letters would be late for the post. You cannot give me a more powerful motive to get rid of any of my awkward ways, than that of your wish that I should do so, so remember, dearest love, that I hope you will always tell me exactly what you think on any subject of this nature or any other. You ask me why I do not ride, I believe the chief reason is that I am such a coward, not naturally one, I think, but in couse-quence of one unfortunate fall which frightened me. However I think I could get over my fears, if I was mounted on a very quiet steed, and had some very good natured person to ride with me, who would not be angry with me for being frightened. Only I should be ashamed to let him see how badly I ride. I used to ride sometimes at Abbeyleix, but I did not like it, because Billy Vesey used to be so angry with me for being frightened, and used to scold me and laugh at me. Do not think I am indolent about taking exercise, for I walk a good deal. I am quite shocked at myself for my forgetfulness in never having mentioned Lady de Vesci's health. I think she seems a little better, and not quite so stiff as she was. This fine weather does her good. We have had three beautiful summer days, quite a wonder at Buxton. We went to the races yester-day, which were reckoned good I believe. Mr. Sitwell is our constant attendant from the time we (or rather Car.) are walking in the grove or on the terrace before breakfast, till the end of the day, that is at all times of meeting, and Caroline gets quizzed by us all on his account. Lord Kilkenny and Miss Bourke are expected to-day or to-morrow, the latter will be a great acquisition to Catherine, as she is a great friend of hers. We have been dancing in the ball-room these last two evenings, which looks very pretty when it is lit up. I am not clever enough to know whether "lit up" or "lighted up" is right. I believe you may send Lady de Vesci her Italian Grammar by the coach. I suppose you will not think it worth while to come here as we do not stay I believe after next Monday fortnight. I wish you would go to the sea if you think it would be of use to you, although if I only consulted my own wishes, I should like you to come here, but you know it is not right to be selfish, so I will wish you to go wherever it is best for you to be. I assure you I feel very much for your present uneasiness, and for your sake, my dearest love, I wish with all my heart that you may soon be relieved from it. But I do not see why you should be so much annoyed about it, and why you say it is chiefly on my account that you lament being worse just now. I lament it very much on your account, and for your dear sake I wish you to be free from whatever is unpleasant to yourself, but indeed I think I love you more instead of less for being in an uncomfortable, though I trust but in a very slight degree, a suffering state ; I hope too, that for the future, my affection and tenderness will be a comfort to you whenever you are the least unhappy in any way. I hope you feel that this will indeed be the case, and that I should love you still more dearly in affliction, than at any other time. Dearest Clifton, we are to be comforts to each other, and should certainly love each other better in sickness than in health. I know hereafter I shall be wretched if I am not able to think that you are the happier for having linked your fate with mine. Do you not think you shall? I trust you will, and I think it is not quite impossible, if you will be content with true and real affection and the most earnest desire to please you. How my pen runs on, and upon looking back, what a number of words have been left out and what must you think of me after all I said in the beginning of my letter about being more careful and accurate. However I flatter myself there is one improvement in this letter; the handwriting is a little better than usual. Will you tell me if you think so? I believe the Halls will arrive before we go. I am very anxious to become acquainted with Mrs. Hall, as she seems by her letters to have formed a just estimate of you. I hope she will not think me quite unworthy of being chosen by you, for I know you are such a favourite with her. Dearest, adieu, I must go and draw, or my lovely Sybil will never be done. Pray go to the sea, for I think it will do you good, and Lady Powerscourt I should think will be delighted to see you. I have got back the Grecian profile, but do not mean to send it. You must excuse this act of disobedience to your orders, for if I let you have it, you would imagine I resembled it more than I do, and when you saw me again, would turn away from me as a great fright, so I will not let you have it at present.

The ponies are very well and very much admired. Your groom is held in great estimation by the Welby party, as he has saved one of their coach-horses from dying, by his skill, when the farrier was too tipsy to be consulted. We are going to Manchester for a day only, next week. I am quite sure you must be tired with all my nonsense, so I will leave off writing and sign myself ever yours most affectionately,

EMMA PARNELL.

You cannot think how I love writing to you, though at the same time I agree with you in wishing that we had no occasion to exchange letters between us, but till that time arrives, pray write very often to me.

Postscript by Catherine Vesey.

My dear Clifton, I think we shall leave Buxton on Monday fortnight, and soon after that I hope you and Emma will be the happiest of the happy. There is a Bride and Bridegroom here, they were spending the Honey-moon at Matlock when we were at that ever to be remembered place. They seem very loving but have left off whispering. Mama says Emma was going to cry when she heard you were not coming here.

Your very affectionate Coz.

KITS.

I think you have begun to scold very soon and suppose you already consider Emma as Lady Clifton as I heard her complain of your lecture on writing badly.

Do not mind Catherine's nonsense.

EMMA PARNELL.

Berkeley Square,
June 11th, 1825.

My dearest love,

As there is no Post to morrow, and as I am the next day going to Cobham with my father, which will prevent the possibility of your hearing from me again before Thursday, I write to inform you that I am going on well, and hope soon to have everything in readiness. I am to go and see the *skeletons* of imperials to day fixed on the Carriage, if they can be got ready. I have made a little sketch above to shew what I propose, and I think I have provided room for a more *exigeante* lady than she is with whom I am to deal. Charles tells me I shall be allowed the small imperial over the boot No. 4 only; so I have added No. 5 for my own convenience. N.B.—we need not carry all these always, but can go without 4 and 5 except when we are *fully* loaded and equipped. No. 1 is a large $\frac{3}{4}$ imperial for *my Lady's* dresses &c., in which I may perhaps have one coat carried occasionally. 2. My Lady's cap-case. 3. My Lady's boot trunk. 4 and 5 already described. 6. A small Portmanteau for servants under the seat (to which also there is a drop box). 7. My Lady's chaise seat. 8. A large leather pocket to carry books, loose parcels etc.

Have the goodness to consult about these and tell me if I have imagined too much room for my wife's effects. You will allow that I have done it on the most liberal and extensive plan, but I am told that no lady ever finds too much room. A lilac dress and a pair of shoes, with two parcels of cambric from Aunt P. go this day by my friend the Regulator. Do, my sweet love, write me every particular about your dear self, and do not be afraid of shocking or tiring me. I like your nice, affectionate, free, ingenuous letters of all things, and hope they will not be given up till we meet which I trust will be very shortly. I cannot exactly fix my plans, but shall not leave this part of the world till I can get everything in order. Tell me exactly, as soon as the day is fixed when you are to quit Buxton. I fear I cannot hear from you till Tuesday, when I hope to receive a letter before I leave Cobham. I hope I shall not be obliged to go to the seaside, which I only wish as it would afford an opportunity of seeing Aunt P. and C. W. Uncle James will not have interrupted you this week, as I believe he is still in Berkshire fishing. I wonder whether you have had fine weather at Buxton. It has been delicious here for three days: quite hot ! Write all about yourself and our friends to your devotedly attached

CLIFTON.

I am going to take lessons in perspective from Mr. Rowbotham.

MISS EMMA PARNELL TO LORD CLIFTON.

Saturday.

My dearest love,

I must just write a little note to say how very glad I am that you are better and in better spirits as the style of your letter as well as your own account of your letter assures me. Your last letter was certainly rather pathetic and I must have been infected by it, for I find on looking over mine in answer to it, that some parts of it partake of the same style. I am quite ashamed to send it, but you need not read it all if you do not like, and remember that it is to be considered a distinct letter from this (inasmuch as it was written yesterday) although it comes on the same day. I like the broach very much, and the lock of hair that is in it still more, for the sake of one, who I believe will hardly thank me for telling him what he knows so well, namely, that I love him better than anybody in the world. I am a little inclined to believe that your sister and Emily are right in their conjectures as to the cause of your secession from gaiety. Are you afraid of meeting Lady Charlotte Osborne? but however my jealousy is not very great even of her. I confess I should like to see her very much. You must not give implicit credence to this page of nonsense except the three first lines which are quite, quite, true. Our ball on Wednesday was very bad, better on Thursday. The quadrille I was in consisted of people who did not know any of the figures, and I was very much amused at the mistakes we all made for I laughed so I could not remember my own part. Yesterday evening was so lovely, I could not help wishing you were of the party. We were out on the terrace till late in the evening. We have a new acquaintance, Sir Thomas Arbuthnot. I am so very glad you no longer fancy yourself ill.

Your own affectionate,

EMMA PARNELL.

I will not send Miss Maria Webster, it is not proper for you to wear her picture. You ought only to wish for mine.

Lord Clifton to Miss Emma Parnell.

Cobham Hall,
June 13th, 1825.

Oh ! My dearest love, how wearily have four or five days passed as by my coming out of Town I have not received a dear letter from you this morning, which I can well guess reached Berkeley Square to-day : I trust to-morrow's Post will not disappoint your faithful Clif. I find that even the pleasure of reading your writing and learning that you were well when the letter left you, are a great pleasure to me when absent.

I cannot say anything positive as to my going to you : it partly depends upon Elizabeth to whom I made an offer of taking her round to Ireland by that way, to which offer I have as yet no determined reply, and partly on my own health, for I am in hopes that I shall be able to present myself to you with a sound skin as well as mind. I hope I am better, dearest ; better I am sure I shall be when I can see you again. I wonder whether you are as anxious to see me as I am to see you. I fear it is too much to expect.

Tell me everything about your dear self, and write me word how Aunt de V. &c. are.

Do not be afraid of shocking the Post Master, but scribble a few lines whenever the thought comes across you.

I hope the trousseau goes on swimmingly.

117

Adieu! I send to Post on purpose to assure you how unceasingly I am

Yours most affectionately,

CLIFTON.

MISS EMMA PARNELL TO LORD CLIFTON.

Buxton, June 13th.

My dearest Love,

I have consulted Lady de Vesci and she desires me to tell you that she thinks you might do with less room, though at first perhaps there will not be too much. In short, that there is no harm in having as much as you mention, and she supposes you are the best judge as to whether it will make the carriage too heavy or not. At first I was rather angry on finding two pages filled up with imperials, but recollecting that they were good things in their way, I forgave you for once. But tell me, why cannot you leave these important concerns and come and see us again. I am sure they will all go on very well without you, and if you don't come now, I suppose I shall not see you for another month. I mean that you might come for a week and then go away again. Now that weather is so fine, Buxton is not so stupid as it was. Lord de V., Car. and I walked to the Lover's Leap and sat there for nearly an hour yesterday evening. I am quite shocked when I think of the long letter I sent off to you on Saturday. I must tell you a secret in order to make you set a higher value on my correspondence, and this secret is that till the present time, I have hated letter-writing, and now I find that it is the pleasantest occupation in the world, and if I did not force myself to stop, I should never recollect that I had written enough to tire even you, although you have so often told me that my letters could not tire you. Is it not very strange that I should change my taste as to letter-writing so entirely? But it is so delightful not to be afraid of telling all one's foolish thoughts. I really think I am very foolish, notwithstanding the *emblem* you have chosen to represent me under, in the *broach* you sent me, which is a *serpent* holding *your* heart in its possession. I suppose you will tell me it was quite unintentionally that you thus designated your foolish Gypsey girl under the emblem of wisdom.

Dearest love adieu. There are visitors come.

Yours affectly,

EMMA PARNELL.

Our friends Mr. and Mrs. Hall of Hollybush— by our I mean Car's. and mine.

LORD CLIFTON TO MISS EMMA PARNELL.

Cobham Hall,
June 14th, 1825.

Oh, my dearest Emma, that you could have looked on this morning when I opened your three dear letters, (dear, affectionate, loving, everything that I could wish) that you might have partaken, as I wish you ever to partake of what delights me, of the heartfelt joy which their arrival occasioned. I was really glad that I had been five long days without a line, so great was the pleasure that I derived from reading at once seventeen well and closely written sides from her whom I love beyond all description. Your letters of Thursday, Friday, and Saturday all reached me together. I conclude that Thursday's was too late for that day's mail which kept it from me three days. I trust that the letter I wrote from London on Saturday was not cross, and did not shew disappointment which has been so amply cleared away by this morning's Post. How kindly you listen to and profit by my suggestion about writing carelessly; it arose from this palpable cause, that as I am notorious for it myself, I wished that she whom I consider almost already as a part of myself should be free from a like disadvantage. I like besides to shew you that I am sincere, and wish to encourage you to object to my failings or inaccuracies, (which last is all I could accuse you of) in the same familiar way. I wish I could flatter myself that by exertion I could make myself a *meet* partner for such a woman as you are, my dearest love! With your assistance however I will try to improve myself, and if you will put up charitably and lovingly with my failings and errors, will endeavour to merit it at your hands. I *am* delighted by your letters, so you must find an excuse for my writing thus. It pleases me so that you should find delight in writing to me; it shews such reciprocity of taste, feeling and affection. Nothing pleases me more I can assure you. I am in hopes that my sister will accompany me to Buxton some day next week, but of this more when I get to Town. And now, my best beloved, I will get out your letters, and answer them regularly. I am glad you like a long letter better than a note, as you shall have one to-day, which will I hope be acceptable after the shabby *drop* of a note which I sent yesterday. I liked what I saw of Uncle Tom: he talked not about institutions or stone meat, or dust sauce; but I believe I would not have allowed him to speak on any subject but one. I hope you and Uncle James will be good friends, as I wish to be on good terms with all the world. He has been very kind about the business, considering his own disappointment. You may be jealous of Emily or anyone else if you think it worth while; I shall be sorry when I give you cause. I think I know my Beatrice better than *mon oncle chanoine*, and I do not apprehend there is a grain of jealousy about her. I fear you and the old ladies must have found the terrace rather warm, if the weather was at all like what it was in London. I am glad you like Captain Hall's book, as it shews your taste; it is *selon moi* remarkably good, and the most satisfactory narrative I ever read. I think I read it when in Ireland before I was at Abbeyleix—dear Abbeyleix.

I hope you went to the Races the second day, as I wish you to amuse yourself, my love, when your poor Cliffy is absent. By the way they are going to build a new Town by Gravesend to be called Clifton in honour (I suppose) of our wedding. I think others might have suspected our match besides Lady Boothby. Do you know Lady Morgan? She was talking about you to my mother the other day, but from what I can gather from her, more as if she was writing a book, than in common familiar dialogue. I suppose it is nearly settled that you should quit Buxton about the 27th. I shall concert plans accordingly when I get to Town.

I hope you will have finished your Sybil before you have to give it up ; indeed before I get to you. I do feel too confident (vain creature) of your loving me better than all the rest of the world, to be jealous or care to whom you send such idle messages, as that to Uncle James. It pleases me.

I have still a mind to run down to Sandgate for a day ; it would I know so please my dear Aunt and Cousin. I shall enjoy partaking of your wildness while gazing at the troubled waves together. There is nothing so fine or so imposing as the sea in a storm. I hope to see many an one with you, and that we may solace ourselves, by drawing a comparison between that and the calm which will I trust ever reign in our breasts. But stay—I see on reading on a few lines farther, that this disposition to gaze upon the works of nature, is one of the "hidden bad parts of your character." Excuse me but I am smiling while I write ! ! But as you are only disposed to be romantic in private and hate making a parade of such feelings I think I am at least a match for you : and now sweet No. 6 go join your fellows in a little bundle within my writing desk : and I take up No. 7, that dear, long, well written, affectionate, loving, much prized letter. Well written it is in every sense. I wish I could say as much of mine, but I have no pens, and no knife that will cut; besides which it is very hot, and I am going to set off soon. Nevertheless, I must go on with the pleasing task of answering your letters in detail, hoping that your eyes will decypher, and your love lend you patience for your task, of wading through a third sheet (now inevitable). The first two pages of No. 7 are occupied by remarks on your own awkwardness which as I do not acknowledge I shall pass over, merely remarking that the desire therein evinced to please me in every respect cannot fail of being most welcome to me, my dearest, best love. As to your riding, I only suggested it as likely to promote your health and comfort, but I care not about it on any other considerations. You will not find me difficult, as I feel that to please you will be my greatest delight, and I am sometimes vain enough to think that I shall do so, as you are so ready to be satisfied, and willing to meet me at least half way in any attempt to render each other happy and comfortable. I am glad to find that you think Aunt de V. better : I sincerely hope that this trip to Buxton will have the effect of curing her : how great an addition would that be to our happiness. We both owe her much : my debt of gratitude began, you know, (as Uncle J. would say) long before you were born. Let me know as soon as Car. and Mr. S. get upon whispering terms, if they are ever so rude. I am glad you have been dancing and amusing yourself and others. I conceive that you were very "clever" as you wrote both "lit up" and "lighted up" which in my judgement (no authority however) are equally good.

Why, my dearest love, are you naughty enough to "suppose" that I shall not think it worth while to go to Buxton, as you only stay till the 27th. Remember once for all that you have such a selfish fellow to deal with that he is always anxious to do what will please him best ; judge then by your own feelings, what that will be—I am only deterred from fixing by my state of skin, which I would willingly improve before I see you, and by my wish to accommodate Elizabeth in my arrangements, as she will I hope go with me. I believe the carriage &c. will be ready this week.

Upon the first two pages of the 2nd sheet of this letter I am totally incapable of expressing myself in terms at all adequate to what I feel. I declare that I am quite overcome by the pure and virtuous love therein breathed. O, my dearest Emma, how can I ever be worthy of such affectionate goodness of heart? Teach me how I can, my dearest love, teach me how I can conduct myself so as to promote your happiness, and I shall be worse than human if I refuse to strain every nerve to comfort and succour you through all the troubles of life. Yes, I do feel, dearest girl, that you will be to me my sweetest solace in affliction, and the greatest possible reason for my happiness. I humbly thank God that having led me through the fearful vicissitudes of my varied life He has at length permitted me to link my fate with that of a woman whose temper, disposition and habits (I must say it tho' it savours of vanity) are so thoroughly accordant with my own, or rather what I wish my own to be. Excuse all this warmth of expression. I never say or write what I do not feel, and if you think it too high-flown and foolish, your partiality will, I know, readily find an excuse. How I delight in remarking that those two pages are written as the sentiments flowed from your heart. You observe upon having left out words ; I am glad to see it, and also to observe that the letters, words, and lines are written with less care than in other parts of your letter, because it proves that you were not thinking of form or ceremony, but that the words express your thoughts. They are indeed invaluable to me, and I know not that I ever experienced greater pleasure, (hardly on the top of Matlock steep) than I do in reading them over and over again. Pray excuse me, but *my* pen does indeed run on, and I am writing shockingly. Your handwriting is very much improved indeed. I hope the Halls will come to Buxton, and that I shall see them there. I am glad you love writing to me, and I will not fail to write very often to you. Now for No. 8. I am glad you like the broach and the lock of hair. By the bye I think I shall draw a little more largely on your curls by and bye to fill a locket I have got. I have not found a watch to please me yet. Lord de Vesci's chronometer is going very well, only a second-and-half in 4 or 5 days. I went with Bep. and Em. on Sunday to visit Ly. C. Osborne, and we met her coming into the Square and shook hands very cordially. She is a nice little girl, but I do not think I could have ever cared about her much, as I met her with complete indifference. I certainly never admired her little diminutive person. I wish I had been at your balls and witnessed and partaken of the Quadrille mistakes, and of your evening party on the terrace. And now " my own affectionate Emma," I have gone through and answered your three dear letters, and have not left room to tell you how delightfully this place is looking, This is a charming day with a fine breeze. I am not sure whether I shall go to Town, or round to Sandgate, just to peep at Lady P. and C.,* it depends upon the wind as I am going in the yacht. You may know, as if I am in Town I will write a line to-morrow, which will arrive as soon · as these sheets. I shall return from Sandgate, if I go, directly.

Yours ever affectionately,

C.

I send a letter from Lady P.· You should open letters you know are for you or other.

I really have not time to read over this scrawl, fond fool that I am to write so much more than any one can make out. It shews, however, my affection and my unbounded satisfaction in receiving your letters. I hope you will not be annoyed by the miscarriage of the first.

MISS EMMA PARNELL TO LORD CLIFTON.

Buxton, June 16th.

My dearest love,

I have just got your dear little note, and am going to write a few lines though it is near post time to tell you that I am quite as anxious to see you, as you can be to see me. I believe you will be rather shocked at such a declaration, but I do not think it will amount to anger on your part even if you should think me very extraordinary. I must tell you that we are this very moment returned from Manchester where we went at 7 o'clock yester-

*Lady Powerscourt and Catherine Wingfield.

126

day morning, and they talked of staying till late this evening, which annoyed me not a little though of course I did not choose to appear so, for I did not like the idea of not seeing your letter which I knew would be here, till the evening. Luckily the plan was changed, and I have got the dear little note in time to write. Pray do all you can to persuade your sister to agree to your plan. Catherine has given me a note ; I think the hand-writing is like Lady Darnley's but I have not opened that nor any of my other letters yet. I believe I will now. I have read it and it is the kindest letter in the world. I can hardly comprehend how she can write so kindly and even affectionately to a person whom she as yet knows nothing of—but it is I know for your sake, dearest Clifton ; she calls you "her inestimable son," and I do not think she has valued you too highly. Ought I to write to her to thank her for her kindness in writing to me ? I think I ought, and yet I had rather that you would tell her from me all that I would express if I could, but I am, I own, a little apprehensive lest a letter written in my awkward style should give an unfavourable impression of me. And yet I must write a few lines, for it would seem so ungrateful not to offer my thanks, (although I fear it will be done awkwardly) for such a very kind letter from Lady Darnley. The weather here has been dreadfully hot for the last week. Catherine will write to Lady Elizabeth to-morrow to endeavour to persuade her to accede to your plan. I need not say how very happy I shall be in commencing an acquaintance with my dearest Clifton's sister, nor do I think it is very necessary to assure him that I am longing to see him again, and that it really does seem about three months since he went away from Buxton. I am sorry to say Lady de V. is not much better. It is very likely though that she may improve if this fine weather continues. I hope she will. Adieu, my dearest love, believe me, I am very anxious to see you, although you seem a little to doubt it, and am ever

Most affectionately yours,

EMMA.

Lady de V. desires me to say that she hopes your sister will be prevailed upon to come, and all the party join with her in that hope.

LORD CLIFTON TO MISS EMMA PARNELL.

Sandgate,

June 15th, 1825.

After the unreasonably long letter which by the Gravesend Post was yesterday forwarded to my dearest love, I shall not occupy her time long in the perusal of what this excellent pen of Catty Wingfield's shall indite. I started from Gravesend at half past 7 yesterday evening, and being very anxious to see my dear relations here, (although the wind and tide were more favourable for London) as there was a fresh breeze I determined upon passing the night upon the wide waste of waters, which you *wildly* love to gaze upon, and after a rough passage arrived here at half past 10 this morning. I shall probably return to-morrow evening which will bring me up to London on Friday or early on Saturday morning. I shall then

128

learn when it will suit Lady E. to put herself into my carriage and her wardrobe into Lady C's imperials and shall hasten to make my dearest Emma acquainted with one at least of her relations that are to be. This place is looking delightfully, and I think you would like it, altho' it is not a great favourite of mine. I think nevertheless I should like a tête à tête with a certain person prodigiously, among the shady walks, and by the banks of the rippling stream, looking ever and anon "on the dark waters of the deep blue sea." Correct this, it is not right ! I had at one time fondly pictured such a train of circumstances, but it was an idle dream. Perhaps however some day or other it may be so. Altho' there is much wind, it is oppressively hot just now : I doubt not but you have your share of heat at Buxton, where there is little shelter from either heat or cold. I am obliged to Lord de Vesci by the bye for taking care that you should not be run away with ! As I had not ordered my letters to be sent here before, I have of course none to-day : I am vain enough to expect one to-morrow, but I shall not be at all disappointed if there is none ; so fully gratified am I by that mass of kindness and affection which pervaded the batch yesterday received. Write as many more such dear letters as you can. Tell me if mine are too long, and tire you ; you say you prefer a long letter to a note, so I wrote you one yesterday to your heart's content ; and I trust that you will see by my general course of correspondence, that I am not a little fond of the employment. I flatter myself also that you are not averse to it, and that we agree in this as well as other things. I am sorry I did not mention Mrs. Forde who has been very ill, but is I hope quite recovered. I believe they leave Town on Monday. I fear we shall not have the Halls at Buxton ; they talk of going to Harrogate. I longed for a dear companion at Cobham, where I always feel most at home, wishing to shew it to her. I know not when that may be, but I hope my dearest love will like it, tho' it is bigger than the cottage at Abbey Leix. Let me hear every particular of your proceedings at Buxton, but do not think it necessary to write in preference to employing yourself in other ways. I have not got you an Italian Grammar because I have not been able to settle which I should procure: I believe it must be the same as Ly. de V's. Veneroni's is reckoned the best. I hope that will have reached her ere this does, either by Tommy or Uncle James. How foolish I am but I cannot resist the temptation of scribbling into a second sheet, altho' I meant this letter to be a very short one. Aunt P. and C. W. are both very anxious to see you, like all the rest of my relations and friends. I hear there are some pocket handkerchiefs coming for you from Paris : I suppose Johnny will be charged with them. I wish you knew that dear fellow, and that I knew all your near and dear relations: this however will I hope soon be the case. Send me Miss M. Webster, and I will promise neither to shew her picture nor fall in love with her. I am fallen so far and so deep already.

"Oh! my love's like the red red rose
That's newly blown in June.
Oh! my love's like the melody
That's sweetly played in tune.

So fair art thou, my bonny Lass,
So deep in love am I
And I will love thee still, my dear,
Tho' all the sea gang dry."

(Which however does not appear likely to be the case, if I may judge by the appearance of the English Channel, which seems quite full).

"Though all the sea gang dry, my dear,
And rocks melt wi' the sun,
And I will love thee still, my dear,
While the sands of life shall run.

But fare thee weel, my only love,
And fare thee weel awhile,
And I will come again, my love,
An 'twere ten thousand mile."

And now, sweetest, for fear you should ere we meet become quite tired of me and my productions, I must subscribe myself as ever, my dearest Emma's most affectionately,

C.

MISS EMMA PARNELL TO LORD CLIFTON.

Saturday.

My dearest Clifton,

Pray say every thing you can think of for me by way of excuse to your mother if she thinks my letter very stiff and awkward. I really feel so much obliged to her for her letter to me—but I did not know exactly how to say so properly. I send you two fair ladies. You *must* not shew Miss Maria. The other you may if you like.

Yours very affectionately,

EMMA JANE PARNELL.

I am longing to know when you choose to honour us poor inhabitants of the Peak of Derbyshire with a visit.

LORD CLIFTON TO MISS EMMA PARNELL.

Sandgate,

June 16th, 1825.

My dearest Love,

I have a note from you this morning and will return one, for I am sure that another letter would weary even your patience. I am delighted to find that you are longing to have me with you; but then only for a week, that I may go back &c. I hope my present plan will suit you better: I will tell you why I have so arranged it. In the first place I thought it better to have every thing done before I again gave myself up to the joy of your presence, so that I may be quite at liberty when we meet and ready when every thing else is settled—and all the parties arrived. I must observe in passing that were I like anyone else, unaffected by rapid (and particularly night) travelling, I would have run down about once a week to see you, but really, my dearest, I suffer so much from those expeditions that I must determine never to travel so again if I can possibly avoid it.

Do you approve, love ? Now I have been, and am still, kept in great uncertainty by my irruptive complaint, which I am particularly anxious to subdue before I am your husband, if possible, which I hardly believe, altogether. It is indeed too bad that I should vex you with my complaints before your time ; my only object is to make myself agreeable to you in every respect. You will be glad to hear that I am better. I am almost afraid of bathing for fear it should not agree with me, but I will perhaps try it. As to the imperials &c. I have been calculating upon foreign travel, when ladies in general require a great deal of room, but it is not at all necessary, my love, to take all the boxes, and I shall be very happy to accommodate you by leaving some behind. Do you mean to take all your smart clothes to Ireland ? Excuse my importunities. What do you mean by walking to the lover's leap ? Surely Buxton does not presume to have such a spot ! I am delighted by your great secret, and hope that your new love for letter writing will ere long be diminished, and continue so for many a day. I should never wish again to have occasion to write to you. Would that suit you ? Do not be afraid of tiring me. I defy you, and think I have shewn that I am at least a match for tiresomeness. I forgot to say before that we were as usual *d'accord* about *the little expeditious plan*, notwithstanding your apprehensions. Aunt de V. did not expect that I should have to read my own foolish verses at breakfast this morning ! Of course this only copy will be burnt. I never know how to end. Adieu, my own dear Gipsy Girl, may you live and be happy with

Your affectionate

C.

I find I have quite misled you about the spelling of Gipsy—and that I have used you very ill by applying such a term to you, as you may suppose on reading the description I find in a Dictionary, to-wit :

Gipsy—a vagabond who pretends to tell fortunes: a reproachful name for a dark complexion : a name of slight reproach to a woman ! ! ! ! !

Do you mind ?

My own sweet Gipsy ?

Miss Emma Parnell to Lord Clifton.

Buxton, June 17th.

What a delightful letter I received this morning ! I was more than satisfied with it ; it was so much more affectionate than I expected, that I begin to waver in some degree, as to a long-maintained opinion of mine, namely that no man ever loves so much or so warmly as most women do. You need not be affronted at my still being of this opinion, as to the generality of men, for I declare that I fully and entirely except you.

I am not very sorry that you were five days without getting any letters from me as it was partly the cause of your writing me such a dear affectionate letter. I don't quite understand how it could have happened for we send our letters in good time in general. I prize your nice long letter most highly, it is by far the most delightful I have

134

ever yet received from you, and yet I shall not be very sorry if I do not get many more, even were they like your last dear letter; I had much rather look out from the windows of the Great Hotel, to see a brother and sister get out of their carriage, and I do not think that this time I shall turn my head away from the brother: and I shall be delighted to see the sister for his sake, but I am afraid she will not come. I am sure you would like to come, so I shall not be affronted if you find you cannot, as it is probable some fair ladies might be. I am writing in great haste and I see I have blotted my paper but if I do not write now I shall have no time to-morrow, as my Sybil requires a great deal of time. My dear little Uncle, George Dawson, has just arrived from the West Indies, and has written to me. He is one of my nice Uncles. I must find one fault with you, you think too highly of me, you ought to think of me rather as of one who wishes in all things to act and to feel rightly, than as of one who really does so. There is a wide difference between my principles and my practice; my views of what should be done or attempted, and the very little that I ever do or attempt. I do not mean to accuse you of having so little penetration as not to have found this out; but I am afraid that in your kind and affectionate feelings towards me, you are willing to think much more highly of me than I deserve—indeed you should not, for your own sake or for mine, because you will be grievously disappointed and I feel that it is possible that my vanity may be increased tenfold, by receiving such praises from you, and you are aware that I am quite vain enough already. You may think me as affectionate as you like, I will not allow that you have flattered me at all in attributing this quality to me. And now I will leave off talking of myself and go on to other people. You say you hope that "Uncle James" and I shall be good friends. I assure you we are so already. Is he coming to Buxton? I am acquainted with Lady Morgan a *little*, for I don't think she ever spoke to me. She and her stepdaughter were with us at Portrane last summer· Miss Morgan is a beautiful girl and a very quiet nice girl, but I do not like Lady M. at all. I am trying to finish my Sybil before you come, for alas! I shall not be able to attend to it properly when you arrive ! But do not think I am in earnest and delay your coming on that account. I suppose you went to Sandgate. I hope you did, for Lady Powerscourt's sake. I am very glad you say my writing is a little improved. I shall try to improve in everything worth acquiring, now, for your sake. Formerly I had no one to please in such matters but myself, and my pleasure was to be as careless as possible. But now, love, it is and ever shall be my pleasure to be what you like, and you are so good-natured, I do not feel much afraid of failing. Why do you talk of my trouble in decyphering your letters? How can a pleasure be a trouble? You should have seen my joy this morning when I saw three sheets all written over. I must thank you again for your most affectionate, dear, nice letter.

Car. and Mr. Sitwell have not begun to whisper. I think she does not like him much now—his stories are all quite old, and he is thrown into the shade by a very handsome, agreeable little man, a Sir Thomas Arbuthnot. I got the letter from Lady P. It is so beautiful I shall keep it to shew you. I hope you will like it ; I mean that you will be pleased with her sentiments, for they please me very much. I wear your broach every day, and am very fond of it for your sake. My curls are at your service, only the lock you want must be cut off by the discriminating hand of some fair lady, who would have too much sympathy with my feelings to cut it off so as to leave my temples unadorned—which you would do if the scissors were in your hand.

There are some nice people here but they go on Monday—a Mr. and Mrs. Allington. They were at Matlock, May 20th, and remember seeing us there. How you will miss "*la belle Welby*" when you come here. So you have been to see Lady Charlotte Osborne. However I am determined not to be jealous of her or any one else. I should not wonder if *you* were to be a little jealous hereafter. Pray tell me do you mean to be so, or not ? Seriously, I do not think either of us will ever give the other reason. And now having settled this point I must leave off as it is near one o'clock, which you know is late for Buxton.

So, farewell, dearest love, and do not forget how much pleasure your epistles give to your
Very affectionate Imogen,
alias
EMMA.

Friday night.

K.

Berkeley Square,
June 18th, 1825.

My dearest Love,

I rejoice that you will have received yesterday (as I judge) my long letter from Cobham, which I know by your own confession you prize above a scanty note. You are indeed a dear good girl for writing so constantly and so pleasantly to me : I think you must be aware, from a correspondent feeling, how very grateful it is to me to receive your letters, and con over their dear contents, and it is this that makes me less scrupulous of sending you sheets filled with my scrawls. I do indeed take the utmost pleasure both in writing to you, and reading your letters ; my heart beats more frequently and more warmly as I write, I.wish you could feel it ! But then there would be no occasion for writing. How I wish there was none. Do not you, love ? Soon I trust such will be the case and I think it will be difficult to tear me away from you again. I hear a vague report that I am to be married on the 25th of July—is it really to be so distant a day ? Have you fixed it ? for really I have not heard it from authority. The sooner, love, the better says your faithful Clif. What nonsense am I writing, and how large a share of your indulgence must I crave : I trust you have an ample store of that commodity as I shall require it, as you will find to your cost. You hear nothing but what is good of me now, but you will soon find out my evil propensities and bad qualities.

I am glad you have been to Manchester. Did

you visit the manufactures? Or were you employed in fitting yourself out. Let me hear whether you will want to stow away any goods in a stranger's carriage, for perhaps one might arrive at Buxton towards the end of next week. It is arranged that Elizabeth should go with me; the earliest day that we *can* go is Wednesday : the latest I can allow Friday. I hope all the party will approve of this arrangement, and forgive me for estranging one of their present companions in consideration of my bringing another. Can you make out my writing always? You will observe that it varies with the pen, paper, time &c. I am going to see your Aunt, Lady Macartney.* My Father and Mother were there the other day. I have not seen your Papa since I returned to Town, but will call to-morrow. You might have observed that I was in Town in time for Post as I franked a letter to Aunt de V.

Why should you be *shocked* when you declare that you are quite as anxious to see me as I am to see you? Do you think I shall be jealous? No, I wish to be in this as in all things *toujours d'accord*. I long for your answer to my two letters from Cobham and Sandgate. I think 18 sides of paper on Monday. You see how sure I make of my Emma's constancy. I hope you have written to my Mother. Do so if you have not. Francis Forde has been here to-day. Tommy Vesey yesterday. I suspect we shall be at Buxton as soon as the latter, as he is going with one of the Talbots to Ingestre for two days, and starts on Monday. He dines with

*Emma's great-aunt, daughter of John, third Earl of Bute.

us again to-morrow. Uncle James talks of going on Wednesday to Buxton; but I think you need not fear any great share of quizzing, apart from me. I am very sorry that the fine weather has failed to restore dearest Aunt de V's health. What makes you think I doubt your being anxious to see me? I fear my letters were written pettishly in consequence of the overtake in the Post. I did not mean it to be so. Adieu! my dearest love.

Your own attached

C.

MISS EMMA PARNELL TO LORD CLIFTON.

Buxton, June 19th.

My dearest Clifton,

I have to thank you for your long letter of the 15th (which if it had been twice as long again, would have been liked still better) and also for the dear little note of the 16th. I am so sorry you travelled all night from Buxton as you say you find night travelling is not good for you. I do quite approve of your determination not to take such rapid expeditions any more. By the bye I think if you have been in London, as I judge by the cover of Ly. de V's letter, you are very naughty not to have written a line to say something more of your plans, or rather of Lady E's plans. However, I believe this is an unreasonable accusation, and I flatter myself I shall get a dear letter to-morrow, and I hope it will be almost the last. Did you never know that there is a rock called the Lover's Leap about a mile from Buxton on the Bakewell road? We must walk there soon. I shall shew it to you, I hope, before very long. We have had such delightful weather for some time past. I only want your presence to make Buxton quite delightful. I think I shall be a little sorry to leave this place. Would you rather be here for some time longer or at Abbeyleix ? I think Abbeyleix will be in great beauty. I hear your brother is come or coming over. Will he be of the Abbey party ? I hope he will, I want to see him very much. Only one thing makes me tremble a little at the thoughts of being introduced to your relations—I am afraid they will not think me half good enough or pretty enough for you, whom, I know they all think so highly of—and deservedly. The copy of verses are not intended for the flames, neither did you expect they would thus be disposed of, I am sure. I have restored them to the original owner. I don't know why you should have supposed we thought so little of your poetical effusions. We are just returned from church. I don't think you will thank me for this stupid letter : to tell the truth I have but one idea in my head just now, and that is on the subject of your coming. And I find it rather difficult to turn my thoughts to anything else. I am sure you will not be displeased to learn that such is the case, although those around me might reasonably be so. I am not affronted either at the dark complexion or the term of slight reproach, or at any other signification of the word gypsey, which has now in my ears something endearing, from the many associations connected with it. Do you remember coming every now and then from your book and your sopha, to examine what progress 1 had made in my copy of the Gypsey ? I remember almost every word and look of yours addressed to me at Abbeyleix, and particularly those pleasant mornings spent in the way I have just mentioned. And how vexed I was with Catherine for taking you out to ride one day. By the bye, I must beg, when we meet again, that you will not think of giving up riding because I do not ride. I know you will not always be so complimentary, so you may as well begin at once. I remember all the time you were here, you hardly ever rode, and I am afraid I was the cause of your neglecting it. I am sure it is best for you to take a good deal of exercise—so if you forget it, I shall put you in mind, and send you out riding every day, and shall only make one request, that you will come back in time to walk a little with me.

> Yours very affectionately.
> EMMA PARNELL.

I have relapsed into bad writing, and almost deserve another little *lecture* on carelessness.

LORD CLIFTON TO MISS EMMA PARNELL.

> Berkeley Square,
> June 20th, 1825.

My dearest Love,

Thanks for your dear letter received this morning. I believe it is now settled that we should leave this about twelve or one o'clock on Friday, and hope to be at Buxton Saturday night. I hope you will not attribute this delay to any indisposition on my part to join you. You little know me if you do. The fact is, that as it is settled that Beppy should accompany me, I have given her the utmost possible time, to enable her to have a peep at Cobham, &c., and she is to come to Town on Friday morning to proceed immediately with your Clif towards Buxton.

I had intended starting on Wednesday, which is the earliest day on which the carriage &c. would be ready, but I am sure your kind and affectionate heart will derive pleasure from a slight sacrifice of our pleasure, for the sake of others. I am delighted that you should have derived pleasure from my letter from Cobham : it was written with a great deal of satisfaction ; tears, I might almost say, of joy, on answering your inestimably precious example of kindness and affection. I am indeed prepared to love with the entire power and capacity of my heart, while I receive a like return ; I leave it to naturalists to determine which is the most capable of affection, the heart of man or woman. I feel that mine is no common love : it never could have been so with any woman whom I was to make my wife : the measure of it depends on the correspondent feeling in a certain quarter, which I never doubted, and which every word I have heard, or read from my dearest Emma strengthens and confirms. I must now go and take my perspective lesson : but I do not get on much. Thanks for the portraits.

Perspective over, but I am so confused in my thoughts that I do not as I hoped pick up the rules, so as to be able to explain them. I should like you to take a few lessons by and bye, if it can be managed. I cannot for the life of me draw a straight line. And now, dearest love, I must go on with the more engaging part of my letter.

Your affection and love will be everything to me as I know they will lead you to do everything that you think most grateful to their object. Do not be apprehensive of my being disappointed by what I find out after I know you better : if I am not disappointed in this particular, if I enjoy your undivided love and affection all other will be minor objects. You cannot think how I long for the time when we may uninterruptedly enjoy each other's society in quiet and comfort. You must not be angry with me for being anxious and impatient, for I do really look forward to the possession of you as my dearest wife with more intensity or anxiety than I describe. I am living on pins and needles all this week, for as the time of our meeting approaches I become more and more impatient.

What a collection of nonsense I have been writing, but your indulgence will, I know, not be wanting. Pray excuse me, love, for it is for your sake that I feel and write so. When I am writing to you, instead, as in other cases, of being weary and anxious to close my letter, I invariably come to the end of my paper without expressing half what I wish to say. Tell me is it delightful to you to have me in this state? I am sure it is, for we certainly (am I too confident?) do reciprocally feel most tenderly towards each other. I do not wish to write in a loaded strain, but I feel so strongly that I cannot help giving vent to the warmth of my affection, and you may at least depend upon my sincerity. It never has been my way to flatter or say a word I do not mean, and least of all should I say so to you. Do you like my moralizing turn?

I shall require your consoling aid, as I fear I am disagreeable to my family in consequence of being absorbed by one subject. My mother was talking to a German woman this morning, of whom she has heard an excellent character. I fancy she has written about her, and your answer must be directed to me by return of Post.

Lady Macartney was at dinner when I called, and I am to go to-morrow with Lord J. Stuart to visit her. I understand that the utmost stretch of voice is necessary to make *our* aunt hear. The account you give of the difference between your principles and practice, is exactly what I feel with regard to myself. With good principles and love for each other I think we shall stand a fair chance of being happy and of improving each other in practice. Uncle James does not mean to go to Buxton. I must bring the Italian Grammar after all. Tommy dined here, and started this morning, but I think he will not be with you before Thursday or Friday. I do not like Lady Morgan, which is very uncharitable indeed, as I never saw her, nor do I wish it. Nothing that I can help shall delay my going to you : I am too anxious even to let the Sybil interfere. I am surprised you had not received my letter from Sandgate before you sent your's off. I hope it will be an excuse for a letter to-morrow. I am not quite sure that I shall be pleased with Lady P's sentiments. I fancy them a little too gloomy and recluse : however I shall be glad to see her letter and be undeceived. I will spare your curls till I can see them. Mr. and Mrs. Alington were spending the honeymoon at Matlock, were they not, on May 20th.

This (June 20th) is a day of a different complexion to me, as on this day 1823 my dear sister died.* Only think of our having been engaged a long calendar month. All but the first ten days has been long indeed—three weeks have appeared an age. I do not think sweet Imogen will ever give me cause to be jealous, and I am not of such a disposition. No Posthumus.—What a hideous cross little face you have drawn ! I was forced to shew both and said you were between the two.

Farewell, my dearest love. Write one more answer if it be but a note to your loving and affectionate

C.

Miss Emma Parnell to Lord Clifton.

Buxton, June 20.

My dearest Love,

So you have made up your mind to come here. I hope you will not delay setting out any longer than Friday, for if you do not set out till Monday, you could not arrive till we had gone many a mile away from poor dear Buxton ! ! !

You think a great deal more about my *trousseau* than I do myself. I assure you I don't know much about it, and never could or can take much interest in satins and silks. I mean to reform in that respect however, and will make myself learn to think as much about it as it is fitting I should. Car. is the good-natured person who has taken upon herself all the trouble of the affair. Your Aunt de V. thinks your head is full of nothing else

*Lady Mary Brownlow.

146

a great deal to handsome .!!

EMMA PARNELL.
Drawn by herself, 1825.

but imperials. Now I will not allow that to be the case, at least if it is, I hope I am the *Crown-Imperial.* You know there is a flower so-called. What nonsense I am writing. I am so glad your sister is coming and I believe I may as well tell the truth and say that I am quite delighted at the idea of seeing you again. I have begun on a note instead of a letter because I don't think I have time to spare.

As to the "vague report" you mention, I don't know whether it is so arranged or not. I should not wonder however if it was pretty near the truth. Why should you care when it is, if you are coming to Abbeyleix with us? Did you not like being there last time as you seem to be in a hurry to get away from it? Farewell till Saturday, which day I suppose will bring you here. Give my love to Lady E. and tell her I am very glad she is coming.

Yours very affecly.,

EMMA.

LORD CLIFTON TO MISS EMMA PARNELL.

Berkeley Square,
June 21st, 1825.

I have only time for a little note to-date, my dearest Emma, in answer to your dear letter just received. I am going to see Aunt Macartney and have various things to do. I wish if you have not before given me information in a previous letter, you would send Samuel as soon as you get this to Leek with a line to say whether you positively leave Buxton on Monday and which line you take. I write this because by a letter received yesterday from Johnny it appears that he is coming over this week and if by waiting a few hours we might have the pleasure of seeing him, I am sure you would not grudge those few hours, and few as possible they shall be if any, dearest love. You cannot be more impatient for the moment of meeting than I am ; indeed I almost fear I am thought ill-naturedly so here ; for I will not give way to any plan for delay, nor have I intimated a thought of staying to see Johnny, but I feel that it would be ill-natured towards Elizabeth, and unbrotherly on my own part to go off just at the moment he is about to arrive. I have to-day not time to answer your letter particularly, but will just read it over a 3rd or 4th time to see whether anything occurs. Why do not you lecture me about bad and careless writing ? I have done—" a word to the wise ! ! " I was in London to frank Aunt de V's letter, but merely because I could not settle with E. about going I did not write. They were out. My brother will I trust be of the Abbey party. Tremble not, my love, at the thoughts of being introduced to my relations ; I take all responsibility on my shoulders. I remember with pleasure all about the dear Gipsy at Abbeyleix. I believe I looked more at the living G. than Mr. Trench's picture. By the way, both John and W. Trench are in Town. Are you getting a habit, because I think the dun pony would be quiet enough to carry you, and I will not scold or quiz, like Billy Vesey. Exercise is certainly good for me, and for you too in moderation. As to my being with you to walk or what not, it is not necessary to

148

make any request, I am too fond of being with you, and too selfish to need it.

God bless you, dearest,

Yours very affectionately,

C.

I am just come from Chiswick much pleased with the handsome old lady.* She promises to send you a note by me. One more adieu! $\frac{1}{2}$ past 8.

I have only written by way of caution, not at all intending to make any alteration in our plans, if I can help it. I am sure you will understand my meaning and give me credit for the most earnest wish to see you as soon as possible, not to part more for a day longer than necessity requires.

C.

MISS EMMA PARNELL TO LORD CLIFTON.

Buxton, Tuesday.

My dearest love,

I have nothing in the world to say, so only write for the pleasure of writing. I hope we shall hear to-morrow from you what day you set out on your journey. I hope your *tete a tete* party will be an agreeable one. I shall ask Lady Elizabeth (when I know her well enough) what you entertained her with all the weary way. Vanity makes me think that I might be occasionally mentioned, when you had exhausted every other subject. Remember that you will not find us here most likely, if you delay beyond Friday. We have just lost the most agreeable people we have ever had here. Mr. and Mrs. Alington. They are really a loss, both such very nice people. I think my dearest cousin

* Countess Macartney.

Tommy is using us very badly in delaying so long to pay us a visit. I suppose he thinks Buxton a very stupid place, and so it must be for young men. Perhaps you found it stupid too when you were here, but if you did, you must be a great hypocrite for you appeared to like this place (to say nothing of its inhabitants) very much. I am longing to see your sister, and hope she will like me. Do you think she will? I must draw now, for I want to finish my little picture before you come. You know it is for your Aunt de V. You must have got Miss Maria, and what I fear you will not value so much as it resembles me more than her, namely the other little portrait. Tell me what you think of it. I know too well how much you admire Miss M. Webster, and am too jealous to make any enquiries about her.

Yours most affectionately,

EMMA PARNELL.

Will you ask your sister or Miss Wingfield to be so kind as to send the enclosed directions to the shoemaker as I find the pair of shoes sent do not fit me quite. Excuse my writing about such things, my dearest Clifton, and believe me ever

Yours most affecly,

EMMA PARNELL.

What do you think of my good old grand Aunt and Godmother Lady Macartney, who added the beautiful name of Jane, to your detestation, making altogether "Imogen."

"EMMA."

There is a parcel of gloves coming for me directed to you, to Berkeley Square. Don't open them, but bring them here *s'il vous plait*. How do you like my own picture and Miss Maria?

MISS EMMA PARNELL TO LORD CLIFTON.

Buxton, June 22nd.

My dearest love,

Many thanks for your long letter, which really made me feel ashamed of myself, knowing that two shabby little notes were the sum total of all that I had honoured you with this week. But then you know, there is a reason, I shall have nothing to say when we meet if I exhaust all my topics now. I dare say you do not fear the danger of a lady's tongue being stopped for want of something to say, as it is their custom in general to talk on whether they have anything to say or not. I wish Saturday was already come, though indeed I do not wish that it had been differently arranged, but am pleased that your sister should have time to go to Cobham. I like your letter very much; it was doubly welcome, on account of yesterday having been a blank day, during great part of which my thoughts were devoted to the consideration of what might be in the letter I expected and received from you this morning. We had everybody in the place here last night. Mr. Spencer, Catherine's friend, said I was in a blessed state of abstraction, so to prove to him that I did not choose to be thought so, I began a most animated conversation with him on poetry &c., as he is a poet himself I thought the subject would please, and we are to go and read poetry with him (that is he is to read some poems to us) on Thursday evening. Lady de Vesci gave me a very pretty book at Manchester which I have lent to Mr. Spencer to look over before Thursday's party. I have not got it by me, but I feel tempted to send you some very pretty lines which I learned out of it, in hopes that you would like them. They will perhaps amuse you on the journey: as I calculate you will receive this letter just before you leave town. You can tell me, not write to me, whether you think them pretty. I am very glad you are learning perspective. I can guess that you are looking forward to becoming a teacher of that most puzzling science, and I suppose also, you flatter yourself you will have a very docile pupil. I remember you told me one day that you thought me very tractable. I don't think I will write any more for the reason I mentioned in the beginning of this epistle. Dearest love, what a naughty girl I am to make such a poor return for 8 pages full of the most affectionate and kindest feelings. But you know the only rival you have is the Sybil, and it is for her sake I mean to resign my pen, as soon as it will be so good as to stop. Your dear Aunt likes it very much, and I shall have great pleasure in offering it to her when it is finished. About the German woman, will you tell your mother that Lady de Vesci desires me to say that there is a person already engaged, Lady Henry has done us this service and from all accounts she is a very good one. I am not very sorry that "Uncle James" is not coming. If you knew how he quizzed me last winter because I would not speak as much to him as formerly, you would not wonder at my being a little in awe of him. I am longing for Saturday night to arrive, you know we go on Tuesday morning. What a large party we shall be altogether.

Yours most affectionately,

EMMA JANE PARNELL.

Will you forward the enclosed to Mr. Mclean, dentist, Stephens Green, North Dublin, as upon his seeing me on Monday the 4th July depends the welfare and beauty of the teeth of Miss Emma Parnell. Dearest Clifton, this is decidedly the very last letter I mean to write to you, so make the most of it and set a proper value on it.

LORD CLIFTON TO MISS EMMA PARNELL.

Berkeley Square,
June 22nd, 1825.

Dearest M A,

I have only a moment to spare, but write principally to say that I hope I may not have occasion now to put off going to you a moment longer than was intended. Beppy is just off for Cobham and is to be back in good time on Friday, when we proceed northwards. I think we shall be late (say 10) at Buxton on Saturday Night, but I will write tomorrow.

I have been to Hounslow to see a Cavalry Review this morning. Thanks for your note and Aunt de V's. I suppose you leave Buxton on Monday. I long to see you, dearest love, I hope 1 shall ere many days are gone by. I am puzzled about your shoes, which I fear will not be well done.

I shall not order so many pair as you mention, as you may do so yourself here or at Paris.

Yr. affectionate,

C.

Buxton,
June 23rd, Thursday.

I believe I told you yesterday that the letter I then sent off should be the last I would write to you, but you see one day has changed my determination and as I have found a good pen, I believe I shall not think it necessary to restrict myself to one sheet of paper, so I hope you will have time and inclination to read a very long epistle. The Sybil is completely finished, and packed up in double and treble layers of silver paper, waiting till Lady de V. can get it framed. I hope you will think it tolerably well done. I feel satisfied with it myself and they all like it, but I had rather hear *you* say it was pretty than any one else. And now you may see the reason of my intentions of writing as much as I please, having no longer any other occupation. I think I have without meaning it paid you a bad compliment in my last sentence, but you must not understand it so, for indeed even drawing (which is you know my favourite pursuit) has not been found half so pleasant as letter-writing during the last three or four weeks that you have been away.

How long is it? I am sure I do not know. I never can recollect anything about weeks, months, and days, I only know that the time has gone *slowly*. I was a little disappointed to tell the truth when I found by your letter that you could not come on Saturday but indeed I could not wish it otherwise if your staying in town will be the means of your seeing your brother. I know very well how

I should feel if I had the least prospect of seeing any of my dear brothers, and I should be very much surprised if you were not anxious to see yours. I did not write to you to-day the instant I got your letter as you desired, because I knew that on Friday morning you would get my yesterday's letter in which I remember I told you that we should set off early on Tuesday morning, so you know my writing this morning was unnecessary. We go by Chester: for your convenience, Lord and Lady de V. say, they will not set out till Wednesday. What do they mean do you think by your convenience? That is my message; and I deliver it faithfully, and I think at all events we may understand from it that on Wednesday morning, not on Tuesday, we shall begin our peregrinations.

I am half sure we shall not see you for about a week, for I am sure you will not be able to tear yourself and sister away from your brother. Naughty Mr. Johnny! he ought to have arrived about a week ago. Don't you wish he had? We were to have gone to Castleton to day but it is put off till Saturday. I don't care much about seeing it for I hear it is more curious than beautiful. We have as yet heard nothing of Mr. Tommy except from you. I am glad you like my old great Aunt. She is a very good-natured old lady. Have you ever found out yet that I never answer your letters. I mean that I do not follow the general fashion of sitting with the letter received open before me, and then regularly setting to work and inventing something proper to be said. I just write on from my head or my heart (which ever it is) and then I like writing;

if you expected me to write a very good letter, I should not like writing to you at all. However I have your dear little note now open before me and I want to know what you mean by saying " a word to the wise " in reference to careless writing? I am afraid you mean that you are not pleased with my careless writing. I have a great mind to be saucy and say you are very hard to please, only that I could not in conscience tell such a story, knowing or at least hoping that you are pleased with me. Miss Kits is greatly delighted with the thoughts of having Lady E. soon with her, but she says that you and I are are no addition to the pleasantness of the party, that we are too much engrossed with each other to think of others. I made her confess all this, do not think she was so communicative of her own accord. She is a dear good-natured girl, and you must not tell her that I told you this. She said she was glad on my account that you were coming. That was very good-natured of her—was it not? How foolish I shall look if it should so happen that you should not receive this letter till after your return here. That would be the case if you set out on Friday, but I suppose it is not now likely that you should. Have you burnt my letters? I think I should be ashamed to see some of them again. I think I have been a little too affectionate in my style of writing to you. I hope you did not think so. I dare say you think me a very odd, unreserved kind of young lady, but you must make allowances for my natural disposition, which whatever faults may accompany it, is certainly sincere. And then you know I have been accustomed to be much less controulled and watched over than other girls, and have done and said what I liked since I was fifteen. I used to make myself very disagreeable at one time by saying too much what I thought when I disliked anybody. I think in my old age I have learnt to restrain my words and looks in this respect, but it is far more difficult to keep them in proper order when the sentiment within is love instead of hatred. It is very odd how one changes as one grows old. I am very glad that I am changed for I do not think you would have liked me formerly. Will you tell me all your history some day or other, I like to know how and under what circumstances people's characters and dispositions and habits become what they are. I will give you leave to embellish it a little so as to make it up into an interesting narration. How beautiful Abbeyleix will look when we arrive there. By the bye, as to riding, I wish I was not such a coward, for I see you would like me to ride, and it must be such a pleasant way of seeing the country : I am sure I should like it after a little time. I hope I shall not hear from you again, and yet I hope you will not forget to write if you do not. Farewell till then and believe me to be yours most affectionately attached,

Emma Parnell.

If my shoes or any other things are done when you leave London will you bring them with you, *s'il vous plait.*

Berkeley Square,
June 23rd, 1825.

Only one letter to-day, and that from my dearest love. How delightful! for I am not fond of
answering Canterbury applications, and to reply to
yours is unqualified pleasure. I expect Elizabeth
in Town by 12 to-morrow, shall order the horses at
one, and be content if we get off by two. Probably
sleep at Newport Pagnell and have 110 miles to do
on Saturday, which with a pair of horses, and *your
imperials* will be slow work. I dare say we shall not
be at Buxton much before 12, so you must order our
rooms to be got ready, and go to bed. We shall see
you on Sunday morning at Church, if not before!!!
Beppy and I provide ourselves with books for the
weary way, in case we should be tired of talking.
You say I am a hypocrite if I do not like Buxton.
Now I never professed to like it but for its inhabitants, and should I think die of the blue devils if I
was obliged to stay there after you have left it. As
long as you stay there it is well enough!! Shall I
take my ponies to Ireland? Or send them back?
How you do rave about Miss M. W. I will answer
for it you will not be as jealous of her as of your own
picture which you call her's! You are a dear good
girl to have written on Tuesday: I did not expect
a letter this morning as I knew that you would have
none to answer. However I have been pretty attentive as far as frequency and length of writing goes.
N'est ce pas? I do not know which will be first for
number of letters, nor do I care so that we are pretty
equal.

I have got the various little things for you, indeed two writing boxes that you may choose; for after I had procured one, I found another which I liked better. You shall have which you please. I have a large box which is intended for you by and bye, but of which the key is kept in this part of the world, so you can only see its case. The workbox is just arrived. Not so pretty as I wish. I will bring the "Crusaders" and "To-day in Ireland." If I hear anything from Paris or have any other news I will write by and bye from the House of Commons or elsewhere. I have to go to the City, and much to do. Ever, dearest Emma, your most affectionate

C.

Lord Clifton and Lady Elizabeth Bligh duly arrived at Buxton on Saturday, June 25th, in the new chariot with all its imperials and boxes which Lord Clifton had been at so much pains in arranging for his beloved Emma's convenience. Early in the following week, Lord and Lady de Vesci and their whole party started on their journey to Ireland, travelling "through the beautiful Welsh scenery" as Emma describes it in a letter written some seven months later from Cobham to her husband during their first separation, he having been obliged to go to Ireland on business. She continues "You were a gay bachelor on your way to a wedding in Ireland when you last went through Llangollen. Do you remember how sick Miss Emma Parnell was and how she made a pillow of your broad shoulder to sustain her head."

This delightful journey was soon over, and in about a week the happy party arrived at Abbeyleix where the engaged couple had time to look through and compare the letters of congratulation which they had received from their numerous friends and relations, a few of which only can be mentioned here. One of the first letters received by Emma was from her sister Mary, who had married Lord Henry Moore in August of the preceding year 1824. Lord Henry unfortunately had fallen into ill health soon after their marriage and was then staying at Bath for the benefit of his health. Lady Henry wrote from thence on May 25th to express her "pleasure and delight, I assure you tears of joy ran down my cheeks yesterday, when I had Papa's letter." Lord Henry, who died in the following August, also wrote—"Weak as I am and scarcely able to hold my pen, I cannot resist adding a few lines to congratulate my dearest Emma, which I do from my soul. As for his lordship, I think he is the most fortunate of God's creatures."

Her uncles George and Lionel Dawson both wrote most affectionately, the latter writing from Brussels, says: "Nothing that we have heard for a long time has made us half so happy." He then refers to her having left them at Dover in the winter of 1823 "I am sorry you should have supposed I could be angry with you for not coming on here with us. You were your own mistress and of course at perfect liberty to please yourself. Your company would have added to our pleasure, and therefore it was selfishness that could alone have caused the slightest displeasure. You talk, my dear Emma, of obligation. You are under none to me whatever, quite the contrary. Your father paid all expenses and you and Mary did us a great favour by living with us. If you were happy at Emo with us as you were kind enough to say, I'm afraid it was the place more than any exertions on my part that made you so . . . You did just as you pleased and the only favour I ask is, if some day or other we should happen to meet in your house that you allow me to do the same. Many thanks for your enquiries after our dear little children, all are well and growing daily, I am sorry to say, more like their father."

Lord Clifton's brother John writes from Rheims, where he was attending the Coronation of Charles X in the suite of Lord Granville, the British Ambassador at Paris.

May 30th, 1825.

Dearest Clifton,

I will not allow the Duke's Messenger to go without a few lines (hurried as I am immediately after escaping from the Ceremony of the Installation of the Knights of St. Esprit) to congratulate you upon what I now consider as certain. May you, my dear brother, be as happy as I wish you, and as, I think, you deserve to be in the new State you are, I hope, about to enter, and I am sure you will be as much so as is given to this sublunary condition to aspire to. I shall be, as you can imagine, most anxious to make the acquaintance of one who is to be so nearly connected with me. I am sure I shall like her as I never would disapprove of your taste. I have not time to enter into any of the particulars of the Ceremonies which I have witnessed these few last days, but must now content myself with saying that the Coronation was a very fine and improving sight, superior perhaps to the religious part of our own. I was disappointed at hearing nothing from home by last Messenger.

Ever your very affectionate Brother,

J. D. Bligh.

Lord Clifton at 46, Berkeley Square to the Hon. John Duncan Bligh at Paris.

June 3rd, 1825.

My dearest Johnny,

Many thanks for your letter from Rheims just arrived, and for the congratulations which I knew would be cordial from my dearest brother. I cannot inform you when or where the ceremony is to take place, but I suppose in about a month or less and I hope at Cobham. Aunt de V. is, I think for Abbeyleix, but it would be settled much more expeditiously and comfortably at Cobham. I have got leave for the Doctor* to officiate—he tells me he expects another brat in ten days. I long to shew Emma to you as well as the rest and hope you will not find it inconvenient or to interfere with the Paris gaieties to be at the Wedding. I want you to send me a pair of shoes, which should be a little larger, and a little narrower than those of the *grande Mademoiselle Powerscourt*, as a pattern ; E. is about the same height, but a little stouter than Emily. I am sure you will like her for her own sake as well as mine. You will be glad to hear that my father with his usual kindness and affection has arranged matters for settlement etc. in such a manner as to expedite the business, and I hope it will not be delayed longer than the time I mentioned. I can tell you no London news, as my attention has been occupied lately elsewhere. I came to Town on Tuesday morning and after attending the Court of K.'s Bench for two days with G. Martin, appeared against an unfortunate namesake who was found guilty of the assault, and consequently forfeited his recognisances so that he may now be shut up at any moment. He was there and looked composed and unconcerned. The cause was very ill conducted by Gurney and Berens, and I was almost afraid at one

*Rev. John Stokes, Vicar of Cobham, familiarly called "the Doctor."

time, and merely through their misconduct, that the Jury in consideration of the weight of the recognisances and consequent punishment, might have been led by his Counsel, Mr. Mereweather, to vote it accidental. How truly so you may judge. However it is all settled now, thank God, and I hope we shall hear no more of it—I hope your Lisbon *attacheship* may prove pleasant. I am sorry you are leaving Paris. I long to see you dearest Johnny.

I am as ever,

Your affectionately attached brother,

CLIFTON.

Other letters give some idea how much Emma Parnell was liked and admired in the North of Ireland. Isabella Bayley, daughter of Mr. and Mrs. Forde of Seaforde, writes: "Emma has always been a great favourite of mine and I need scarcely say her marriage with a cousin I love so well will not diminish that affection. Clayton desires his kindest congratulations, he is a great admirer of Emma's; there were *many* to dispute the prize with you. I am sure Emma will be a great favourite with all your family."

The Rev. John Brownlow, writes from Lurgan: "I must consider that you are a very fortunate fellow, for Miss Parnell's accomplishments, mental as well as personal, are a theme of admiration, and from all I know, I can but say that Lady Clifton will be the happiest of her sex. Alicia begs her kindest love to you and begs me to say that she coincides in all I have said."

To this may be added a missive from Elm Park, Armagh: "Congratulations to our much loved Cousin on his approaching happiness which we hope may be long and lasting. As none of the daughters of Eve ever possessed before so much beauty or so much virtue, we feel at a loss for words sufficiently poetic to express our admiration of the fair object of his affections. Signed by Catherine Brownlow, Anna Elizabeth Close, M. Brownlow, Kathne. C. Brownlow, Isabella Elizabeth Brownlow, Francis Brownlow, M. Close."

Few details have reached us about the wedding, but we know that among those present were the Viscount and Viscountess de Vesci, the Earl and Countess of Darnley, with the Hon. John and Lady Elizabeth Bligh and also Sir Henry Parnell, his daughter Caroline, and the Hon. and Rev. William Wingfield. The marriage was solemnized on July 26th, 1825, in the old church in the grounds at Abbeyleix, long since disused. The ceremony was performed by the Rev. John Stokes, Vicar of Cobham, who had been tutor to Lord Clifton, and who was till his death the valued and loved friend of the Darnley family. The happy pair went off in their new chariot to Clifton Lodge to spend the honeymoon.

Several of the members of the wedding party tried their hands at verses for the occasion, and though not marked by any great poetic merit, they help us to picture the happy and affectionate family party.

LORD CLIFTON TO VISCOUNTESS DE VESCI.

Could I command Golconda's mine
Or gather all the gems that shine
    Beneath the trackless sea ;
However they might deck thy dress
Little would all combined express
    The love I bear to thee.

This trifling token of that love
As well as jewels rare may prove
    How dear to me thou art ;
To my beloved Aunt as well
This unassuming brooch may tell
    The feelings of my heart.

Such kindness as is known by few
From childhood's earliest hour I knew
    Since first my tongue could spell ;
Mid boyhood's mirth, in manhood's prime
More than can be expressed in rhyme
    Thy worth I've known right well.

But now increased a thousandfold
How can my debt of thanks be told
    Since to a hundred more
Thy kindness adds the last, the best
The boon that's dearest to my breast
    Than ought I knew before.

Yes—to my Uncle dear and thee
Aunt Fanny, ever twin'd shall be
    My debt of gratitude :
As long may Emma's gentle mind
Such friends to value feel inclined
    And on their kindness brood.

Amid glad scenes of mutual love
That here begin, O, may we prove
    Our gratitude to you ;
And through each year of waning life
May both the husband and the wife
    In wedlock prove as true.

                Abbeyleix, July, 1825.

By Emma Parnell.

I will not say I love the well
    Too plainly that these eyes declare
What these fond lips so often tell,
    Useless it were to vow or swear.

I will not say thou art more dear
    To me than all the world beside
Nor wish to thee unfolded were
    My thoughts of thee, my love ! my pride !

I will not say how fondly still
   I'll love thee till life's day is o'er
I will not say that grief and ill
   Shall only make me love thee more.

I will not tell thee I am blest
   To think how true thy love for me
Nor say to heaven how oft addrest
   Dearest, my prayers have been for thee.

But I will bid thee love as well
   Thou could'st not *better* love than me
And oft let looks of kindness tell
   That I am loved, dear Clif by thee.

                   July 18th, 1825.

SONNET AND VERSES BY THE EARL OF DARNLEY.

When youth and beauty bless the nuptial bed
And Cupid reigns in Hymen's sacred bowers,
How sweetly glide away the fleeting hours.
Th' enraptured pair nor care nor sorrow dread,
To lasting bliss by flattering fancy led.
Yet oft a tempest on the sunshine low'rs :
And oft a serpent lurks beneath the flowers,
By hearts perverse, and minds corrupted bred,
But when pure hands are joined, when passing show
Pure hearts reciprocate esteem approve,
When mild religion sanctions ardent love
And human ties seem ratified above
Love's flowers can never fade, must ever blow
Such bliss—may Edward and his Emma know !
                        D.

Let others sing the siege of Troy
   Or celebrate the Golden Fleece
Far better theme my muse employ
   She sings the praise of Abbeyleix.

A sister and a brother there
   Two nephews and a little niece
Must all in turn her homage share
   Whene'er she sings of Abbeyleix.

But chiefly they, the Lord and Dame
   Awake her kindliest sympathies
Who knows them well, can never blame
   A song in praise of Abbeyleix.

What though no Gothic splendour there
   No sculptured forms of classic Greece
Though little ornament appear
   Yet all are pleased with Abbeyleix.

How like its owners long has stood
   This mansion of content and peace
Plain, unobtrusive, useful, good,
   The hospitable Abbeyleix.

How like them in each neighbouring glade
   Appear the widely spreading trees
Protecting all beneath their shade
   The fostering care of Abbeyleix.

And see the calm and silent Nore
   That flows unruffled by the breeze
To fertilize the neighbouring shore
   The flowery meads of Abbeyleix.

M.

The flocks and herds along the plain
  Full of the pasture stretched at ease,
See loaded with the ripening grain
  The well tilled fields of Abbeyleix.

Or rather to yon Village stray
  And higher praises sing than these
For there appear in full display
  The happiest fruits of Abbeleix.

There wealth attempts no vain parade
  Of ostentatious charities,
But comfort and content are made
  To mark the site of Abbeyleix.

Learning with industry combined
  Each visitor delighted sees
And learns to love with me, the kind
  And gentle pair of Abbeyleix.

By time exalted and refined
  Long may their happiness increase
And long may I a welcome find
  As heretofore at Abbeyleix.

But I must check my rhyming strain
  Or these dull lines will never cease,
So farewell till we meet again,
  My kind dear friends of Abbeyleix.

                                    D.

Abbeyleix, Monday, August 8th, 1825.

CHAPTER IV.

Honeymoon and Afterwards.

Lord Clifton at Clifton Lodge to Viscountess Powerscourt at Sandgate.

August 6th, 1825.

Dearest Aunt P.

Only think of my ingratitude. Here have we been ten days, and I have not thought of writing to my very dear relations at Sandgate. Indeed it is not through want of affection and love, of which I think they may be assured without my telling them, however I must trust to them to find a cause for this neglect, as well as for that of my dearest wife, and I think they will not attribute it to ennui.

To enter upon a history of my happiness would only be a repetition of an old story, nor could words do justice to my feelings, so I will let it alone. Suffice it to say that every hour's experience confirms me in the prudence of my choice, and I am more and more anxious to present my Emma to those I love, and who, I know, will love her for her own as well as for my sake. It was the source of no common satisfaction to me that she was approved of by her new Papa and Mama, of course the anticipation of the first interview was not unattended with anxiety, on that head I had ample reason to be satisfied. They are to come here on Monday. Of course we shall be most happy to see them, but I think the few days we have passed here have slipped away surprisingly quickly. We have entirely relinquished the idea of going to Italy this winter, so that I hope we shall meet at Cobham in the autumn. If not, we will go and see you, if you will have us. We shall probably, when we leave Ireland in a month or six weeks, go to Bath to see Lady H. Moore. Her situation, poor dear, is very critical, as in addition to her confinement which she expects daily, Lord Henry is in a state, I fear, almost desperate. I apprehend he is nearly in the last stage of consumption, but she, as is common in such cases, knows nothing of his danger. Give my affectionate love to Cat. and Em., undiminished by the intensity of that which I feel for my dearest wife.

Addio, carissima zia, dal nipote amantissimo,

CLIFTON.

The happy honeymoon period of solitude passed only too quickly, and on August 8th Lord and Lady Darnley, Beppy and Johnny joined the young couple at Clifton Lodge. The latter says in his journal, "arrived at Clifton Lodge where we found Clifton and his Emma quite well and I hope as happy as they appeared to be."

Early in September, Lord and Lady Clifton went to Harrogate, and on September 10th were again joined by their family on the way to Bishopthorpe for a Musical Festival in York Minster. They stayed at Harrogate until October 7th exploring the surrounding country ; a map drawn by them is still preserved. They then proceeded to Cheltenham to visit Lady Clifton's sister, Lady Henry Moore, whose husband had died in August a few days after the birth of their child (Henry, afterwards Marquess of Drogheda). Lord Clifton wrote thence to his brother at Cobham.

LORD CLIFTON AT CHELTENHAM TO HON. J. D. BLIGH AT COBHAM.

October 10th, 1825.

My dearest Johnny,

I regret that it did not occur to me yesterday that a letter then written would probably reach you on your birthday ; as it is, I am sure you will think that my congratulations, though a day too late are not the less sincere ; nor is it necessary, my dear brother, to assure you how very truly I wish you every happiness that this world can afford, (What I now look upon as the greatest earthly happiness) I hope you may in good time be as happily married as I am. I hope we shall be with you about Friday, as we talk of leaving this place on Wednesday next, to return in November. I suppose you have been entertaining H.R.H. Prince Leopold last week, and I conclude have had a scrimmage or two in the preserves. By the way do not let Puckle Hill be hacked if you can help it, as I wish to entice Boghurst's birds in that direction.

I bought a horse at Harrogate, which will I think be a clever one if I have any luck with him, which I have not often in the horse line. Mr. Samuel will arrive in London towards the end of the week, I hope with knees etc. safe. Give my duty and love as usual, Emma sends her's also. I like my newly seen sister very much, she is very tranquil and composed. The baby is a nice one, and I hope our treasure is well, but I am rather huffed with Beppy for not writing one word about her paragon of infants.*

Addio, carissimo fratello. By the bye I have asked my other brother John to go to Cobham on his way to Edinburgh. Will you tell them so?

Your affectionate brother,

CLIFTON.

On October 14th, Lord and Lady Clifton arrived at Cobham for the first time since their marriage. Lord and Lady Darnley had taken great trouble to fit up some rooms for them in the north wing of the house and welcomed them most affectionately. They did their best to make Emma, who had never had a home of her own, feel that Cobham really was her home, and they constantly invited her relations to stay there. The first to come were her aunts, the Ladies Louisa and Anna Maria Dawson on October 27th of this year. Lady Louisa Stuart says about

---

* Their niece, Mary Brownlow.

COBHAM HALL.
From an old Engraving.

this visit; "Louisa and Anna did not leave Lady Macartney till the 26th, when they paid their niece, Lady Clifton, a visit at Cobham, Lord Darnley's, and were received by Lord and Lady Darnley with a cordiality highly gratifying."

With the exception of a short visit to London the Cliftons spent the rest of the winter at Cobham, the brothers and their father shooting every day with various friends. In February, Johnny left for St. Petersburg, having been appointed to attend the Duke of Wellington on a special mission; Lord Clifton was obliged to go to Ireland, leaving his wife at Cobham. He left on Thursday 23rd, put in an appearance at the House of Commons, posted a letter to his wife and reached Shrewsbury in the "Wonder" Coach at midnight on Friday.

LADY CLIFTON AT COBHAM TO LORD CLIFTON AT CLIFTON LODGE.

24th Feb., 1826.

Friday—just before dinner, for which I have just made my toilette.

My dearest darling Hubby,

Your sweet little letter was joyfully received by me this morning, although its appearance excited a great deal of laughter amongst the rest of the family; but I was so pleased with you for it. I think you will receive this at Clifton Lodge. How pleasant it will be to pass another honey-moon or moons there this summer. What a fine day for dear Cliffy's journey thought I to myself this morning, and I hope he will have a continuance of this fine weather till safely arrived on the shores of Green Erin, after which arrival you know you must expect rain in abundance or Erin would be Green no longer. I wonder whether you were very much interested in the debate on the Silk Trade last night, and whether there is any chance of my eyes being greeted to-morrow morning by an eloquent and appropriate speech delivered by that accomplished young nobleman Lord Clifton. I am quite sure that he could speak both eloquently and appropriately if he would take pains to do so.

Your Mama very kindly wanted me to take up my abode in the most inhabited side of the house, but I refused, and would not accept Emily or Beppy's offers either. So the faithful Windsor* and I passed the night very comfortably. Lord Darnley was so good-natured he would escort me to my room, although I told him not.

I have been busy at a certain little picture this morning, and have taken a good walk. Dinner is ready, I fear I cannot write much more. How I shall long for another letter. Dearest darling, pray take care of yourself, and don't put yourself in the way of getting chilled. I have a fire in my bed-room to supply the absence of caloric. May God

---

* Windsor was Lord Clifton's favourite dog, who always slept in his master's room, not altogether with Lady Clifton's approval.

JOHN, 4TH EARL OF DARNLEY; ELIZABETH, COUNTESS
OF DARNLEY; AND LADY CATHERINE BLIGH.

From miniature paintings after portraits
by John Hoppner, R.A.

bless and protect you, my dear love, and bring you back safe to your loving wife. Good bye, love, I don't know how to stop writing, but am your very affecte. Wifey.

EMMA CLIFTON.

LORD CLIFTON AT SHREWSBURY TO LADY CLIFTON AT COBHAM.

Midnight, 'twixt Friday and
Sat. (Feb. 1826).

My darling sweet and pleasant, here I am, *Wonder*fully conveyed hither, having by John Connor's assistance as nearly missed my passage as possible.

I will write from Holyhead if I can get a better pen.

Your most affectionate husband,

C.

Quite well, boils broke. I must wish myself many happy returns as my birthday is coming. God grant I may improve. Off at 5.

Mr. Vandeleur was one of my "Wonder" companions. I wonder what mischief he is bent on !

LADY CLIFTON AT COBHAM TO LORD CLIFTON AT CLIFTON LODGE.

February the 25th, 1826.

My dearest Cliffy,

I wish you many, many happy returns of your birthday my own dear love, and I will try in my prayers to-night to pray to God that every succeeding day and year of your life may bring you nearer to Him ; that so, through His grace, you may be found walking in the strait and narrow way which leadeth to life eternal whenever you are removed from this world. How much happier I am this 25th February than I was last. I had no kind affectionate husband then to make me happy with his fondness and affection. And I think that you are happier too, and that both of us have great reason to bless Him, who is the Giver of all good Gifts, for our happiness. Let us, dearest love, try to shew our gratitude by an earnest endeavour to live to God's glory, and for the good of our fellow-creatures. This has been a most beautiful day—I hope it has been so with you, particularly while you passed through the beautiful Welsh scenery. You were a gay bachelor on your way to a wedding in Ireland when you last went through Llangollen. Do you remember how sick Miss Emma Parnell was, and how she made a pillow of your broad shoulder to sustain her head ? I wonder whether you will cross to-morrow or not. I suppose I shall get a letter in a few days. I know there is no post to-day, but I am writing because I only mean to write a short letter to-morrow. Miss D'Arcy is still here and has drawn Beppy and Catarrh,* neither of them are favourably represented but both very like. Darling little Mary** is looking very pretty, and wished Uncle Kif many happy birthdays this morning. So did all the party in a most affectionate manner. Long John made a very nice little speech to me on the occasion, as I went into the luncheon room. W. W.*** went to Sandgate this morning.

*Catherine Wingfield.
**Mary Brownlow.
***William Wingfield.

Lord Darnley escorted me again last night, I mean to try and prevent him to-night, for I know it is very wrong and foolish to mind walking about the house alone. He goes to town on Monday. I believe your Aunt P. and the Wings have postponed their departure till Friday. I should like to be with you at the Lodge but I know you will get through your business much better without me. Pray remember me to Mr. Disney. You never told me whether your Father settled to have the house improved by a new staircase. Pray tell me and will you have some baskets of roses made on the plots of grass behind the house. Good bye my dear Hubby till to-morrow. I have dressed early that I might have a few quiet moments to write to you. I have let Emily* see the *darling* picture that I hope will be like you, and she thinks it all like but the nose, which does not project enough. I meant this for a very good likeness but see it is not.**

Your affectionate and dutiful Wifey

EMMA CLIFTON.

LORD CLIFTON AT BANGOR TO LADY CLIFTON AT COBHAM.

Penrhyn Arms,
Bangor, Saturday evening,
Feb. 25th, 1826.

I am sure my dearest Love will be glad to hear from me sooner than she expected, and I think she will approve of my reasons for halting here. It blows hard, and there is every prospect of a rough

*Emily Wingfield.
**A pen and ink sketch of Lord Clifton on a page of original letter.

passage, and I shall not lose any time if I pass through Dublin as I intend on Monday. Besides which I shall have an opportunity of examining my *beau-père's* bridge,* and most of all I shall be able to go to Church instead of spending my Sunday at Sea, which probably I could not have done at Holyhead as I do not think there is any English service; indeed I am not sure there is here, but I suppose the Cathedral will not be without it.—I have met with no mishaps on the journey, and got three or four hours sleep at Shrewsbury, and a good deal in the Coach—when I was stepping into it this morning who should appear but Francis Forde, just arrived from Oxford : who accompanied me this far, and is gone on to Holyhead. I mean now instead of sleeping a night in Dublin, to pass on to Clifton Lodge if I have a tolerable passage. You shall have a line from Dublin. I have just taken out and kissed my little locket, but I have not opened Miss D'Arcy's drawing, nor shall I till I have finished my letters, as the post is soon going out. I must write to Trefusis and Disney. Write me word if you wish me to do anything at C. Lodge in the way of flower garden or otherwise.

God bless you sweetest—My duty and love to those who expect it. Ever dearest,

Your affectionately attached husband,

CLIFTON.

* Sir Henry Parnell had been much concerned in the House of Commons with the promotion of the scheme of the road from Chester to Holyhead which comprised the Menai Suspension Bridge, erected by Telford.

Sunday, February 26th, 1826.

Mr. Stokes sends his love to you. We have had
a most beautiful day here. Mr. Stokes preached
one of Cooper's Sermons. I hope if you got to
Dublin to-day you went to hear Mr. Matthias preach
at the Bethesda. How very happy I shall be when
my *Presh Hubby* comes back. Mr. and Mrs. S. both
say that it is quite worth while to be separated in
order to know the joy of a re-union. I don't agree
with her at all. I opened Dr. Achat's letter thinking
it was a *bill* but I have read it and advise you not
to pay all the rent as he wishes, I think it would be
very inconvenient; his reply to the aspersion of
dirty which you cast on his house is quite spirited
and indeed I think it is rather our own fault in
trusting John Connor and his spouse. Baboo has
just given a sweet kiss for dear Uncle Kif. I wish
I could deposit it on the lips for which it is meant.
Good-bye dear darling love, and write soon to your
own little wife who is most affectionately yours.

EMMA CLIFTON.

February 26th, 1826.

I have been to Church, dearest love and have
dined and am just off for Holyhead. The Coach is
waiting for your

affectionate hubby

C.

Monday, Feb. 27th, 1826.

There has been a gay party of fifteen dining
here in honour of dear darling Hubby's birthday,
and also of Mr. Stokes', the old lady came here and
paid me a visit, and sent her most affectionate love
to her dear Clifton. Edward* dined with Miss
Brownlow, who is in great health and beauty and
sends a kiss to Uncle Kif. I love her so much, dear
little thing, and I think she has grown prettier and
nicer since you went. Perhaps it is that I have
more time to look at her, my eyes not being always
rivetted on your darling face. Indeed, I think if
you were as beautiful as Adonis, I could not like
looking at you more than I do now. Dearest Cliffy,
though you are away, I am very happy, often thinking what a blessing it is to have you for my own
dear husband, and how pleasant it is to meet daily
and hourly with so much affection and kindness as
is constantly shown me by your dear mother and
dear Beppy, not forgetting Lady P. and the Wings.
How delightful it will be to see you again, darling
Cliffy, and I am sure you will be the happiest man
in the world when you return to me, as I shall be
the happiest woman. The boys are in great spirits,
they had all manner of good things at dinner and
afterwards we all drank Lord Clifton's and Mr.
Stokes' health. There was a beautiful tower of
cakes and sweet things in the middle of the table
on which was a C with a coronet over it, and a long
streaming flag, composed of Canterbury silk, being

*Edward Stokes.

the gore of Beppy's gown which Mrs. Treadaway is now in the act of making I suppose. I shall be so glad when a letter comes with an account of your safe arrival in the city of Dublin. I conclude you are this evening at Clifton Lodge. We had another most beautiful day, and I was out a little, but not a great deal as I tired myself yesterday. I must confess that I think the time goes very slowly in dear hubby's absence. I have been busy at your picture to-day; Miss D'Arcy has promised to paint you in a brooch for me some day, she is a very good-natured unaffected person, but she would not be always a very pleasant companion for she talks so much. She says the whole place rings with Lord and Lady Clifton's happiness, And indeed in *my* opinion they are a very happy couple. Dearest Cliffy, how I do long to look at you and talk to you, but I know you are well employed. If I have not already subscribed to the Flax Society will you have my name put down, and will you enquire how the Scholars that Miss Warner teaches are going on. I assure you I mean to be very much interested in all these things when we go there in the Summer. The boys are making a dreadful noise, which rather confuses me.

Good-bye dearest love, may God bless you now and for ever, my dear dear husband, is the most sincere wish and prayer of your affectionate Wife,

EMMA CLIFTON.

ci-devant Emma Parnell.

Mr. Stokes' love.

9-30 p.m. Feb. 27th, 1826.

I am safe over the water, my dearest little wife, and have received your dear letter written the day I left you : to-night or to-morrow morning I hope to have another. I hope also that tho' short have been my letters you have had constant intimation of my movements since I left you. I am staying here with my friend Trefusis, and start to-morrow with Mr. Disney for Clifton Lodge. We had a rough passage of 11 and a half hours to-day, but I have eaten a good dinner and am quite well, thank God. I like your dear little letter very much, and present or absent delight in my precious wife, and thank God for so sweet a boon. I hope I may improve by your dear example, precious love. I am glad I staid yesterday at Bangor as altho' I may not have done much good by so doing, there is a pleasure in reflecting that you have at least endeavoured to do right. I will write from Clifton Lodge, but you will probably not receive my letter for two or three days after this, not till Sunday.

Adieu my dearest love, may God in His mercy protect you now prays your affectionate and loving husband,

CLIFTON.

LADY CLIFTON AT COBHAM TO LORD CLIFTON AT
CLIFTON LODGE.

Feb. 28th, 1826,
ten minutes past six.

My best beloved Hubby,

Having kissed and read your two dear letters at intervals during the day, I have settled myself very comfortably being first and alone in the library, to enjoy the pleasure of writing to my own sweet Cliffy. In the first place I must tell you that I was very much delighted and surprised this morning by the sight of your letters. I am indeed pleased with you for writing both nights to me, for I am sure you must have been very tired each night, and I would not let myself expect you to write, as I wished you to go to bed the instant you arrived. I greatly approve of your having halted at Bangor, and hope you heard a good sermon at the Cathedral. Also that the vol. of Cooper's Sermons was not neglected. I am afraid you must have had a rough passage yesterday. I took a walk soon after break-fast and I remember that although the day was very pleasant and sunny there was a good deal of wind. I hope to hear an account of your safe arrival on Thursday. I hope my sweet love takes his *medecines etc.* and I hope that he takes proper care of himself in every way. You know you *ought* to take more care of yourself than formerly as you are my darling husband. Beppy desires me to remind you of the sad condition of that boys' school in Athboy for which your Pip is at much expense and which owing to the infirm and stupid master it has got cannot do much good. Ask your father to have a

N.

master from the Kildare Street School. I wish you would call on Mrs. Warner and her daughter who have been so attentive to the schools. You know you ought to shew that we are all pleased with them for being so good about it. As to the flower-garden I think it would be a great improvement to have one, but you are a much better judge than I am how it would be best done. Miss *Dare-say* has drawn a striking likeness of Lady P. and of Emily and she is working at a likeness of your Mama which promises to be very like. I have been out to-day, a most delightful day it was. Beppy has had a very bad face-ache. I am afraid Lady P. and the Wings are going this week. My dear love, I don't recollect any news and so will here conclude, assuring you that I love you most dearly, and long for the happy moment when I shall see you again.

Your most affectionately attached Wife,

Emma Clifton.

All send their love to my dear *presh* hubby. Which room do you sleep in? the first we slept in or the second? does Mrs. Gunning supply you well with apple-pies and *Charlotte de Pommes.* We had what Beppy calls a Clifton de Pommes to-day, and I ate some in honour of you. Once more, adieu. Windsor performed a very ingenious feat last night. I had turned the arm-chair with its face to the wall in order to keep him from getting in. And in the morning I found that he had managed to climb up and was lying very comfortably.

Wednesday, March 1st, 1826.

My dearest love and Presh Hubby,

I got another little letter this morning dated Bangor and am now in great spirits at the idea of getting by to-morrow's post an account of your safe arrival in Dublin. I am very well and in great spirits, which I know you will be glad to hear. There was a fine long letter from Johnny this morning dated from Berlin. He arrived on the 17th at 5 o'clock in the morning and pulled Lord Castlereagh* out of bed and breakfasted with him. He did not see much of him however but was to meet him at dinner at Lord Clanwilliam's. Lord C. is coming back with Lord Clanwilliam in May. Lord Clanwilliam invited Johnny to stop at Berlin on his way back and proceed with them via Paris. Lord Fincastle arrived at Berlin after incessant travelling and fatigue. Johnny dined with the Duke of Cumberland, and the King and Royal Family were there. Prince George, a funny little boy like the Duke of Clarence. Johnny is in very good spirits, but finds it cold enough already. Nothing can exceed the attention paid to the Duke of Wellington by the Prussians, all along. Everybody crowding to see him at Berlin. Johnny went to the theatre and to two great balls besides, and left Berlin the 20th so he must have been busy enough when he was there. Miss D'Arcy has drawn a really lovely and faithful picture of your Mama. She has drawn me in colours, I think if you would give her your pencil

* Lord Darnley's nephew, son of his sister Catherine.

187

drawing she would give it to you.   To-morrow, dear
love will have been absent one long week, and
therefore his return is one week nearer.   I wrote a
long letter to our new housemaid yesterday full of
instructions.   I hope she and fair *Squint-eye* will
not fight.   There was a letter from Aunt de V. this
morning, she is afraid Aunt Minny has beat her
niece, as she looks like it.   Mr. J. B. has a bet upon
me against Mrs. Burton.   She was Miss Power,
close to Abbeyleix and was married the week before
we were entered into that happy state.   A most
happy state we have found it, have we not, dearest
Cliffy ?   I am afraid I cannot write any more.
Hubby's picture grows every day more and more
like.   I am in spirits about it as Miss D. thinks it
very like.   May God in His great mercy and love
bless you, my dearest love, and may you every day
become more and more anxious to obtain His favour
and His blessing.

Your loving Wife,

EMMA CLIFTON.

Beppy's love, kiss from the dear little chick.

LORD CLIFTON AT CLIFTON LODGE TO LADY CLIFTON
AT COBHAM.

March 1st, 1826.

My dearest Wifey will be I know glad to hear
from her Hubby from this place, which he is
endeavouring to beautify for her reception in the
Summer ; indeed my hands are rather cold with
setting out the garden fence, etc., which must
account for my bad writing, as I have not time or
patience to wait till they get warm.   The day is so

EDWARD, LORD CLIFTON.
Fron a drawing by Enna
Lady Clifton.

bad that I think we shall not get out beyond the domain, and there is some doubt of our getting anything for dinner as Athboy Market will supply no meat. However, Mrs. Gunning promises to procure some. I have seen none of the natives beyond the walls of the house yet, but I suppose I shall have that felicity soon. I felt rather lonely last night in our *nuptial* bed, where Mrs. Gunning has placed me : indeed I have before that often longed for my sweet *compagnon de lit*. I fear you will hardly make this out, particularly the French part, but you will be ready to guess. I find everything much *in statu quo* (Latin too) having come down with Mr. Disney in a *chaise-de-poste*. I have already had some petitions, and have set a man or two to work. The broken stones are still at the gate, but I have not re-embodied the ragged regiment. I feel so fully occupied here in body and mind that I do not pine at all for our separation, which will I trust not exceed three weeks. If you were with me I think I should not desire to leave our sweet home. I think we shall be comfortable enough ; I have settled nothing about the alterations in the mansion but must do so soon. I shall endeavour to have the fences put in order to keep out the cattle which are great intruders and eat all our shrubs, rare as they are and precious from their rarity. The house appears warm and comfortable, and I think the Gunnings have been exerting themselves. The trees are fewer than they were, as more are blown down, as I predicted, having seen how the Divine improver bared their forlorn roots. The water has been a little in the cellar, but it soon receded. I hope we shall have a few fine days to ride about and inspect the property, but I feel that my chief attention must be directed to the house and grounds. I hear the Ladies Flax society is given up or altered in some way : I shall enquire into it, and subscribe, etc. for you. My precious Darling, how I do long to have you here, and spend honeymoons as you so rightly call them ; thank God our Honey days have not been confined to a poor Moon, and I pray for a continuance of that great happiness which He has vouchsafed to me in the inestimable gift of my own sweet Emma. Adieu, my best beloved! I will write again to-morrow I trust more legibly. My duty and love at Cobham, ever dearest Wife unalterably yours.

C.

Lady Clifton at Cobham to Lord Clifton at Clifton Lodge.

March 2nd. 1826.

My dearest love,

Thank you for your letter from Holyhead, and I now hope certainly to-morrow to hear of your safe arrival in Dublin. I am so glad you recollected Miss Emma Parnell, she recollects very well all the circumstances of that very pleasant journey. As for home news, your Pip is returned ; our carriage has arrived this evening, I don't know whether by his or your order. There was a letter from William Brownlow this morning, and one from Lady Amherst, in which honourable mention was made of Arthur Forde. Lady A. said that thousands of the natives were dying every day of the Cholera Morbus.

Very few English. Lady Amherst has been so fortunate as to be the means of the recovery of several hundreds by a peculiar medicine which has been never known to fail. There is to be a large dinner-party here on Saturday. Miss D'Arcy has introduced a Dr. Skey here, at least I suppose that such is the case as I never heard of him till she came. He is we all think an odd, pleasant, well informed little man. He has very good-naturedly promised to go and see the Toffields; the man is very bad with a kind of St. Vitus's dance that he is subject to, the woman who is my laundress, with the ague. How dreadful it is to see the poor man. We went to the school and to the Toffields, and Mrs. Cutcher with William* to-day and you can hardly imagine how well and how suitably he spoke to the children and to the people. It was quite an improving thing to hear him, he explained to the children the part of Scripture they were reading, in the most interesting and impressive manner. And then he talked so beautifully to old Mrs. Cutcher on all the most important subjects of the Bible. Or rather she talked to him about them and very feelingly. I wish you had been there to hear them, it is so useful to hear those talk on religion, who know and feel what it really is in their hearts. I will not tire you, but I will just tell you that I could not help remarking how much (in all the visits of this kind in which I have been one of William's companions) the people were delighted and pleased with him for talking to them in the way he does, and some of them had tears in their

*William Wingfield.

eyes as they thanked him for his delightful conversation. There is indeed much to delight us and
make us happy, to be found in the Gospel if we
seek to understand it by praying to God to enable
us to do so. I hope I have not tired you dearest
love, but my heart is full of many impressive things
which I heard to-day. And I am sure that if it was
only for the good it may do to ourselves we ought
to go about among the poor people, and take an
interest in talking to them not only about their
body's but their soul's welfare.—I suppose you are
very busy at Clifton Lodge. All here are very well
not excepting your own little Wifey. Good-bye my
dearest husband, may God graciously bless you and
protect you.

Ever your affectionate Wife,

EMMA CLIFTON.

I usually write to you after dinner or just before.
I fancy there is an idea of Lady Davy's being here
the end of the month.

LORD CLIFTON AT CLIFTON LODGE TO LADY CLIFTON
AT COBHAM.

March 2nd, 1826.

My dearest wife's letters on Saturday and
Sunday arrived this morning, and I regret that
visits from Hopkins, Cusack, Dr. Dronson, etc.,
together with a projected tour to Portlester prevented my writing at large. I am very busy about
the place improving and have a dozen men
employed. I will write at length to-night for
to-morrow's Post which is my only chance of having
time, the gossoons require so much attention.

Thanks for your darling remarks on my birthday.

Adieu sweetest, dearest and most beloved of wives.

Your affectionate hubby,

C.

LORD CLIFTON AT CLIFTON LODGE TO LADY CLIFTON
AT COBHAM.

Thursday night, March 2nd, 1826.

My dearest darling wife,

How busily must I be employed when I assure you that I feel neither lonely nor melancholy without you, my sweet girl. Do not be affronted, for I am looking forward so earnestly to the pleasure of being with you here that I forget our present separation in anticipation of the future. I will not say that there are not moments during the 24 hours when I very much long to clasp you in my arms, but I hope that I shall do so ere many nights have rolled over our heads. I have more to do here than I expected and think I must stay a day or two after the Assizes, which I did not intend. If so I hope to be in Dublin on Saturday the 11th and to sail on the 13th which would bring me to London about the 15th, the anniversary by the way of my first seeing Miss Emma Parnell, at all events I will try to compress my absence within three weeks. My Mother talked of coming up to Town on that day; perhaps wifey will come too to meet her dearly beloved husband. Your sweet commands about the rose beds shall be obeyed and I will go over to the Nurseryman to-morrow or next day to select some, and other shrubs. I hope I shall be able to make the place look a little comfortable for you. The architect comes to-morrow but I shall settle nothing on that score till I go to London and consult Repton. I have laid out the garden, and they have begun to make the fence round it. I did not consider when I wrote you a hurried note this morning that there was no Post to London; so that you will probably get this at the same time. I did not see anybody in Dublin altho' I hear that Uncle Francis and his family are there. I did not even ask for Uncle Tom or the Thos. Fordes. I have received a letter from Uncle Tom Bligh asking me to Brittas, perhaps I shall go on Friday in next week for a night in my way to Dublin. I will write a line to-morrow to tell you how we go on.

Adieu sweetest and dearest wife.

Your affectionate hubby,

C.

LADY ELIZABETH BLIGH AT COBHAM TO HON. J. D. BLIGH AT ST. PETERSBURGH.

March 2nd, 1826.

I find that there is an express going off to you to-morrow, therefore, "here I am to torment you" with the task of deciphering some of my scribbling. But joking apart, my own dear Johnny, I am very happy in this opportunity of addressing you, and hope you will not regret in hearing from Sister Bet. Our party is reduced to six " Filles" and two "Gossoons," and will, I am sorry to say, be still further reduced on Monday, when three of the "Filles" and one of the " Gossoons" purpose taking their departure, and then we shall remain Lord and Lady D., Lady C., and Lady E.

Aunt P. has protracted her stay much longer than she intended, but I suppose she will positively go on Monday. W. W. went to Sandgate on Saturday on purpose to do duty for Mr. Glennie. Papa has also been away for a few days and returned to-day for dinner. Yesterday was the first "Antient."* I am not sure whether we are to go up for the next. Charles is coming on Sunday to set off again on Monday towards Ireland.

Emma has had a billet doux from Holyhead but none yet from Dublin, her good man expected to be at the lodge on Monday. I believe I told you that Kate D'Arcy had been staying here and taking all our portraits, she has succeeded remarkably well with Mamma, I think it much the most like I have ever seen of her, and I have the satisfaction of knowing that it is my property. Em has a capital one of old Clif and there are one or two very good of herself. Kate stayed on and on till to-day, when Mamma took her over to Chatham, attended the Chatham Meeting, and paid several visits. We are to have a turn out on Saturday. Deans, Hothams and some Colonels to dinner. We have had pleasant weather but not particularly warm. I have been riding and walking a good deal, and have been pretty well except face-ache which has been rather troublesome. The Doctor has a cold and got W. W. to do duty for him this morning. He and all his dined here on Monday to celebrate his own and Olif's birthday, we had a very jolly party. Little

*Weekly concerts of classical music.

Dawson is a fine little fellow and quite a character. The dear little old woman eat her dinner here and paid a visit to the Darling, she seemed to .enjoy herself and talked of you much, she certainly loves you as her own. The dear Pet is dearer than ever, if you can imagine that possible, she still retains her affection for Uncle Da Da, and often desires to write to him, to send him kisses, etc, She seems daily to increase in health and strength, God be praised. A letter received to-day from Wm. Brownlow, he seems going on very well. He wants Mamma to apply for a staff appointment for him. Mamma had a letter from Lord Amherst praising George Brownlow and A. Forde very much. I have not attempted any but private news as whatever public there may be, you are sure to see in the " public prints."

We were delighted with your letter and obliged to you for writing so much in so much bustle my dear. God bless and preserve you. I cannot end this *griffonage* better than with this my constant anxious prayer.

Ever yours dearest truly affectionate.

ELIZABETH BLIGH.

When deary was just now asked if she liked some person present, she said, " Like Da Da."

LADY CLIFTON AT COBHAM TO LORD CLIFTON AT
CLIFTON LODGE.

Friday, March 3rd, 1826.

My dearest love,

I was most happy this morning when I read your dear letter, and knew that you were safe on shore again, and I try to be thankful to God for His great mercy in preserving my dear husband safe to me, and for having helped me with such a true and dear friend. Indeed, dear Clif, you have been very good about writing, and I have felt it a great comfort to know how you were going on. I hope you are not heated by travelling, if you are you know Dr. Adams is at hand, and can give you some little cooling thing. I suppose old Bijou was not very sick as he does not mention it, but what a tedious passage you had. However you were well enough to do justice to Mr. Trefusis's dinner it seems and I daresay you slept very soundly after your tossing. Do you ever dream of Wifey? I will tell you what I have settled you had better do about your shirts. In the first place your Uncle Francis and Lady Catherine are in Dublin, and you might ask her to choose two pieces of fine linen for you, and send them to the Orphan House, Circular Row. You must send a pattern shirt, and then they will cut them out and make them exactly like the pattern. Your Aunt P. is one of the Governesses and she says the King had an immense quantity of shirts made there when he was in Dublin. Do, dear love, do this for I think it would be a good plan, and I am sure it would be no trouble to Lady Catherine or Louisa Forde if she was in Dublin. Have you ever had any answer about the nice-looking coachman? There was a letter from Mrs. Macneil to-day to Lady P., she talked of being in treaty for us about a footman, but does not mention the coachman. I shall be sorry if he has engaged himself elsewhere. The footman is I believe good-looking and reckoned a good servant, but William heard his Uncle (with whom this man lived) say that since he left him he had been at Mr. Byng's and at the Duke of Northumberland's where it is supposed he got spoiled, as a Gen. Campbell, to whom he offered himself, would not take him, and told Col. Stratford that he heard he was a lazy, drunken footman. So I am afraid he will not do. I begin to think it is a difficult matter to get a good servant. Perhaps you might hear of some good footman in Ireland. So much for household affairs. I think they have put other things out of my head, and the rest of my letter will be stupid. Pray remember to send Johnny's letter back, as Lord D. did not half like sending it you for fear that in your great hurry of business you might forget it. It does Johnny credit I think. The dear child is very well, pretty and funny, often talks of Uncle Kif, dear Uncle Kif, how I wish he were coming home to his loving wife, and all that he loves here.

Good-bye, my sweetest, dearest husband.

Your most affectionately attached Wife,

EMMA CLIFTON.

Love from all. Mr. Stokes has asked W. W. to preach again this next Sunday. I fear Lady P. goes on Monday.

LADY CLIFTON AT COBHAM TO LORD CLIFTON AT CLIFTON LODGE.

Saturday, after dinner, 4th March, 1826.
Dearest darling Cliffy,

The important affair of dinner being over, I seize on a few minutes to scribble to you. We went out walking about two, and walked to Shawn, and came back by the high ground, where we chased old Bijou one day on horseback. We had a delightful walk. Little Wifey has grown quite strong and stout and does not feel tired after walking. I was told this morning that it was impossible that I could have a letter from you, but I look forward to that pleasure to-morrow. Dean and Mrs. Stephens, Mr., Mrs. and Miss Hothams, the eldest Miss D'Arcy and Miss Kate, and three officers, one who sat by me, Col. Hay, was very pleasant I thought; Col. Lindsay, Col. Savage, Major D'Arcy, and Dr. Skey. William W. filled the bottom of the table.

What a cruel death the poor elephant has come to. I think it will be rude of me to sit here any more, so adieu till to-morrow, my own dearest husband, and think often of your affecte. Wifey,

EMMA CLIFTON.

LORD CLIFTON AT ATHBOY TO LADY CLIFTON AT
COBHAM.

Darnley Arms Hotel,
Athboy, March 5th, 1826.

My dearest Love,

I have just heard an excellent sermon from Mr. Nangle, who would preach better if he wrote out his sermon instead of doing it extempore. However he is very impressive and takes pains. I wish we had him instead of Mr. Dronson who is a regular drone. Thanks dearest love, thanks for your delightful letters, absence only makes me love you more and more, and I long for the day of our meeting again. I used you very ill yesterday by not writing, but I went out without thinking of doing so and when I returned it was too late. I have been in Church nearly three hours as there was Sacrament, and the sermon an hour long. I go to Trim to-morrow and will write to-night, and from thence will finish my letter. There is a great deal of business.

My duty and love, dearest of wives. May God Almighty evermore preserve you, prays your faithful and affectionate hubby.

C.

LADY CLIFTON AT COBHAM TO LORD CLIFTON AT CLIFTON LODGE.

Sunday, March 5th, 1826.

My dearest darling Cliffy,

I was very much delighted with your sweet affectionate letter, this morning received. And I have thanked the Giver of all good, this day in my prayers for having blessed me with such a kind affectionate husband. I will write more at large to-morrow; I am very busy just now, it is about or near five, and I want to copy out W. W.'s sermon of to-day for Hubby to read. Lord D., Mr. Stokes and everybody else said it was a very good sermon. I am sorry to say I fell asleep at Church, so W. was so good-natured as to lend it me. About the time for afternoon Church, there came on a violent shower, which prevented my going. The day has cleared again, the sun is shining, and everything looking very pleasant.

(After dinner). Charles Brownlow and Fred are here. I am sure I should like Charles very much indeed if I was intimate with him. Little Mary looked very pretty and seemed very glad to see her Papa. He made many enquiries about you, but he tells me what I did not know, (but it is impossible I am sure, as you have so much to do), that you told him you would be back next Saturday. About the middle of the week after this I look forward to seeing my dear husband again. Catherine and Emily send their love to you as they are going to-morrow ; I am very sorry they are.

Did you get any dinner on Wednesday I expect to see you very thin after such short commons. I can enter into your feelings the first night at Clifton Lodge, I felt something the same my first night *sans* you here. I am so much obliged to you for taking so much pains to beautify and make comfortable our house. I think we shall be very happy and comfortable there and I enjoy the thoughts of our honey-moons there very much. Is it true that the election is to be after harvest? If so will it interfere with our residence at Clifton Lodge. Tell me dearest, what you think about it. How very much we love each other, darling hubby, don't you think so? I send you a little prayer which I wrote out from something I read the other day. I hope you will like it.

May God bless you, my own sweet love, is my very earnest prayer. Your most affectionate little Wifey.

EMMA CLIFTON.

Is Miss Gunning as pretty as ever?

LADY CLIFTON AT COBHAM TO LORD CLIFTON AT
CLIFTON LODGE.

Monday, March 6th, 1826.

My dearest Cliffy,

I did not get any sweet letter from you this
morning there being no post, but such a precious
one as I got yesterday may well do to feast my eyes
and heart on for two days. I look forward to the
happy moment of our re-union with the greatest
joy and delight unmixed with impatience, because
I feel convinced that it is your duty to be at
Clifton Lodge just now, and I like to think that
my dearest husband is usefully employed and
therefore I have no doubt happily. To be useful to
our country by conscientiously fulfilling the duties
of our station, must always add to our happiness, at
least I think so. I have been very much amused by
thinking how many little odd circumstances there
must be in your establishment, in which the fair
Gunning fills up all the different parts in her own
person. Has she bestowed on your Lordship's head
another shower-bath similar to that with which she
greeted you on your wedding-day ? I am glad you
are making fences to keep out the cattle. I think I
recollect some shrubs too good to be spoilt by the
cows. As to the alteration in the mansion, you
never told me whether Lord D. has empowered you
to make any. I think the new staircase would
make the house very comfortable. The darling
child said she would go to Ireland to see Uncle Kif,
and as there was a horse in view, she said "ride on

202

horse to Ireland see Uncle Kif"—she was in great spirits before her Papa to-day, who took much more notice of her than he did last time, and seemed to admire her very much. He and Fred went out riding with Beppy to-day, we walked to Shawn and were caught in a shower of rain coming back. Your mama thought I was tired and would make me lie on our bed, which I did like an obedient young lady. Major Brownlow tells me that you did not approve of the coachman because he would not answer the purposes of coachman and postillion both. When should we want a postillion, love? I don't understand why a coachman would not do. Your father told me yesterday that he thought we should be in town the time you came back as Lady D. wishes to go to the Ancient Music that week. Now, dear hubby, if this is the case am I to go prepared to remain in town, and shall I bring up whatever things you have here? You were talking of going to town to attend your parliamentary duties when you returned; now, if I meet you in town perhaps we had better not return. What do you think about it dearest? If you write directly you get this perhaps I may get it in time to act accordingly. Shall I leave Windsor here? He is getting terribly fat. You know I have the carriage as Lord D. brought it down. Good bye, my sweet and precious husband, how I do long to see you, in the meantime I am your very affectionate and fond Wifey,

EMMA CLIFTON.

Monday Night, March 6th, 1826.
My dearest best beloved, most loving wife.

Pressure of public as well as private business
has so taken up my time that I have used you most
shabbily in the way of letter-writing, which I feel
the more sensibly in consequence of the continued
darling letters I have received from you. Oh!
what pleasure it gives me to read them at such a
distance from my sweet wife; how I look anxiously
for the arrival of the Post. The business of the
Assizes is heavy, and they will probably last for
four days. I shall get from them however as soon
as possible that I may finish the work I have to do
here. In consequence of my having employed a
few hands on the improvements, the gate was beset
this morning by 40 or 50 wretches with spades, etc.
seeking for employment which I was unable to offer
them. Alas! we have much to go through in
witnessing the distress of this poor country, but the
more we have to endure and the more difficult is
the task we propose to ourselves, the more I feel
assured we shall through God's assistance rejoice in
overcoming difficulties and being of some use. I
need much the assistance of my darling wife who
will, I doubt not, administer comfort to her hubby
and her neighbours together. I like that you
should take pleasure in talking on religious subjects
to the poor, and I hope you will practice it with me.
How pleasant our honey-moon may so prove. Mr.
Disney has been in and interrupted me so that it is
now twelve o'clock, and I must be up very early, so

that I will finish this at Trim. I saw Mr. Bourke there whom you know, I believe, at least he enquired for you, and I think I have heard you speak of him. He is brother I believe to Miss Bourke who was the Lady Kilkenny. I saw Mr. R. Ruxton also.

Tuesday, 7th.—Here I take up my pen again, in the midst of noise and tumult occasioned by the dispute who shall have most road jobs. I think however there is a chance of getting over the business sooner than I expected as we have got through over four Baronies, and shall probably dispatch 8 or 10 more to-day. I am perfectly bewildered by the noise, and am unable to finish as I wish. You have no conception of the noise. I suppose I shall have to dine with the judges to-day, if not I shall go home and have plenty to do there, I assure you. Mr. Disney is not satisfactory in all things—he has sent me here to-day totally uninformed of very material circumstances, relating to the Lune presentments. God bless and preserve you my dearest wife, persevere in your pious and religious feeling, and be by God's grace instrumental in improving your devoted hubby.

C.

LADY CLIFTON AT COBHAM TO LORD CLIFTON AT CLIFTON LODGE.

Tuesday, March 7th, 1826.

Just before dinner for which the table is set out in the far end of the library. Lady D., Beppy and I are all.

Dearest hubby's letters arrived this morning to

the great joy of his Wifey who likes very much to receive such sweet and affectionate proofs of his love to her. It makes me very happy to think that you have not felt lonely or melancholy; I do not think I have felt so either and yet I have missed you and often, often longed for your sweet society. I should be very selfish indeed if I could wish you to be melancholy when away from me. And oh, what a joyful meeting will ours be, I will not think of it lest I should get too impatient for it to arrive. God has richly blest us in giving us to each other who seem so well adapted to each other. Let us try and be thankful to Him. Dear Baboo would write and when I asked what she would say, she said what you see here written by her own tiny hand and then she drew Uncle Kif's portrait.* Her Papa went this morning, so did Aunt P. and the Wings I am sorry to say. I suppose they are at Sandgate by this time. Dearest Cliffy, will you grant me a boon? I think if I know you, you will. And now I will tell you what it is. I wish you would kindly allow me to act according to what I think right, in the matter of going out. Surely you will not wish to make me unhappy by making me do what I think wrong. By making I do not mean forcing but over-persuading. I hardly know how to give my reasons for entertaining this wish, but I think it is because I think entering into worldly amusements must draw the mind away from meditation on serious subjects and from the desire of loving and serving God. I think that entering upon a course of

*In the original is Mary Brownlow's childish drawing and writing.

frivolous pleasures is inconsistent with that state of watchfulness and preparation for eternity which it is our duty as well as our interest to cultivate. And on the ground of late hours I do not think it right as late hours at night must be followed by late hours in the morning, and thus the time usually devoted to reading the Scriptures and to prayer, would be consumed in bed. Now on all these grounds I think what is called going out must be dangerous to the soul's welfare, at all events I feel that to mine it would be dangerous. And yet, indeed dear Cliffy, I do not wish to lay down a general rule, nor do I think it such an essential point as many others which I could name. Nor do I think that there is any merit attached to those who abstain from those things. If we could do everything that we are commanded we should still be unprofitable servants. But I do wish very fervently that I might be excused from acting against my conscience, and to be saved from the pain of acting a double part, which I should feel myself to be doing if I appeared to like what in my heart I disapprove. You must know that last Sunday your father came and talked to me for some time on this subject. He said it would grieve him very much to have it said that Lady Clifton was so good she would not go to a ball ; but indeed with such a corrupt heart as I have I need not be afraid of being too good, or rather it is impossible for anyone to be so. My own sweet Cliffy, I hope you are not tired of my letter. I am sure you will think in a kind and considerate way about my feelings on this subject although they may differ from yours. I am sure we shall never regret the time spent in seeking for God's blessing and praying for a renovation of heart and life. My own dearest husband, forgive me if I grieve you by thinking differently to what you do. May God in His mercy bless you and bring you safe home to me. Beppy sends her love. There was a letter from Lord Castlereagh to-day, I should like to see him.

Good bye, my sweet love,

Your very affectionate and loving Wifey,

EMMA CLIFTON.

LADY CLIFTON AT COBHAM TO LORD CLIFTON.

March 8th, 1826.

My dearest Cliffy.

I can only write a line to-day being very much hurried as the history of myself will be interesting to you, I will tell you what I have done to-day. Read and painted till 2, went out with Beppy a very hot and oppressive day did not come home till 6. How happy I am to think of seeing my dear and precious husband, I hope in a week's time. I believe we go up on Wednesday. You will find your own little Wifey in our own little room at Bruton Street. I believe I am to be under the paternal roof the first night I am in town. What a happy meeting ours I hope and pray will be. May God in His great mercy bless and protect my sweet husband and restore him to the arms of his very loving wife, his own little Emma Clifton.

O how delightful it is to think that a fortnight (save one day) of your absence has passed away.

Mind you are not to sail in a storm. I think

you will get this letter on Sunday. I hope you will go and hear Mr. Matthias. Pray remember me to your Uncle Francis's* daughters whom I know a little.

Grand Jury Room, Trim.
March 8th, 1826.

The business is not nearly finished, and I have left a cargo of plants at C. Lodge undisposed of, to which I shall hasten as soon as possible. I have only dined one day with the Grand Jury and suppose they will dine together again to-day for the business will hardly be over by night. I have received a dear letter this morning which ought to have been over yesterday had not the wind detained it. I hope the letters will soon give way to the more delightful intercourse by being together which was so many months unbroken, and which I hope will be again unbroken for very long when we meet. I am so confused in this room of confusion that I know not what I write, and you must excuse the very unconnected scrawl which I have sent you. Mr. Disney still remains at C. Lodge. I purpose going to Brittas Friday and on Saturday to Dublin, and I hope to sail on Monday. I have still a great deal to do before I get away, among other things I have invited the Tenantry to meet at Athboy on Friday morning to consult about employing, the four roads, etc. God bless you my sweet love, prays constantly your affectionately devoted hubby.

C.

* Francis Brownlow, brother of Lady Darnley.

March the 9th, 1826.

My own dearest love,

Thank you for your nice little letter from the Darnley Arms and for all the kind and loving things in that and other letters. I think you have been very good about writing, for you appear to have been very busy. I am glad you heard Mr. Nangle. It would indeed be a delightful thing to have him at Athboy instead of the worthy but alas ! lazy Dr. Dronson. I do not think, being as you know very dull in comprehension of many such things as posts going out and coming in, that this letter will reach Dublin till (we) you I mean, leave it. I am so identified with you that the word "we" would come instead of "you." I hope your passage will not be very rough. I think that we must stay in Bruton Street for some little time, (after that happy re-union which we both are longing for) because we must really exert ourselves and try to get servants. Perhaps we could come down here again in Easter Week, but I think it will be necessary for us to stay a little time for the purpose I have mentioned. We have had another sultry day, and have enjoyed it very much and been out a great deal. I and Beppy have it now in our power to get very well acquainted. I am very glad to have her for my sister, and think she is full of amiable qualities and kindness. How much I regret that I never saw your dear sister Mary, I am sure I should have loved her very much, for her own sake as well as for her darling brother C's sake. The sweet child is very well and blooming, and improves every day. What a treasure the dear little thing is, and will continue to be more and more, I hope. I have very nearly finished your picture, my sweet love, if I could get the mouth like, it would altogether be very like you. I often think of you my own precious and beloved husband, and I leave you to judge by your own feelings how delightful the anticipation of next Wednesday is to me. Beppy sends her love. Ever dearest, your affectionate and loving wife.

EMMA CLIFTON.

I fancy that I shall see you first at about 12 o'clock on Wednesday night in our own little drawing-room 20, Bruton Street. I hope I shall not be disappointed.

LORD CLIFTON AT ATHBOY TO LADY CLIFTON.

Darnley Arms, Athboy.
March 10th, 1826.

My sweetest darling wife; best of correspondents, a thousand thanks for your dear letters, which I have constantly received. I do indeed look forward with the greatest pleasure to seeing you in a very few days. I hope to reach London on Wednesday but not till late, as I do not like to venture travelling in the Mail. My present purpose is to go to Dublin to-morrow and spend next day there, and sail on Monday. I would go to-day were it not that I prefer setting out from Dublin after Sunday in which you will agree with me as to the propriety tho' it keeps me two days more from you. Indeed my darling I long for our reunion. Will you

meet me in London ? I know you will, and we will
return to Cobham or not at Easter, as they and you
like. I fear we shall not be able to set you out
smart till after Easter as we have no Footman or
Coachman. I can get a Coachman and horses
directly however, but I calculated on your not being
much in`Town till after Easter. I have been all
day at a meeting of the Tenants which I convened,
and which passed off well. The object, the employment of the Poor. It has detained me so long that I
cannot write much. Yesterday there was no Post
to London but I hope that with the exception of one
day you have received my scrawls regularly. I
must now hasten home to direct the planting.

Adieu ! dearest love, more dear each day to
your affectionate and devoted husband

                                        C.

LORD CLIFTON AT DUBLIN TO LADY CLIFTON.

Bilton's Hotel, Dublin,
March 12th, 1826.

I have received since I arrived in Dublin last
night (as I supposed too late for the Post), two more
delightful letters from my beloved wife, for which,
and all the rest of them ten thousand thanks, my
dearest love—oh how precious are your letters to
me when we are parted. I hope however now so
soon to see you that I can expect no more letters
nor shall I probably write any. This will I suppose
sail with me to-morrow, and I hope only precede
me by a few hours. I am sorry to say that altho'
for some days after my arrival in Ireland I was
better and clearer than usual, within this last day

or two I have had a sudden and rather violent attack of my old eruption, and I should have been this day the better for a little sponging like that I got from certain maidens at Abbeyleix last Summer. It is just possible that I may be induced on this account to travel slowly, in which case I shall not arrive before Thursday. If I arrive on Wednesday it will be before 12, after which do not expect me. I trust I may be with you and clasp you in my arms before that hour. If I am detained on the road I will write so that you may hear on Thursday morning. I found my dear Aunt Theodosia Bligh* and her family here, and have been dining with them. Lady C. Brownlow† and her daughters and John‡ also have I seen. Uncle Tom Parnell is out of Town, and there is no parcel left at Lady de V.'s for Caroline, as for the shirts I shall have them made in London for reasons which I shall explain.

God bless you sweetest love, and bring me safe back to your loving embrace. My heart's delight, Good night.

Your devoted hub.,

C.

LORD CLIFTON AT HOLYHEAD TO LADY CLIFTON IN LONDON.

Holyhead,

March 13th, 1826.

Here I am, dearest wife, after a roughish passage of 9 hours, not sick. My poor head bad but

*Daughter of John, third Earl of Darnley, wife of Thomas Bligh of Brittas.

† Wife of Francis Brownlow, daughter of Earl of Meath.

‡ Afterwards Dean of Clonmacnoise, married Lady Elizabeth Bligh in 1833.

I am going to Bangor to-night. I hope to reach London on Wednesday night, but if I do not arrive attribute it to my taking care of myself.

Ever dearest wife, your loving hubby,

C.

Lord Clifton at 20, Bruton Street to the Hon. John Duncan Bligh at St. Petersburgh.

20, Bruton Street,

March 17th, 1826.

My dearest Johnny,

I really have used you very ill, having so long neglected to write to you, whereas you have been as usual so good a correspondent, giving us such constant accounts of your proceedings, I have just read a letter from you from Riga, and hope soon to hear of your arrival at Petersburgh.

I returned from Ireland Wednesday last, having come in the course of the day from Shrewsbury. I suppose at least 200 Versts, *i.e.* 155 miles. I wish you could get over the ground as expeditiously, but I think neither horses nor roads are so good in that part of the world. I hope you have found yourself on pleasant terms with the Great Man's suite, for altho' it must be a great bore being left far behind by reason of bad horses, pleasant companions occasionally must make a great difference to you. I suppose you will probably stay a short time at Berlin on your return, and perhaps return with Frederic etc. There appears to be nearly as much mercantile distress in Prussia as there is here. There is a difference as to the probable event of things. Some say the prospect is brightening, some that we shall see much worse distress than heretofore after awhile. I confess that though I speak ignorantly on the subject, I have the greatest confidence in the resources of the country. I was so exceedingly busy in Ireland that I could hardly find time to write to anyone. The business at the Assizes was unusually heavy and I had much to do at Clifton Lodge. The potato crop proved rather a short one, and the prices are high, but no great rise in price was anticipated, but the distress among the poorer classes is very general, and we endeavoured to suggest some means of relieving it at a meeting of the Tenants at Athboy partly by the joint contributions of Landlord and Tenant, which would be a much more efficient way of employing the poor than indiscriminate employ-ment from my father at so much per day, as there would be persons on the spot interested in the out-lay of the money. I think we may hope for improve-ment, and there is certainly ample room for it. Mr. Disney has pretty well settled the farm of James-town which Cussack had to manage, with but little success. I saw Uncle Tom, Aunt Theo, four girls and Edward in Dublin. They are living for the most part at Brittas and Mrs. Edward is laying out a flower garden. I planted a few shrubs at C. Lodge, and shall get her to assist me some day, and I hear she has great taste. Poor Tom is I fear dying. My father met him at Crosse's yesterday on his divorce business. Madame is living somewhere in London.

It is indeed an unpleasant business and know-ing as we do the difficulties of the Law where there are no intricacies, we cannot see the way out of this difficulty. I hope all may go well. What a black villain L. W. is. Does your great Captain ever say anything on the subject? I suppose not. The Worthy and Independent Freemen of Canterbury resident in London have been bestirring themselves to get a third man (*quemcunque, mode tertius sit*) but hitherto without the smallest success. They have applied to several who said that if they could obtain a certain number of promises that they would stand, but who on enquiry have given it up as a bad job. Our friends at Canterbury are firm, and all the newspapers deprecate and ridicule the idea, so that I think we stand pretty well. I will enumerate some of the people they have applied to. Sir. G. Webster was at Canterbury beating about the bush for some days, and finding a cool reception, returned to his London friends, and resigned all pretension. Sir M. Inglis—something of the same sort—Sir R. Farquhar—declined and stands for Hythe—one of the Watsons—I know not what answer he returned. Barclay, Perkins and Co. have also been in requisition; I suppose they treated the worthies to strong beer, and at last I believe they mean to apply to Cobbett as a last resource. They say the King is very ill, but a Bulletin this morning pronounces him better, I trust we may not have Frederic 1st yet awhile. I had the happiness of finding my dearest wife, parents, and sister quite well and I hope that before very long you will join the happy family circle. They go to Cobham to-morrow, and I suppose we shall go in the course of next week. Adieu! my dearest brother. May God evermore preserve you, prays

Your affectionate brother,

CLIFTON.

CHAPTER V.

𝕽eligion and 𝕻olitics.

LORD and Lady Darnley were always most kind to their daughter-in-law. In later years she often spoke to her children and grandchildren of their consideration and affection for her, especially of the care they took to make her happy and comfortable during Lord Clifton's enforced absences in Ireland. It is evident, however, that they found it difficult to understand the narrowness of the creed which led her to condemn every form of amusement as sinful waste of time, if not worse.

The Earl of Darnley had a great idea of the duties and responsibilities incumbent on rank and position, and politics had for him a paramount interest. He was a regular attendant at the House of Lords, where he spoke frequently and used all his influence to promote tolerance and moderation between opposing parties. Although himself a Whig and an active promoter of Catholic Emancipation and Electoral Reform, he was at the same time a personal friend of the Duke of Wellington, with whom in private he often discussed political affairs.

His interests however, were by no means entirely centred on politics ; he had travelled much and spent a great deal of money in collecting pictures, sculpture and *objets d'art* for the adornment of his stately home. Both Lord and Lady Darnley lent every encouragement to the contemporary revival of classical music and were regular attendants at the "Antient Musick" concerts, often going on from them to the balls at Almack's, which always took place on the same evenings. In this way they became acquainted with many interesting people outside their own immediate circle, and among those who enjoyed their hospitality both at Cobham and 46, Berkeley Square, were Mrs. Siddons and her daughters, Patty being an especial favourite on account of her beautiful singing ; this much appealed to the music-loving family at Cobham and is constantly referred to in Lady Darnley's letters.

Very friendly relations existed between the Darnleys and the Royal Family ; the Prince Regent and the Royal Dukes were frequent guests at Lady Darnley's parties in Berkeley Square. The Duke and Duchess of

Clarence paid more than one visit to Cobham Hall, and a very genuine friendship with the Duke and Duchess of Kent led to an interesting and important connexion between Lord Darnley and a certain historic event. In 1819, when the Duke of Kent was making arrangements to travel back from Germany to England in order that the anxiously awaited confinement of the Duchess might take place in England, a temporary embarrassment occurred owing to the lack of the necessary funds to meet the immediate expenses of travelling. The difficulty was removed by Lord Darnley advancing the money and thus enabling the Duke and Duchess to come to England shortly before the birth of the future Queen Victoria. It may indeed be recorded with some interest that this event took place only a few days after a visit to Cobham Hall, where they rested for a night on their journey between Dover and London. The gratitude of the Duchess of Kent and her brother, Prince Leopold (afterwards King of the Belgians), was expressed on more than one occasion subsequently.

In the intervals of his political, artistic and social occupations Lord Darnley devoted himself with untiring energy to wholesome recreations such as riding, shooting and yachting. It seems probable that he hardly left enough time for the careful management of his property, and that his open-handed way of living considerably embarrassed his estate. But for about forty years the Earl and Countess of Darnley occupied a conspicuous place in London society, and it is greatly to their credit, that during the dissipations and excesses which brought the period of the Regency into such disrepute, no breath of scandal or reproach seems ever to have reached the family of Cobham Hall and Berkeley Square. In every department of life Lord and Lady Darnley discharged their duties with exemplary rectitude, in home life, fashionable society, politics and religion, and their social influence at this period must have been for the good of all.

It was upon this brilliant stage that the young Lady Clifton made her appearance in the family circle. Emma was a complete stranger to fashionable London and knew nothing about the circumstances in which she now found herself. She approached life from an entirely different point of view. To her always, right was right, wrong was wrong, and no question of relative values were possible. In after years however, she did sometimes admit that she regretted that she had always been so confident that she was right and her parents-in-law wrong. Obstinacy of conviction and incapacity for seeing the point of view of other people were the chief faults of a character which was, in other respects, singularly free from blame. We see in some of the literature of the time, especially in books intended for children, such as Mrs. Sherwood's "Fairchild Family," that Lady Clifton's views were characteristic of certain new and extreme religious doctrines of the day, the growing popularity of which may be attributed to a reaction against the loose and decadent morality which had so long been prevalent in the upper classes. In her case these ideas were fortunately accompanied by equally strong convictions of the feminine duties of love and submission to lawful authority. In daily life she was ever kind, gentle and amiable ; she was also very humble and tolerant and we may fairly say that her life was more truly Christian than her creed. The following record of a conversation between Lord and Lady Clifton at this time, gives us some idea of the simplicity and earnestness of the latter's character.

March 19, 1826. I had a long conversation with my dear husband this day, upon the subject of going out into the world. We talked it over a long time, as we have often done before, and neither of us could bring the other to a conviction that what that other maintained was wrong. As my dear husband seemed to think very strongly that my youth and inexperience disqualified me from forming a correct opinion, I at last promised him that I would refrain from giving out my opinion till such time that I was convinced it was a well grounded one, and that I would go wherever he should propose this Spring, and make my remarks first in silence on each amusement that we entered into, and afterwards to him and thus talk and think the matter over together. And my dear husband has also promised on his part that he will not avoid those whom without intimate knowledge of them, he suspects of cant and hypocrisy, and that he will willingly when opportunity offers, make their acquaintance and judge for himself. And may God in his great mercy give unto each of us grace not to lean on our own understanding, but to acknowledge Him in all our paths, and to seek His blessing and direction on all our undertakings. " Redeeming the time, because the days are evil." (Ephes. v, 16.)

Lord and Lady Clifton settled in 20 Bruton Street for the London season on April 9th, 1826, Emma's sister Caroline being their guest. John Bligh returned from Russia on April 21st and the Cliftons celebrated his return by a family dinner next day, at which were present, Lord and Lady Darnley, Beppy and Johnny, Sir Henry and Caroline Parnell, Tom Bligh of Brittas, also Clifton's and Johnny's great friend Frederick Gascoigne.

Parliament was dissolved in June. Lord Clifton was again returned for Canterbury, and he and his wife, with Caroline Parnell went to Cobham after the election was over. Here they remained until July 1st, when they started for Ireland; they spent most of the rest of the year at Clifton Lodge.

June 23rd, 1826 (Cobham). I intend to give a good deal of time to reading and to music when I am at Clifton Lodge. I wish to read some Universal History through, either Rollin's or Mavor's. I propose taking in the Christian Examiner and Church of Ireland Magazine. Also to get Gillie's Narrative of an Excursion to the Mountains of Piemont, Cecil's Remains, and "May you like it," by a Country Curate. I hope also to learn to be useful to the poor around. I intend to pay attention to the schools and to visiting the sick. I hope I shall not forget when in London to get those useful plaisters which E.B. recommended. Also a Medicine Chest. I got up at a quarter before eight to-day, Lord C. at nine.

June 28th. Beppy showed me some very pretty verses that she had written on the eve of Clif's departure for Ireland last February. I was very much pleased with this token of her kind feelings to both of us. Got a letter from Uncle Tom to-day, in which he seems to accuse me of taking no interest in the improvement of the condition of my poor countrywomen; he does not know how anxiously I wish to be of use to them, but I feel obliged to him for reminding me of my duty, and for exhorting me to walk in the right way. May I indeed by God's grace helping me, throw off my natural idleness and exert all the powers that He has given me in His service. On the 26th a sad accident happened here to the blacksmith, Lamb, giving us a striking lesson of the insecurity of the health and strength of man.

Thursday, June 29th. We went in the " Elizabeth " [Lord Darnley's yacht] from Gravesend to Sheerness, where we landed and walked about. We saw an immense building for the purpose of forging Anchors—they were forging one while we were there. Then we were shewn the foundations for a great storehouse which they are in the act of building. Then a mast-house of a great size, and afterwards we were taken to see the docks which are very fine. We saw some ships "in ordinary" near Sheerness, which means a temporary house being erected over the deck, for the purpose of preserving the deck and everything appertaining to the ship from the influence of the weather. The Howe was one, the Téméraire another. Sheerness is on the island of Sheppey; the convicts are employed there. Near the mouth of the Medway we saw the Regent, a magnificent ship on service.

[John Bligh also describes this day in his journal, and adds: " Dined on board, sailed to Rochester Bridge where horses and vehicles met us to take us home. Delightful !]

July 17th, Bangor. This is the first day I have found any spare moments to employ in writing my journal. On Saturday, July 1st, we arrived in London from Cobham. We arrived at Leamington the Saturday following, July 8th, and found the dear baby very much improved and grown. [Lady Clifton's eldest brother, John Parnell and her widowed sister, Lady Henry Moore, with her son Henry, afterwards third Marquess of Drogheda, were staying at Leamington, and Lady Henry Moore accompanied the Cliftons to Ireland.] I was very much pleased with observing how much religion seems to be the uppermost subject in the minds of John and Mary. Some people call them enthusiasts, and blame them for what they consider irrational and over-zealous conduct, but why should these terms be applied to those who make it their chief end to glorify God, to serve Him and obey His commandments and to enjoy His free mercy here and for ever? I feel convinced that such is the aim and desire of my dear brother and sister. They both seem deeply impressed with a feeling of their own guilt and helplessness, both seem to look with the eye of faith unto the Lord Jesus Christ for salvation and to feel most thankfully the great mercy of God in providing a way of salvation for fallen sinners . . . and both prove the reality of their faith by being zealous of good works, endeavouring in all things to conform to the *one rule* for the conduct of Christians, namely the Word of God. They seem very anxious to do good to the souls and bodies of others. At the same time I must take notice that in some little instances I think

John is unnecessarily and unscripturally particular. He thinks it is wrong to dress like any other gentleman and that that degree of attention to dress which is common in our rank of life is sinful. He thinks it necessary too to be stern and harsh in his manner when he thinks he is in company with irreligious people. I hope to see him give up these peculiarities, and be more like Edward and William Wingfield. I admire both John and Mary for their sincerity and Christian courage in acknowledging freely their opinions and their hopes before those who I am afraid would ridicule and deride them.

We went to see Warwick Castle and saw the beautiful Vase which was found among the ruins of Adrian's Villa, and brought to England. We saw (on our journey here) Mr. Thomason's Metallic Vase which is a copy of this. There are some fine pictures at Warwick Castle, I think we remarked that it was peculiarly rich in Vandykes. We left Leamington on Tuesday, slept at Shifnal, Wednesday at Llangollen, and went to see the "Ladies," (Lady Eleanor Butler and Miss Ponsonby), they took a great deal of notice of Mary and made many enquiries about the child. They told Lady C. Brownlow, who succeeded us in visiting them that they had seen a pretty little widow, as fair as the Parnells and as black as the Moores (alluding to her dress). Thursday night we arrived here very late, having been delayed several hours at Kapel Kerrigge (Capel Cerig) for horses. Found here a large family party. I admire the country very much.

LADY CLIFTON AT CLIFTON LODGE TO THE HON. J.
D. BLIGH, TOURING IN WALES.

August 22nd, 1826.

My dear Johnny,

With many apologies for not writing to you before, I intend now writing you as long an epistle as I can put together considering the great scarcity of news in this place. Your letter was quite a delightful one, it was so long, and you write such a very easy hand to read. I conclude you and Timar are now wandering together, and I hope you will not fail to give us some account now and then of what you are doing. I should enjoy a tour in Wales very much I think, if women could travel in the same independent manner that men can, but whenever we do make an excursion of that kind, I shall propose Scotland, as I have never yet seen anything of that country. I have been making acquaintance with your cousins at Brittas. We went there early last week and Clif went to Dublin after spending a day there, and I stayed two or three days more. I was at first perplexed about their names, and was afraid to mention any one by name, for fear of mistaking. I like them very much, they were all very good-natured to me and I spent my time very pleasantly. What a fine girl Bessy is, she would be very handsome I think if she had a prettier mouth. Clifton and the two Squire Hopkins' were out on the bog yesterday. They killed a good many grouse. The neighbours are very attentive to us in making

227

us presents of fruit. Old Nic brought us a dozen
peaches, but it is supposed he did so to please his
young wife, who is said to be the very reverse of
what he is as to spending money. She is furnish-
ing Balrath all over, and making great alterations
in his style of living, and made him set up a very
fine equipage. The Featherstones and Macveaghs
have sent us fruit too. William Tighe and Mr.
Hamilton are coming here this day week to *rough it*
here for a few days. We do not think ourselves
able to entertain any ladies. Nevertheless my
sisters have promised to pay us a visit but have
fixed no time. I have been gardening with Gunning to-day, and I think he seems to take an interest
in flowers. We are in hopes that just about the
house will look a great deal prettier the next time
Lord and Lady Darnley come here. Gunning
promises to get all sorts of flowers from his friend
Sir T. Chapman's gardener. The China roses that
Clifton planted against the house in the spring
make a very good show already. You can't imagine
without being on the spot how much he did in the
fortnight he was alone here in the spring. The
little lawn is very well mowed and looks really very
pretty in *our* eyes, and the flower-beds in it every
here and there make it look very different to what it
did this time last year. The garden wall is getting
on very well, but the men will not work unless they
are very closely watched and I am afraid Clif
worries himself too much about them. Do you
know of a good Scotch steward ? For Clif begins
to think such a personage will be requisite here.
We had an ample fall of rain last night and this

CLIFTON LODGE,
Co. Meath.
From a Photograph.

morning, which I think must have been of great use. I had a letter from Beppy the other day written in very good spirits, so I hope she has quite recovered from the effects of her illness. I am sure we have both acquired a *brogue* already, for I find I do not think Mr. F. Hopkins's way of speaking near as extraordinary as I used. Clifton will certainly get it in the greatest degree of the two, as he has a better ear than I have. Now I hope I have not tired you with my prosing. I must tell you that Dr. Dronson preached a Charity sermon last Sunday and the *on dit* is that he told someone that he had entertained some thoughts of asking the Bishop to come and preach it, but upon consideration it appeared to him that he could fill the pulpit quite as well himself. The collection was a pretty good one I believe.

Now, dear Johnny, believe me

Your affectionate sister,

EMMA CLIFTON.

FROM LADY CLIFTON'S JOURNAL.

Friday, Sept. 8th, 1826. [Clifton Lodge.] I hope God will give me grace to endeavour to devote all to his glory, as to money, I mean from to-day to put by the 10th of all I receive, for charitable purposes, and after spending some of which may remain in necessary expenses, to use the rest of it in promoting the good cause also. [This was her unvarying rule throughout life.]

Sept. 25th, 1826. Mem. That it is my duty as mistress of a family to attend to the spiritual welfare of my servants, I ought to endeavour to contrive time for each to read the Bible. I purpose having Cawdell [her maid] up to read to her every day after breakfast when we get to Cobham, where I am sure she must be exposed to many temptations to neglect religion. Where there are so many servants, and many perhaps destitute of serious concern for their souls. I think I ought to begin here with her and with Eliza. And poor Peggy! I ought indeed to try to bring her to some knowledge of God, and Oh may He who alone can give the increase, bless my humble endeavours, for His Name's sake.

During the autumn of this year, Emma Clifton, probably owing to her state of health, seems to have fallen into a morbid habit of dwelling on her spiritual state, and her journal contains many pages lamenting her want of holiness. A few passages only are given here.

I had hardly any sense of God's presence and majesty at private prayer or family prayer this morning; this is a besetting sin of mine. Oh how often I am quite irreverent and careless, and have my thoughts full of worldly matters. I am not respectful or kind enough to my dear husband in my manner and words, when endeavouring to point out any error which I perceive.

October 2nd. I indulged my body too much this morning at the expense of my soul, I did not get up till a quarter of an hour after the time when I might have done so. I was very censorious on the subject of my sister C.'s faults, and dwelt upon them in an unkind manner. The Scriptures say, "Judge not." . . . The contrast between my situation and that of the poor hard-working girl downstairs who is so anxious to learn and to read the Bible, and who has hardly any opportunity, made me feel very much ashamed of my own unthankfulness for the great and rich blessings that the Gracious God has poured down upon me. . . . I was guilty of great selfishness in my heart this day, about coming back from Athboy, feeling most unwilling to give up my own gratification to the comfort of all the party.

Oct. the 16th. It is now between 11 and 12 in the forenoon and I have been already guilty of many sins, I loitered and wasted time in dressing, I turned the blessings of God into occasions of committing sin, for I gave way to needless anxiety on the subject of catering for the family. Instead of being thankful to Him who so constantly crowns our table with abundance, I was filled with care and anxiety so much so that I suffered the matter to intrude on my thoughts at family prayers and afterwards I was peevish and querulous towards my dear husband on the same subject.

Her husband was not without sympathy with her views as will be seen by the following letter written to her when visiting his brother-in-law, Charles Brownlow.

LORD CLIFTON AT LURGAN, TO LADY CLIFTON
AT CLIFTON LODGE.

October 10th, 1826.

My dearest darling Love will be happy to hear that I am well. I received your letter of Saturday this morning. I should have had much pleasure in my visit here had I not been most forcibly reminded of the change since I was here 3 short years ago. Then everything was saintly and ceremonious, religious, nay evangelical: now alas! nothing appears to be thought of but electioneering. I hope I never may be placed in such a situation as I find poor Charles in at the present moment. I confess it shocks me that persons (parsons I might say) who were 3 years ago preaching to me to renounce the world and all its vanities (as others may be doing now) should appear now slaves to the world. It was at that time John Brownlow* gave me Bickersteth on Prayer, which copy you have. Now I see him playing hazard, blind hooky, billiards and doing anything rather than—but I do him wrong and am uncharitable— surely however this could not have been so if my beloved sister had lived—but God in His Mercy has spared her that pain. May He preserve her darling child and may she learn that to Him alone can she look for support and assistance in this world of trouble.

I know not when I have been more melancholy than I have been this day. I returned not long since from the spot where, when last here, I saw the

---

* Rev. John Brownlow, afterwards Vicar of Sandgate, brother of Charles Brownlow, afterwards 1st Lord Lurgan.

mortal remains of one I tenderly loved consigned to earth. Poor Charles is overrun with relations who influence him, I think, against his better judgement; I think it would have been otherwise had Baboo's darling Mother been alive. Perhaps, dearest love, being absent from you adds to my melancholy ; but I hope to see you, my best beloved, on Saturday with the blessing of God.

I go to Narrowwater tomorrow, and on Friday as circumstances shall direct either to Dublin or Brittas in my way to Clifton Lodge.

God bless and preserve you and yours, dearest love. Thanks for your text.

Yr. most affectionate

C.

FROM LADY CLIFTON'S JOURNAL.

November 2nd, 1826. I have for some days given way too much to the sensual love of ease. Every morning I have got up later than the morning preceding. I have partly thought it right to indulge more than usual on account of my weak back, but I have carried this indulgence to a sinful degree, as this day we got up so late that we both neglected prayer. And I have thus sinned myself and led my husband into sin also. I must pray earnestly to be able to overcome my sloth. . . .

I ought to note down that from what my maid has told me, I fear my example has been very injurious to her. It appears that she was tempted to join in many things that she knew were wrong, according to the strict rule of Scripture, although not reckoned so by the looser estimate of sinful

Q.

men. She joined in all these things against her conscience, and reaped the bitter fruits of inward disquietude, and a loss of peace of mind. She felt also a worldly spirit steal on her by degrees, and a deadness as to religion. All this I felt also, and may the Lord in His tender mercy keep both her and me from again walking in those ways. May He change the briar into a myrtle tree, and by the sanctifying influence of His spirit on my soul, enable me to glorify Him with my body and spirit, as one bought with a price. May He give me grace to set an example of obedience to His will to this young creature who is committed to my care. I hope when at Cobham to be able to have her to read with me an hour or two after breakfast. I had better get Adam's explanation of St. Matthew for that purpose.

November 17th. I am sorry to remark that I have indulged very much lately in the sin of sloth. I have wasted the talent of time. How much more I might do towards the care of my own soul, and the welfare of others, if I was dressed only half-an-hour sooner. I feel that I have been committing a great sin. It is indeed a very low and sensual sin to prefer the indulgence of lying in bed, to the discharge of all those duties which would amply fill up my time if I got up.

LADY CLIFTON AT CLIFTON LODGE TO CAROLINE PARNELL AT ABBEYLEIX.

November 22nd, 1826.

PRIVATE.

My dear Caroline,

Permit a sage old matron like me to enquire

234

what you and that good looking young gentleman who came over from Balrath to see you here, were about? Is it you or Catherine who is his attraction at Abbeyleix? And what do you think of him? I will tell you what I think, which is, that *if* he likes you and would be allowed by papa *to propose* (which I very much doubt) that you would be very unwise not to be willing to have such a good husband as he would most likely prove to be. At least I have always heard that he is very amiable and very much to be liked.

* Pooh! Nonsense! Car. will never marry! because she is too particular.

I think I should like him for a brother-in-law very much. However, I must remain in the dark I suppose as to whether there is any chance of his becoming so.

I have lost two of my young ladies, the Miss Disneys, who went away with their papa yesterday. Mary and Theo. Bligh are still here, and I believe remain till Monday. The latter regrets your absence, as she thinks you would walk with her and jump drains, &c. Poor dear Mrs. Macneil has only just recovered from a miscarriage which I believe she had about three weeks ago. I hope she will go to Abbeyleix, I should like them to be better acquainted with one another. She is very much to be liked I think. I have not much to say, so I will not scribble any longer, but with love to all, am ever your affectionate sister,

EMMA CLIFTON.

Both the Miss Blighs send kind remembrances to you.

*These words in Lord Clifton's handwriting.

Christmas found Lord and Lady Clifton back again at Cobham, and Emma seems to have been in a happier state of mind. She writes in her journal on December 31st, 1826.

This is indeed the last day of the year and I cannot but take notice that it has been to me a year crowned with blessings. I would thankfully acknowledge that God's tender love and fatherly care have been extended to me. I have enjoyed great health and all the comforts and luxuries of life have been mine. I had formerly no settled home (although through the mercy of God, I never suffered any uneasiness on that account but found a home oftentimes in the houses of different dear friends and relations), but during the last 17 months, thanks be to God, I have found rest in the house of my husband as Naomi wished that Ruth and Orpah might. Oh! how I wish that I were more thankful to God, for that first and best of all earthly blessings the kind, loving and most precious husband that He has given me! Every day I do but perceive what a treasure I have in my dearest C. and no woman can be more happy in her marriage than I am. As to spiritual blessings I have enjoyed a large share among which I do not reckon least the great advantage of having had between 4 and 5 months retirement at Clifton Lodge where I had much more time for reading the word of God than I had for a long time and where I was blest with the religious society of my brothers and sister Mary, and I acknowledge with thankfulness that my brother John's example and conversation were of great use to me, although I do not think his very Calvinistic views are desirable.

January 9th, 1827. I have during the week or ten days been becoming later every morning. When we came here I persisted for some time in getting up before 8, so as to have quite done my washings by half past eight, but now when my cup of tea comes at that time I am generally in bed. I feel that it is very wrong to encourage sloth and idleness in this manner, and I know I shall have to give an account of my time as of every other talent entrusted to my care.

Monday, Jan. 15th. I indulged shamefully in lying in bed this morning, and I fear that my idleness was in fact the procuring cause of the absence of three persons besides myself from family prayer. The sin of indolence does indeed easily beset me.

Sunday, Jan. 21st. So much snow that we did not go to Church. After prayers I went to my or our sitting-room and was agreeably surprised by my dear Cliffy's following me there. We read the 55th and 56th Chapters of Isaiah, and afterwards one of Mr. Close's excellent lectures. The subject was family religion.

January 28th. I hope and Pray that I may happily have formed a wrong opinion of many who are near and dear to me, especially my dear father and mother-in-law. Of these, my dear husband's parents, I have tried in vain to persuade myself that they have embraced salvation through Christ, but I greatly fear that these two dear persons are still relying on their own righteousness. Most exemplary are they as husband and wife, as father and mother and as heads of a family and in every duty among men, but what will this avail them if they are not found in Christ.

Lord and Lady Clifton on leaving Cobham went to a house that they had taken in Harley Street, where their eldest son, John Stuart, afterwards the 6th Earl of Darnley, was born on April 16th, 1827.

Emma Clifton's journal speaks of the pleasure she enjoyed during the time she was expecting this happy event from some visits beginning April 4th, 1827, " from my dear old friend Kate Browne."* She has so much information and learning and so much strength of mind and sound judgment, united with so much humility and lowliness and is most truly affectionate and kind. Many and many a kind thing she has done for me and many a kind though grave reproof has she in old times administered to me, and I think even in those times I deeply felt the value of such friendship and now that I am older and have many other dear friends, I prize it more and more. This is the first time that I have

* Mrs. Peter Browne, eldest daughter of Emma Clifton's cousin, Mrs. Puget.

had any comfortable conversation with her for nearly four years. We were talking of my approaching confinement and she asked me whether I dreaded it or was afraid of dying. She said many persons would say that it was wrong to talk of death to a person in my situation. She thought it a point of duty to remember that "although the generality of women recover, yet that some die in childbirth, and we should remember that there is a risk of death, and endeavour to prepare ourselves for it." Some pages follow of what Mrs. Peter Browne said ending with her offer to come to Lady Clifton at the time if Lady Darnley was not able to come. This conversation seems to have led to the following letter being written by Lady Clifton in case matters went wrong with her.

LADY CLIFTON TO LORD CLIFTON.

April 4th, 1827.

My own dearest most beloved husband, I have often thought that in the probability of that event which must sooner or later happen to all, befalling me at the time of my confinement, that it would be a comfort to you to find a few lines from your own beloved wife addressed to yourself. I do not know however whether I shall be able to write or not, for the idea of such a separation quite overwhelms me, and I cannot refrain from weeping when I endeavour to think of it. I do indeed feel bewildered when I attempt to think that perhaps in a very short time our sweet and inexpressibly tender union may be dissolved. I have not courage to consider the subject fully—I ought not to let myself be agitated, I think; and I feel that to suffer my mind to dwell upon this most painful idea would infallibly agitate it. I do however mean to make it a subject of daily prayer that God would be pleased for His dear Son's sake to give me grace, to acquiesce with meekness and resignation in His will, if this should be the case. And to you also, my dearest Cliffy, may this grace be granted. I will endeavour to remember that our Heavenly Father knoweth what is best for us, and that if He should be pleased to take me away from you, it would no doubt be for the good of your soul, and might be the means appointed by God to bring you nearer to Himself, and to lead you to seek more entirely for all your happiness in the Fountain of Living Waters, whose favour is better than life itself, and in Whose presence there is fulness of joy for evermore. I wish so much that I could tell you how much I love you. It is however in vain to attempt to express it, unless by referring you to your own heart, that dear treasury of love and tenderness. And oh! how I grieve to think that I should often have grieved you and treated you unkindly as I know I have often done by giving way to peevishness and a fretful temper. Dearest love, I am quite sure you never were angry with me, nevertheless; and I dare say you hardly recollect the incidents I refer to. I will put off finishing this till another quiet opportunity offers, for I find I am not fit to write, and should perhaps give you an idea that I am melancholy which is not the case; for thanks be to God, few women are so richly blessed as I am. I do not mean that I am glad there are so few in a similar happy situation, but that I am thankful that I am one of the few on whom God has been pleased to pour out peculiar blessings.

EARL OF DARNLEY AT COBHAM TO LORD CLIFTON AT HARLEY STREET.

[Birth of John Stuart, afterwards 6th Earl of Darnley, April 16th, 1827,]

Dearest Clif,

Your letters received this morning at Sandgate occasioned various lively emotions, among which joy and gratitude you will easily believe were predominant. Most heartily we congratulate you, and hope to do so in person to-morrow.

Let good accounts meet us in Berkeley Square at or before 2, and your carriage if quite convenient, I shall send to Rochester for the letters to-night.

With kindest love to your Dear Mother,

Your most affectionate,

DARNLEY.

All Well. We leave Beppy and Itty here.

[Endorsed by Emma Clifton after Lord Darnley's death, " My dear Lord Darnley's most kind letter about myself and little John.—April 20th, 1831."]

After the birth of their son, Lord and Lady Clifton remained in London until after the christening of the child, which took place in London on Sunday, May 27th. Mr. Stokes came up from Cobham to officiate, and John Bligh notes in his diary that there was a family dinner at the Cliftons that evening, and another family dinner in Berkeley Square on the following. On June 4th Lord Clifton went to join his parents at Sandgate for the wedding of his cousin, Emily Wingfield to the Rev. Frederick Twisleton, which took place at Cheriton Church. On June 21st the Cliftons were present at a dinner party in Berkeley Square, at which the Duke and Duchess of Clarence and the Duke of Sussex were guests. On June 26th or 27th the Cliftons took their infant son down to Cobham, when he had his first sight of the noble home, which was destined to be his own personal property for more than sixty years. There was a large and gay party as usual at Cobham, and the yacht "Elizabeth" was in great request at Gravesend. On July 3rd, among other guests, came Mrs. and Miss Siddons, and the great actress gave recitations from Shakespeare on two successive evenings. Lady Clifton no doubt did not find this gaiety congenial, but she remained at Cobham until July 11th, when she and Lord Clifton left with their child for Ireland.

Emma seems to have persevered in her determination not to go to parties. She writes two pages in her journal on May 30th, 1827, on that subject, "finding that attending them and maintaining a watchful and devotional state of mind were incompatible," and also that it interfered with family worship in the evening. "Clifton does not see the obligation we are under to attend to these two points so clearly as I do" she observes sadly, "if he did he would think otherwise about evening or rather nocturnal parties."

Emma also reports a somewhat disagreeable conversation she had during this visit to Cobham with an unnamed person (probably Lady Darnley's brother, James Brownlow). She writes " B. has been talking to me in a manner which shows how closely those who are careless of religion observe the conduct of those who make a profession of it. He said, 'you make a point of keeping away from what is bad, but what good do you do? You say that you wish to make the most of your time but you idle all day long.' I attempted to defend myself by admitting the truth of what he said, but declaring that were I at home, I should act differently, but I could see that he looked to my actions and gave no credit to my words. However, I know that I have not willingly spent this week in idleness and I have been unhappy in my mind all the time. I have joined in all these things from the fear of displeasing Lord and Lady D. and from thinking that it would seem rude and unkind if I did not do as others do. How difficult it is to know what one ought to do in such a house as this! And what a pity it is that the master and mistress of it do not think more of improving the talents of time and influence committed to their care! If they did, they would not, in mistaken kindness, be willing by promoting a constant round of various amusements and by late and irregular hours, to induce their children and friends to neglect such great salvation as is offered to them in the Gospel. We have been spending a week in enjoying this lovely place and delightful weather, we have had sailing parties and music and poetry and pleasant and lively conversation, and it was very agreeable to spend the time thus, that is agreeable to self, this last week I feel that I have not lived unto God and that I have by my inconsistent conduct been a stumbling block in the way of one who scoffs at religion. I think it would be well another time to make a rule of remaining in my own room till two o'clock."

August 2nd. "Since we came here my

dear C. has been very punctual at family prayers at nine and appears determined to persevere. I was very late this morning, let me take care lest my irregularity should induce him to fall back into the same sin and so I should be a stumbling block in his way."

Lord and Lady Clifton did not go to Cobham for Christmas this year but Lord Clifton went over in January to attend Parliament, to see his parents and to have a little shooting. Lady Clifton and the baby remained at Clifton Lodge. We have only one of her letters this time but most of Lord Clifton's to her have been preserved. He arrived at Cobham on January 19th and found there a letter from Sir Henry Parnell saying that he and his daughters (Caroline, and Lady Henry Moore) would arrive at Cobham that evening from Dover; they seem to have staid there some days. Uncle Tom Parnell had kindly gone to Clifton Lodge to keep Emma company; after he left she went to Brittas to stay with Mr. and Lady Theodosia Bligh. (The latter was Lord Darnley's sister who had married in 1790 her cousin, Thomas Cherburgh Bligh, of Brittas).

Lord Clifton at Cobham to Lady Clifton at Clifton Lodge.

Jan. 19th, 1828.

I wrote no more to my dearest love but I put 3 covers into the Post at Shrewsbury, Birmingham and London to mark my progress. I arrived here at a quarter before 12, and found all, thank God, quite well. I should have been in time for breakfast but that the Mail was 2 hours later than usual. I just recollect that there is no Post to-night.

Jan. 20th. I found a letter from Sir. H. announcing their arrival at Dover and intention of being here yesterday evening which accordingly happened, and I am glad to say they all arrived in good Health. Henry grown a great deal, Mary much *in statu quo* and Car. thin from her raking. Her bonnet is not larger than yours, petticoats short. Sir H. goes to Town tomorrow to return Tuesday or Wednesday: the sisters of course stay. I found a letter from Tom Vesey declining to go, which I believe I told you. We had a good passage of 7 and a half hours which I now recollect I also told you. I am not a whit the worse for my expeditious journey and found the few hours sleep at Bangor of much use, and came in here as fresh as possible, and joined the shooting party after getting some breakfast. I wrote my dear a few lines yesterday and hope to have a nice little letter from her to-morrow or next day. I expect that I cannot hear from you till Tuesday as there is no Post from London to-morrow. Pray dearest love, write me all particulars about your dear self, mentioning your cold etc. and let me hear exactly how J. S.* and his nurse are getting on, kiss the sweet baby for his old Papa. Only think of Parliament's being put off a week †—had I known it and of Tom Vesey's determination I need not have left you so soon. I did not fully feel the loss I for a time sustain, till last night when I retired for the night and had time to reflect and meditate, I had been so hurried before that that I had hardly time to think.

God in His mercy bless and preserve you. I hope dear kind Uncle Tom has gone to you, he is really a friend of ours.

Your affectionately attached,

C.

LORD CLIFTON AT COBHAM TO LADY CLIFTON AT
CLIFTON LODGE.

Jan 21st, 1828.

My dearest Love,

I have but a few moments to write to you but just sit down to say I am quite well. Your Papa went to town this morning and returns to-morrow. Mary was supposed to be in *petite santé* this morning and did not come down to breakfast but she seems very well now. Car. is in force, and Henry very nice. I am longing to hear from you, and to-morrow morning's post will be expected with great impatience as I hope to have two letters. My darling, I hope you have not felt your lonely situation very much, and that you forgive my cruelty in leaving

---

* John Stuart Bligh, their little son.

† In consequence of Lord Goderich's resignation on January 8th, Parliament was prorogued until January 29th. The Duke of Wellington became Prime Minister.

you. I trust that Uncle Tom went down to you. Let me hear what you are about with the other Uncle Tom. Give me all particulars about yourself and others. Sir Henry Blackwood (the Port Admiral) and his son are come here to dinner, and I expect the butler to announce it—I had a very nice little letter from Itty dear this morning, which I will send you if I can find it. We have been out shooting of course, and had good sport. Johnny is the commander in chief. The Tighes are here, also Mr. Rich and his sons. Kiss my darling baby for me. God bless you both my very dears.

Your affectionate hubby,

C.

Lord Clifton at Cobham to Lady Clifton at Clifton Lodge.

Jan. 22nd, 1828.

O my dearest love, what delightful sensations did your two dear letters inspire as I read them this morning in the fields where I was attending Johnny in a shooting match, to kill a quantity of partridges, in which he partly failed, but got 42 birds which was pretty well. I am delighted by your last letter and the account of our dear child. Notwithstanding the little interruption which took place in the 2nd night of his weaning, I think on the whole he appears to have gone on wonderfully well. I hope poor nurse is quite recovered by this time. How very kind it is of your Uncle to go to you during your loneliness at the Lodge : he really shews his affection when it is wanted, which very few will do. I hope you will thus be rendered somewhat more comfortable during my absence. How I wish I could say how short it should be, but alas! I cannot. I have great hopes however that it will not be very long, and you may depend upon my slipping away the moment that I decently can. No one seems to know what the final Ministerial arrangements will be, and no party is satisfied; at least so I hear. Your Papa returned from Town to-day, but brought no particular news. You amuse me with the account of your visitors; Miss Talbot must be a curious creature. I hope you will take Post horses whenever you feel inclined to go out as it is quite right that you should go during this fine weather, and enjoy yourself a little. I have been forced to postpone writing till after dinner as I was out all day. Adieu! sweetest, dearest and most precious of mortal beings. May the Immortal and Almighty Giver of all good gifts rain down upon us the blessings of His grace and Providence. How grateful ought we to be and how dreadfully the reverse, at least I am. This morning I might have had a serious accident as my horse fell with me in the road, but thank God, I was not a bit hurt, shall we ever take warning of our frail state?

God bless my dearest wife, kiss my baby for me tenderly, my sweet love, and let me have heaps of your precious letters. Miss Wilkinson came to-day and is now singing with E. Bligh. Mr. Rich sends his remembrances, and a kiss to J. Stuart. I regret to say he goes to-night.

Your loving husband,

CLIFFY.

R.

January 23rd, 1828.

I find that sister Mary has written to my dearest Wife to-day and I hope she has given a good account of us all ; she amuses herself principally with drawing which she does very nicely, having taken lessons in Paris. I had a very good account of you and baby and nurse from Dr. Adams to-day ; God grant that you may all continue well, and that I may see you again safe and well as soon as possible. I suppose I shall go to Town on Tuesday for the meeting and return here for a day or two while the Ministerial arrangements are making and before the work of the Session begins : it will be a few days probably before I can conjecture how long I may be detained. We have shooting here every day much as at Abbeyleix. I endeavour to follow your injunctions as to reading a portion of the Scriptures daily, but I have not read much yet except for an hour or two on Sunday. Pray for me, dearest, for I want your prayers ; I am a very sinful creature, and I fear incorrigible. Kiss my dear Baby for me. I feel no ill effects from my fall.

Adieu, dearest love,

Your affectionate husband,

C.

January 27th, 1828.

I have received a very nice letter from my sweet wife, on the eve of her departure for Brittas for which many thanks. I hope you are comfortably settled there now and that you may enjoy yourself with my aunt and cousins. Pray without scruple write us all about your *sejour* there, and how you are received, entertained, &c. ·I am much obliged to Mr. Chambers for communicating what you state and I will endeavour with God's blessing to rectify it; it is unfortunate that I should get the credit of neglect of my poor suffering neighbours in the County of Meath, as my greatest object in residing there is to improve their situation. It will be my business to endeavour to cultivate the kind feeling of the people about my father's estate. I have heard nothing of what Gunning etc. are about, as they do not write as I desired them.

We are all well here. God bless you my dearest love. Kiss baby dear for me.

Your affectionate husband,

C.

LORD CLIFTON AT COBHAM TO LADY CLIFTON AT BRITTAS.

Jan. 29th, 1828.

My dearest love.

You will perhaps be surprised to hear from me still from here, but the reason of my not being in the House of Commons is that I have just enough of gout in my big toe to prevent my lending my assistance to the great Council of the Nation. It feels as if it would not be a fit—or continue—which I scarcely hope will prove the case. It would be very uncomfortable to be laid up far away from my dearest wife and child. I hope the dear

Bairn has not suffered since the first night you got to Brittas from whence I had the pleasure of receiving a letter this morning. I must insist upon your sending for Cawdell or Betsey if there is any difficulty about carrying him, as air and exercise are indispensable for the continuance of his health. Pray mind this injunction, as I should be very sorry to think that any too nice delicacy of feeling should be in the way of your comfort or baby's health. Your Papa went to Town this morning for the meeting of Parliament. My Papa and Charles Brownlow, who came on Saturday, went yesterday. No one seems to know what is to be done in Parliament and I confess I am not very eager about Public business. It needs not your rhetoric to convince me of the disagreeableness of Electioneering; I am fully convinced of it, and have no taste or inclination for it, beyond the performance of a duty. Your sisters are staying here still I am happy to say: they did intend going to-day, but my Mother asked them to stay. They seem to enjoy themselves; Mary appears very fond of music, of which we have had abundance. Miss Wilkinson went to-day; Edward Bligh* is not nearly so great here with her, as he is in Ireland when he has it all to himself. I am glad you have the society of his wife, who is a very sensible person and I should think a good companion. This is delightful weather for her garden; pray take hints, plants, or anything you can get. I feel my widowed state very much. This is the first day of cessation from the feverish excitement of shooting, singing etc. Kiss darling

* Edward Bligh of Brittas, known as " Pipes."

baby for his old gouty Papa, I wish I could see you both.

God in his mercy bless you and your sweet child prays.

Your affectionate hubby

C.

LORD CLIFTON AT COBHAM TO LADY CLIFTON AT BRITTAS.

February 7th, 1828.

My dearest wife,

I have received your long sermon-letter and altho' I am ever averse to doctrinal argument which the religion of such as you always if discussed involves, I cannot refrain from making some observations upon it, and at all events expressing my delight, that, however we may differ upon many points to which I do not attach the same importance as you do, you are influenced by so pure a spirit of Christian love, and pious devotion to God, manifested by your every word and action, and that at all events I most heartily concur with the sentiment with which you conclude, "may the Lord in His great mercy make the light of his glorious Gospel to shine into both our hearts, and make us to know more of Him."

What I most complain of in those with whom Faith is all in all in Religion, is, that they impute infidelity to those whose Faith is in fact much more comprehensive than that which would prescribe to the Justice and other infinite attributes of the Almighty, which in the nature of things are unsearchable, and not to be named by the limited capacity of man. I believe, I must believe, if I acknowledge Him to be in all respects infinite, that God is just, and that however it may please His all wise Providence to disguise from poor weak Man the perfection of his omnipotence, it is the height of presumption in the perishable creature to question his Creator's justice or other attributes ; and what is it but questioning this same, if we think it necessary to reconcile to our finite capacity, the workings of His infinite goodness, before we can set our seal to the Religion God has enjoined, that it is true. I believe, at least I hope I believe ; but I cannot think it necessary that the Belief I profess should depend upon an argument in my poor weak mind upon the justice etc. of the Almighty. The great doctrine of the atonement I believe as fully as you can, but if I did not suppose that the measure of my fruition of its advantages, should depend upon my own endeavour, with the Grace of God preventing me in common with all who will avail themselves of it, I do not see why I should strive to obtain it, as the sacrifice has been full and sufficient for all Mankind, and leaves it perfectly consistent with God's Justice to pardon whosoever it may please Him to pardon, and destroy whom He will destroy. I have drawn this case to shew you the danger of Calvinistic doctrines. If the person imbibing them takes a pious and devoted turn, well and good ; we cannot be too religious and I would not quarrel with him for the degree of piety with which he is devoted to God ; but conceive the horrible state into which a man may be brought if he supposes that as the decrees of the Almighty are fixed and immutable, and that as all are sinners, and Christ Jesus a sufficient ransom for all, it matters not what steps he may himself take towards Salvation. But no more of this—I rejoice, my sweet love, to see the pious bent of your thoughts and actions, in this respect I truly have no reason to complain of the doctrines you profess, my invaluable wife. The sincerity of your love to your Maker, makes the happy creature to whom your fate is most closely allied, most confident in your love to him, and fills him with the most delightful sensations of affection and esteem. My heart yearns for you, like a weaned child, and I look forward to seeing you again soon, if it shall please the Almighty disposer of all events so to bring us together again. Would that I were truly grateful for all the blessings I enjoy.

LORD CLIFTON AT COBHAM TO LADY CLIFTON AT BRITTAS.

Feb. 10th, 1828.

My dearest Love,

I received your dear affectionate letters yesterday and to-day, and am delighted by your account of yourself and baby. You may be sure that no proposition of yours can make me angry or approaching to a state in which I hope I never was and never shall be when you are the object; and you need not have hinted at the possibility of such a contingency. I am much pleased moreover by the Christian spirit of kindness and true charity which prompts you to take care of your deceased

Aunt's children,* but I fear that there are difficulties in the way which you do not seem to have considered, and which in our present circumstances appear to me to preclude us from doing what we might wish. In the first place, the fact of our having to move backwards and forwards 400 miles every year, you know already entails considerable expense, and that we are sufficiently crowded— how would it be if we had another child of a different age from our own who would require another nurse, at least I think so. To Mary it is quite a different thing, she has a child of the same age for whom a companion is desirable, and the same nurse will do for both and she does not expect more children. You will say, but suppose we should have more children ourselves, we must take care of them; granted, but at the same time as such a contingency is possible it behoves us not to saddle ourselves with another person's till we know how we can provide for our own. If we once take a child in that way of course we must keep it till provided for, and I really think you would be loading yourself unnecessarily under existing circumstances to undertake such a task. However, I am open to conviction and desirous that you should be kind to, and assist your cousins. I have just directed a letter from Mary to Mr. Erskine, I suppose on that subject. And now sweetest, I must tell you that I mean to go to Town to-morrow, and if I can possibly get through the business of Parliament this week, to start on my return early

* Lady Harriet Erskine, née Dawson, died December 16th, 1827, leaving eight young children.

the next. My Father talks of going with me, but has not decided. If I go as I suppose I should hope to be with you at the end of next week, would that suit? I may report myself well except that the toe which was lame at Abbeyleix is still so, and Mr. Beaumont* says the nail will come off, and that it will not heal for some time. Adieu! dearest, kiss my sweet baby for me, and give my love to all at Brittas.

Your affectionate and loving hubby,

C.

LADY CLIFTON AT BRITTAS TO LORD CLIFTON AT COBHAM.

Monday, 18th February, 1828.

My dearest love,

I am very glad your toe is in a fair way of recovery. I do not wish you to have too much confidence in medical advisers, but I think you can hardly justify your conduct if you do not follow the dictates of reason and common sense, in a case like yours of a tendency to inflammation (i.e. Gout) and irruption or humour in the blood. And I cannot help thinking that common sense dictates great carefulness about diet and abstinence, and frequent doses of innocent medicine (i.e. rhubarb and magnesia). I am rejoiced to think of your return as likely to take place soon—I think Lady Theo. expects you to come here, and I would suggest your writing a pretty little letter as you well know how to do, to tell her when you have fixed the time, and to thank her for all her very great kindness to me

* The family doctor.

and baby. She has been truly affectionate and kind to me and him, and I think she is a person who sets a high value on little attentions, and is quite delighted with any little expression of kindness. I am afraid she is equally disposed to be affected by the least appearance of neglect or forgetfulness; but indeed I cannot help suspecting that your Mama has given her formerly some reason for complaint, in having neglected her when living in London. They seem very sore on the subject, and therefore as they have been very kind to *us*, I should wish to shew our sense of it. I am sure you would be pleased if you knew how attentive and kind one and all have been to me during my stay here. And they are quite delightfully so to baby which you know is a sure method of winning a parent's heart. I am very glad to think that I shall have my sisters' company, but I wish Car. could go to some place where she would enjoy herself more, as she did not seem to like Clifton Lodge.

I am afraid of being late.

Your affectionate Wife
EMMA CLIFTON.

Lord Clifton went to London as soon as his gout permitted him, for affairs in both Houses of Parliament were exceedingly interesting and important. The chief measure of this Session, the Repeal of the Test and Corporation Acts* was introduced by Lord

*The Test and Corporation Acts, passed in the reign of Charles II. required that all persons, before sitting in the legislature, or accepting office under the Crown, should qualify by receiving the Sacrament of the Lord's Supper according to the ritual of the Church of England.

John Russell in February, and though the Government at first opposed the proposal, it was eventually supported by the Duke of Wellington in the House of Lords and carried in both Houses by large majorities, including Lord Darnley and Lord Clifton. After this was settled they both went to Ireland, and on April 25th Lord Clifton brought his wife and year-old son to 3, Mount Street, for the Parliamentary season. Lady Clifton still remained obdurate about sharing in amusements as will be shown by the following pages of her journal and a letter from her father-in-law.

FROM LADY CLIFTON'S JOURNAL (1828).

On Friday 25th of April came to town. On Wednesday 30th, went to hear Mrs. Fry give an account of what had been done since 1816 up to the present time for female prisoners. Was much interested. Hope I may find it practicable to visit Trim Gaol with Mrs. Hamilton and perhaps Lady Dunsany. Striking anecdote of the importance of family prayer. Young woman just before execution spoke to Mrs. Fry and entreated her to warn other young women never to live with irreligious ladies, imputed her own untimely death to the bad effect on her mind produced by the ungodly, worldly life of her mistress.

Thursday, May 1st. Met Mr. Calthorpe who said that he thought the strongest reason to be brought forward against any amusement partaking of the nature of an assembly was the infinite harm done to the servants of those who attend. In order to obtain shelter, they enter the public-houses, where they meet with the most abandoned characters; depravity and profligacy among servants is perhaps the inevitable consequence of the gay assemblies of their superiors, many of whom would be shocked if they had any conception of the temptations to which they expose their servants.

I fear that my endeavour to shew my sense of my obligations to my Reedeemer by obeying His injunctions of coming out from the world and being separate from it and not conformed to it, has been sullied by a great deal of pride, vanity and folly. I fear that my errors, follies and sins have been and are stumbling-blocks in the way of my beloved husband and others. But I do not think it would be right to renounce the duty, from fear of the consequences of my errors and sinful failures in it; the same motive might induce me to forbear discharging any duty which is peculiarly exposed to the observation and remarks of others. Rather let me remember that with God all things are possible, and that He can and no doubt will in His own good time, give me grace and strength to walk worthy of the vocation wherewith I am called.

During our stay in London I went to the Meetings of the British and Foreign School Society, the Naval and Military Bible Society and the Reformation Society.

Beppy said if I did not go to the Ancient Concert on Wednesday, all the fine people, when they heard the reason of my being absent, would turn up their noses, and be filled with contempt for religion. She said also that she thought that it was the devil who put it into people's heads to give up worldly amusements and society, in order that he might make religion appear unamiable and prevent others from embracing it. Query. Who are those who would thus scoff and ridicule, and be disgusted with religion ? Are they not, however amiable and pleasing, yet walking according to the course of this world, according to the prince of the power of the air, the spirit that now worketh in the children of disobedience ? Is not their standard of right and wrong that of the world, and not that of God ?

EARL OF DARNLEY AT 46 BERKELEY SQUARE TO LADY
CLIFTON AT 3 MOUNT STREET.

Sunday, May 4th, 1828.

Your letter, my Dearest Emma, so far from offending me, has only raised you in my opinion, and you may rest assured that neither my Religious nor Political Principles will ever lead me, directly or indirectly, to attempt to force the conscience of any one.

As to your quotations from Scripture " Set your affections on things above " etc. " Love not the world " etc. So say I—but I must still maintain that between setting affections on and loving and using moderately and occasionally, as recreation from more serious matters, there is a wide and important difference, and I know not how this can be better exemplified than by the illustration (which I believe I borrow from Clifton) in the difference between drinking a glass or two of wine and getting drunk.

Your opinions may be correct, but I trust they are not, as they consign to eternal perdition the great mass of Mankind, including

Your most affectionate

DARNLEY.

P.S.—Though you will not come yourself, I hope you will allow that lost Sheep, your Husband, to partake of what I must still think our innocent recreations on Wednesday.

Parliamentary affairs at this time were in rather a curious condition. An undoubted Tory, in the person of the Duke of Wellington, was Premier, and a very strong Premier too. Still he kept his place only by favour of the Whigs, who abstained from factious opposition though not openly supporting him. He had already passed one of their measures, the Test and Corporation Acts, he was next year to make what appeared at the time the most extraordinary *volte face* ever known in politics and to pass the Catholic Relief Act against which, he himself and every member of his party were heavily pledged. At the time his conduct appeared almost inexplicable and there were few who understood his motives. Memoirs which have since been published more than justify his conduct and we now know that in all probability his good generalship alone saved the country from the terrors of civil war. It was as a general rather than as a statesman that the Duke achieved his end. Having made up his mind that the thing had to be done, he carefully concealed his real intentions from everybody until the moment came for action. Then he rushed it through, probably the only way in which it could have been done. We know now that at this time (May and June, 1828) the Duke was deeply considering the case for the removal of Catholic Disabilities and allusions to conversations with him in Lord Darnley's letters are extremely interesting.

Many changes had followed the secession of the "Canningites" from the Duke's Government. Vesey Fitzgerald, who was appointed President of the Board of Trade, had to seek re-election in Co. Clare ; O'Connell, the leader of the Irish Catholics, opposed him and won the seat. As he was unable to take the required oaths he could not take his seat and a deadlock resulted which, it was perceived, would be repeated all over Ireland.

The Duke sat silently by when Lord Eldon, at the Pitt Club dinner, proposed "One cheer more for Protestant Ascendency," he was equally silent while Lord Darnley and

Lord Winchilsea wrangled in the House of Lords over the great Anti-Catholic meeting of Pennenden Heath; and in December, 1828, when the Roman Catholic Primate of Ireland and the Lord Lieutenant (the Duke's old friend and comrade, the Marquess of Anglesey) attempted to force his hand, he removed the latter from office. A few weeks after this summary action, the Catholic Relief Bill was brought in and rapidly passed through both Houses of Parliament.

Lord Clifton's visits to Ireland in July and November were probably connected with the disturbed state of that country, as well as with the alterations at Clifton Lodge. Lady Clifton passed the summer at Cobham and Sandgate. Lord Clifton joined his father at Cowes for a few days yachting in August and after that the whole family met at Sandgate.

The death of Simon Taylor, John Bligh's greatest friend, from a fall from his horse when riding in Hyde Park, was a very sorrowful event at this time. Lord and Lady Darnley were full of sympathy for their son and cheered him by a visit to Paris, staying in the Rue Royale from September 19th to October 17th. They then returned to Sandgate where the Cliftons had remained during their absence.

Lord Darnley attended the Anti-Catholic Meeting on Pennenden Heath in Kent on October 28th, but Lord Clifton, more prudent than his father, kept clear of it. The Whigs were in rather an awkward position on that occasion, as they were embarrassed by their Radical allies. The meeting produced no result but a great deal of talk.

EARL OF DARNLEY AT 46, BERKELEY SQUARE TO HON. J. D. BLIGH AT PARIS.

Friday, June 6th, 1828.

Thanks for your letter of the 26th. It pleased us much to find you were so comfortably *domicilié chez son Excellence*, but we fear the late changes may dislodge you. I cannot however learn for certain whether Lord Granville goes or stays, but I think the former opinion preponderates among his friends, and after all you will know it better and sooner than I can tell you, however uncommunicative he may be.

I thought the late changes might afford to the Great Captain an opportunity of putting in execution the favorable intentions he had expressed towards you at the beginning of the year, and therefore reminded him of them. But as I told him distinctly that I feared it would be out of my power to give any parliamentary support to his

Government, and that under those circumstances it would be for him to decide how far it might be possible for him to give effect to his kind intentions towards you, and as I have not heard a word from him on the subject, though I have met him more than once in the House of Lords, I conclude nothing will or can be done. I do not however see how the change here or at Paris (if it take place) can affect you if you like to remain. If Lord Granville goes, there seems to be little doubt that his successor will be Lord Cowley and that Lord Stuart will go to Vienna. At all events you are at perfect liberty to take your own line, or to follow your inclinations, as I can have no object but your comfort and advantage, and by no means wish you to do anything that does not accord perfectly with your own feelings.

As to the state of things here, I am still inclined to hope, notwithstanding the untoward circumstances of the Pitt Club (as it is impudently and falsely called) that the Premier will not shut the door upon Catholic Emancipation à la Eldon, but that our debate on Monday will be of a conciliatory nature. This will be very much my touchstone with regard to the present Government, and induces me rather to suspend my judgment than at once to adopt with Charles [Brownlow] and others the tone of violent opposition and calling it a military and anti-Catholic Government. That it partakes of both those characters is certain, but I trust not to the exclusion of more free and liberal principles. Time will show. As to foreign politics, if they are to be really à la Metternich they must be bad, and I confess my opinion of the present Foreign Secretary [Earl of Aberdeen] is not very high, nor do I think those who call him a humbug (and there are many such) are very wrong.

Your mother and sister are gone to a School meeting, and have left me the sole task of conversing with you, at all times a very pleasant one, and which I should perhaps extend by scribbling on much more, if I did not wish to study the often repeated question in which I must take some part on Monday or Tuesday, for it seems generally thought that we must have two nights of it. It will be very interesting on many accounts. Wellesley intends to give us an oration, and to judge by the soreness manifested yesterday by *Old Boys* in answer to an attack (in rather bad taste, as usual) from King, *he* will show some sport.

I am under the strict discipline of Rich's doctor who swears he will cure

Your most affectionate,
D.

EARL OF DARNLEY AT FOREIGN OFFICE TO HON. J. D. BLIGH AT PARIS.

Friday, 4 p.m., June 13th, 1828.

Dearest John,

I have just come here from over the way, where I have had a long talk with the Great Captain, who told me amongst other things, that he did not care a farthing for my letter, but was determined to provide for you at home as soon as he could. He talked of Under Secretary of State, but that the Finance Committee had left and was leaving so little Patronage to Government, that he did not like to say when or how he could do anything, but of his good dispositions towards you I might rest assured. He also informed me you were to have your old Master, Stuart, where you are. [Sir Charles Stuart, lately created Lord Stuart de Rothesay].

We had also a long discussion of the Catholic Question, on which I find him quite reasonable, but denying any pledge. In short his view is very much what I thought it would be. He is very anxious to see it settled, but cannot at present see how it can be. He said it was always present to his mind, going to bed, getting up and dressing, and that there was a wide difference between wishing to do a thing and finding the means. The violence in a certain quarter he described as excessive. Quite a Passion. I informed him I had written a strong letter to Killeen on Wednesday begging forbearance and abstinence from irritating language, and that Charles Brownlow who went by the same mail (on matrimonial affairs*) and who is now I conclude in Dublin, promised to exert himself to keep them quiet if he could. I think I have in great measure converted the said Charles Brownin and made him as much a Wellingtonian as I am disposed to be myself. Sure I am that while this reign lasts, he is the best Minister we can have, provided he keeps clear of ultra-Toryism. By the bye he defended himself about the Pitt Club,

*Charles Brownlow, afterwards Lord Lurgan, widower of Lord Darnley's daughter Mary, married secondly, July 15th, 1828, Jane, daughter of Roderick Macneill, of Barra, Inverness-shire.

where he says he always went, and thought it would be shabby to have been absent now.

The papers will inform you all about the debate in the House of Commons yesterday. Surely the thing stands better than it ever did before. The first day in the Lords is remarkably ill given in the Times. I spoke for an hour, and I think not ill for a rare skirmisher. I will endeavour to send you a more faithful report, as I have this day taken time and pains to correct that of the Mirror of Parliament which was also less correct than usual.

I intended to have gone to Cobham to-day in the " Bet " which is at Greenwich, but must defer it till Sunday morning, when I hope to hear the Dr. [Mr. Stokes].

Lady Stuart has just been at the door, and expressed herself very kindly towards you, so I flatter myself your situation, if you remain, will be at least as good, and if you come away, much better. And now for Committee.

So addio Caro

D.

COUNTESS OF DARNLEY AT COBHAM TO HON J. D. BLIGH AT PARIS.

July 11th, 1828.

Dearest Johnny,

Your letters of the 4th and 7th arrived to-day ; your constant remembrances of us are most cordial to our hearts, as they so perpetually prove that we are so much in the feelings of a heart so much and so justly valued by all who have and do know its value. The little " painted things " are very pretty and the Bonnet I very much like, both as pretty and convenient. Aunt P. and Cata went to Addington yesterday, and I believe go to Town Monday to arrange about taking possession of Watton. I hope it will answer their expectations, and I believe it will do so from what I have heard. There is as numerous a neighbourhood as need be wished. The Glennie family will probably be their first visitors. If dear Beppy is well, we, Lord D. and I, intend (D.V.) dining to-morrow at Bromley Hill at 3 o'clock, and sleeping in London. Lord D. proposes that we should sleep Sunday night at Staines or thereabouts, and going next day to see Windsor Castle, which will put us out of the way of dear Charles' wedding if it actually takes place Monday, of which I believe the only doubt is Colonel Macneill's not being returned from Scotland. But Charles must go with or without Jane, so as to be in Ireland Thursday. I am sure we all wish him happiness in every respect; and with Jane he has, I think, every prospect of it. This in haste to your bag.

E. D.

Remembrances to Timar [John's friend, Simon Taylor, who was staying at Paris.]

Lady Clifton at Cobham to Lord Clifton at Clifton Lodge.

Wednesday, July 24th, 1828.

My dearest love,

The time has appeared very long since you went, and it is very sad indeed not to see you all day long. However, I trust your absence for a short time will be productive of much future comfort to yourself and me, little J.S. etc. He is very well, had a good night, and I try not to spoil him. I am afraid to write much as it is late. Your father and mother are very kind to me, making arrangements to go to Sandgate.

May God bless and protect you my darling.

Ever your affectionate wife,

E. CLIFTON.

My dear, I am so sorry not to write more.

LADY CLIFTON AT COBHAM TO LORD CLIFTON AT CLIFTON LODGE.

July 28th, 1828.

My dearest love.

You will be glad to hear that Simon Taylor arrived here yesterday, bringing an excellent account of Johnny, who is however much annoyed at being obliged to give up his rooms.* Papa is going to town therefore I write by him, to gain a day. Your parents and Beppy are annoyed by finding that the Brighton races begin on Wednesday (30th) the day on which they intend going there. I am so afraid you must be very uncomfortable at Clifton Lodge without anything to eat, or any one to wait on you. I am pressed for time, so will only just say that the dear boy looks and is very well. I wish you would take the subject of the linen into consideration. I greatly fear Eliza uses it. Could you not inspect?

Your affectionate Wife,

EMMA CLIFTON.

Papa is in a hurry.

*At the Embassy in Paris.

Tuesday night, 29th July, 1828.

My dearest love,

I neglected to write in time for Eastwood who
went earlier than usual therefore send a few lines
by Tom Vesey who goes early in the morning. I
and dear baby are very well, and I endeavour not to
spoil him. I am a good deal frightened by the rats
just now, who are squeaking under the bed. I was
very much pleased this morning to find you had
arrived in Dublin. I hope you are tolerably comfortable at the Lodge. Pray write me an account
of the flowers and shrubs, pyramidal yew-tree etc.,
also of the show of fruit in the garden, of which eat
with moderation. Ask Peggy Marly if she ever got
her money. And do think about the linen. If you
decide on having it over, pray tell Eliza to put my
babylinen and napkins up in the trunk. Cawdell
says that ten shillings a week is the general charge
for linen at a watering place. Perhaps if we do *not*
have a house in London, we can do without it as
then our own would lie by, that is unless the
Gunnings use it. We do not leave this till Saturday.

Ever your affectionate Wife,

EMMA CLIFTON.

I shall be very glad to have you back again.

COUNTESS OF DARNLEY AT BRIGHTON TO HON. J. D.
BLIGH AT PARIS.

August 4th, 1828.

My dearest Johnny,

Beppy having finished a letter to you this morning, will of course shorten my letter, and I hope she has expressed how sorry we all were that you have been a post or two without a letter direct from the family.

Simon Taylor in his short visit made us happy, by saying you were so, and that you enjoyed your Boat, which must indeed be badly manned, as he said *He* was next best, and the Duke de Fitz-James one of your crew. I should suppose you could turn them all round. Simon took the Bonnet for Lady L., as it was one of my reasons for asking you to send it to make him a visitor at St. James' Square, which will save him and you all future trouble about Almacks etc.

Matt,* we flatter ourselves gets on, and would more so if he made more exertion, but this fine sea air braces him, and he enjoys it in long and frequent drives. We have quite a storm on shore, and the full benefit of sea breezes in this house on the marine Parade, in so much that a door and window cannot be opened at same time, the waves were so strong that I really think Tom Vesey had a narrow escape when bathing, he was saved by one of the sailors, who attended the machines, but he says he had lost his breath and another young man really was insensible for a minute or two. This is a very good house, and we are well lodged, also three Bayleys and Tom Vesey all day long. Your father did not sail from hence, he went on horseback to Worthing or Bognor where he expected to go on board the " Bet," but as it was the beginning of

*Her nephew, Mathew Forde.

273

this storm, I think it likely he went by land to Portsmouth.

Sandgate will not be improved by this wind, for Emma, and the two dears, but I hope they arrived there safe. We shall leave this, D.V., Thursday, and if Lord Arran chooses it I intend him a visit to dine and sleep and then on to London Friday. I must be there some days, but if it can be arranged I wish Beppy to be at Watton, and then I would go there. Lord D. wishes me to wait for him there, or go to Ashridge! But I should prefer going to Sandgate. Prince Leo is coming here, and the Duchess of Kent to Tunbridge.

God bless you, my dear Johnny.

Yours always very tenderly,

E. D.

I have forgot to tell you that I sent to Coutts £11 for you that I may not be in your debt if I give you any more commissions. Lady L's Bonnet goes of course to that account.

EARL OF DARNLEY AT COWES TO COUNTESS OF DARNLEY AT 46, BERKELEY SQUARE.

Friday, August 8th, 1828.

Though I have not won the Cup, I never was better pleased with your namesake, who did wonders. The two first got such a start, that there was little or no chance of catching them, though I came in close to the second and beat the Ann after (I should think) the best race that ever was seen between two vessels. After having been run foul of by her, and losing my top-mast early in the race by the collision of one of the others. Pray communicate all this to Johnny. If I had had a fair start with the Julia and had not lost my mast I might have beat her, though I am inclined to think I should not, but I am sure I should have been near her and beat all the rest. The 13th I am to have another race with the Ann at Portsmouth. Adieu Dearest, I will endeavour to collect my thoughts and will write at length to-morrow. Clifton was with me and much delighted. Both "kite ell," [little Mary Brownlow's way of saying "quite well."] I fear I shall be too late.

D.

LADY CLIFTON AT SANDGATE TO LORD CLIFTON AT COWES.

Saturday, August 9th, 1828.

Thank you, dearest love, for your kindness in letting me have daily accounts of your progress. The great wind here to-day and the roar of the waves at this moment, combine to excite in me an anxious thought as to your degree of prudence about sailing, whether it is sufficient to keep you from trusting yourself on the water in a storm. I pity the poor vessels who are out at sea, for the sound of the tempest is tremendous. As you said in the letter I received this morning that you would perhaps come here to-day, I could not help expecting you a little, although I knew it was more probable that you would not come till next week. Mr. Madden has made his preparations as valet in the new room downstairs, and Mrs. Andrews has got some extra lamb chops ready to dress in case you should arrive hungry and Mrs. Jones said she thought she had better put a second pillow on her Ladyship's bed. I have been making very arduous researches into your road book, and the result is, that I think you cannot come in one day as I calculate the distance from Fareham to Hythe to be 123 miles, by Rye, Hastings and Brighton. In the little set of maps at the end of the book containing the Road from Margate to Southampton, the line of that which I have mentioned between Hythe and Fareham goes by Rye, Eastbourne, New Shoreham, Chichester, and Fareham, but I do not know where to find it in the book, as all the references give one the first mentioned line of road. Let me know exactly what day you are coming that I may have a fine, large plum-bread ready for you. I begin to find my solitude rather too much, and believe it is not good for woman to be alone, any more than man. I have been made a little nervous by the fear of Windsor's going mad, his eyes have looked very fiery and wild the last day or two, but I believe he is only a little indisposed by over-eating! There have been people coming up to the house with different things to show or to sell whose appearance rather frightened me. Yesterday, an Italian with images, to-day a great Frenchman with white mice, Savoyard boys who came about an hour afterwards, and either just or before them, a great stout beggar-woman and child. I am always afraid of these idle strollers who are seldom good sort of people. I believe Lady D. was to be in town yesterday and was afterwards going to Watton to visit Lady Powerscourt, Catherine, etc. I am becoming exceedingly sleepy so I may as well conclude. I shall be

> Ever your very affectionate wife,
>
> E.C.

Sweet very nice and well.

Sunday. I received yours of Friday. I am very glad you are enjoying yourself and would not be so selfish as to wish you to forego your favourite amusement for my sake. Pray continue to relate the affairs of the " Bet," for I assure you I like to have an account of what goes on. I have just heard Mr. Glennie preach a delightful sermon. I think you will be here about Friday. I had a letter from Beppy dated London this morning where they are to remain some days.

LADY CLIFTON AT SANDGATE TO LORD CLIFTON AT COWES.

> August 11th, 1828.

My dearest love,

I hope you will stay as long as there is anything going on that you particularly wish to see, although I wish much to have you with me. I am conscious that I am a very bad companion for you in the evening, which I lament much, but you know it is not my fault, but that of Mr. Morpheus. We are all very well and comfortable but as baby suffered very much last night with his teeth, I have sent for Mr. Hutchinson and hope he will not disappoint me. I am sorry the Elizabeth did not win a prize as I am sure you and your father would have been delighted if she had. I do not understand how you have settled about Clifton Lodge, but you will explain all when you come.

Ever, dearest,

Your affectionate Wife,

Emma C.

I shall scold very much if I discover any of my letters loose among your parcels etc. when you come.

Pray do not get a very lonely cottage, I like the cheerful sound of human voices round me. I do not wish to be like my collateral ancestor's Hermit. [The poet, Thomas Parnell.]

Lord Clifton at Cowes to Lady Clifton at Sandgate.

August 10th, 1828.

From the same place whither I have repaired from the same cause as yesterday. I am quite disgusted with Cowes which is dreadful when one is forced to remain anchored. I have been quite knocked down since Church by the melancholy intelligence of the death of our friend Simon Taylor, poor fellow his pony fell with him and he was kicked on the head in getting up and never spoke afterwards. In the midst of life we are in death indeed, and this is a dreadful warning at this moment, when I am witnessing and I fear by my presence abetting a life of thoughtlessness and attachment to temporary objects, beyond what one is in the habit of meeting with. Our dear Johnny will feel this blow most severely, as S. T. was the greatest friend he had, they were quite like brothers. I am already heartily sick of Cowes and longing to be with you even before this melancholy intelligence reached me : of course it has added to my disgust at what is passing before me : there is a bad set in the yacht club and I probably shall never, unless casually, join them again. I have heard from Mary* this morning, and she declines a plan I had formed that she should come over, and live in the same house with us somewhere near the sea. I have heard of a cottage near Ride, but I think it might be too much for us alone. I am determined not to take a house here, for it is [unfinished.]

LORD CLIFTON AT PORTSMOUTH TO HON. J. D. BLIGH AT PARIS.

August 11th, 1828.

My Dearest Johnny,

I have tried several times, but can hardly write to you so shocked am I by the catastrophe, which must have still more shocked and grieved you. Poor dear Simon ! Little did I think that I was never to see him more ! ! ! Oh what a lesson is this to us, dearest brother, may the great Giver of all things grant that we may profit by it. I know well your kind heart will feel the loss of your most intimate friend. I came to Cowes on Wednesday from Clifton Lodge, which I left on Monday morning, by Bristol, where I was at two on Tuesday.

The Bet was third for the cup and sailed beautifully, beating everything but the Julia with which she had no trial, as from the start and an accident which deprived us of our top-mast she was never within a mile and a half of us.

*Lady Henry Moore.

Goodbye dearest Johnny, I would have written other particulars were not my heart so heavy.

Your affectionate brother,

CLIFTON.

We beat the Ann fairly.

Good accounts from Sandgate.

My father desires me to say that he felt he could not write to you and has requested Trefusis to do so for him.

LADY CLIFTON AT SANDGATE TO LORD CLIFTON AT COWES.

August 12th, 1828.

My dearest love,

I am indeed greatly grieved to hear of the death of poor Simon Taylor, and especially as it was so sudden, and, might alas, have found him unprepared. Oh may it be a warning to you and me and all who hear of it to endeavour to be ready, to watch and pray, for we know not when our hour may come. Poor young man, he is taken away just when everything seemed to smile upon him, and has left for ever all those things that gave him so much satisfaction. Dearest Cliffy, let us pray to be enabled to have our treasure in heaven, and that we may have grace to seek for our souls' salvation while we are spared. We do not know but what we may have but a very short part of our time before us. Oh! do not let us think it too much to devote what does yet remain to seeking diligently for the one thing needful.

Dearest love, I do not know why we should go to the Isle of Wight to live there, if you find it disagreeable already. Perhaps we should be more comfortable somewhere else. I should like to go somewhere where there is a good preacher, for why should we not seek advantage for the soul as well as the body ? I think I have heard there is such a one at Hastings, what sort of a place is that ? I am inclined to think that you are not really kind to your father when you encourage him in his yachting, which by your own confession leads to a life of thoughtlessness and attachment to temporary objects. Besides you know I cannot approve of any steward of God's property spending as much on a toy (read yacht) for himself, as would build a small church and maintain a good minister to preach the tidings of salvation to perishing sinners in it. If I could get it into my clutches I should like much to turn it into a floating church for poor ignorant sailors at Portsmouth. Such are called Bethels, and I dare say you might go and hear service in one of them next Sunday at Portsmouth by a regular clergyman of the Church of England.

I fear you think I have been unkind about letter-writing. You have been very kind indeed and have written constantly. I have written more letters than you have yet received. I wrote on the Saturday I came here, and on the Monday and Tuesday afterwards and directed to C. L.; on Wednesday in that week I got your letter saying you intended leaving C. L. on the Monday, then two days past. Then I thought it better not to write till I heard from you at Cowes and I believe I wrote to you on Friday and Saturday, and yesterday also. I

did get your letters from Brighton but after some
delay as I was from Thursday the 31st July till
Tuesday the 5th, I think, without hearing from you,
and then got two letters a day for three days. If
you should come late on Friday or Saturday I think
it would be more comfortable for you to dine on
the road, as of course we do not have much meat in
the house. I shall indeed be very glad to see you
again, and I hope and pray it may please the Lord
to preserve you, and bring you here safe and well.
Darling boy had his gums lanced yesterday with
your gum-lancet. Mr. Hutchinson had none with
him so it was fortunate I had it. I consulted him
about my bathing in sea, and hinted my situation,
and he said if in the family way I ought by no
means to bathe in the sea, and that it would be
running the greatest risk in the world. But that
sea-air was always strengthening. Both children
are very well, as is also your very affectionate wife

EMMA CLIFTON.

LADY CLIFTON AT SANDGATE TO LORD CLIFTON AT CANTERBURY.

August 14th, 1828.

My dearest love,

I hope you are as comfortable at Canterbury as
circumstances will admit of, and that you endeavour
to *employ* the young attendant you took with you,
and to keep him out of mischief. There was a
letter from Lady D. this morning to little Mary, and
in it she said that they hoped to come here on
Tuesday next. I went down *toute seule* to the
village yesterday after dinner, and paid a visit to

Susan Hogben and her mother, whom I found in her bed, and very much pleased to have a visitor. Had I known of the poor old woman's situation before, I should not, I think have remained so long without going to see her. However it did me no good in a bodily way, as the daughter's room having a fire heated me very much, and I felt chilled in the mother's room which was comparatively cold and airy, and to this chill I attributed a pretty severe fit of face-ache during the evening. I also went down on the beach after visiting the Hogbens, but did not enjoy it as if you had been with me and on my return home I met to my dismay a fierce-looking mastiff and a drunken man as I thought. I intended endeavouring to please you again to-day by going down to the beach, but a shower of rain came on at one o'clock and I waited till I thought it too near dinner-time to go. However this afternoon I made amends by getting Hartley and her charge to accompany me a little way on Lord F.'s road. I have only sent you this long account of myself because I wished to show you that I have been attempting to follow up your system. The dear boy has been very well to-day, but suffered a good deal last night. Miss B. [Mary Brownlow] very well also. I must tell you that I have bought a very nice pair of screens exactly the same color as those I wished to replace and I have most ingeniously mended the others with strips of gold beaters' skin, put on in the way that a wound is closed with adhesive plaster. It was a great amusement to me when I was in pain yesterday evening. I shall be rejoiced to see you my beloved Cliffy, and hope it may please God to preserve and bless you, here and hereafter,

Ever your affectionate wife,

E. CLIFTON.

Very Morpheusious !

I opened a letter the post-mark of which was Devonport, which I believe, means Plymouth Dock, thinking it might be from Henry, but alas, it was from R. Disney. I send you all your letters to read in the carriage. I see by to-day's paper Friday, H.M.S. the Glasgow has arrived at Portsmouth. How shall I know if my brother is in it ? I know Papa has been manœuvring to have him kept out in some other ship. Will you, dearest go to a haber-dasher's and buy me a short gauze or crêpe scarf shaded with different colours. It is not to be very long, but just long enough to hide shape, pink and brown or lilac.

EARL OF DARNLEY AT WATTON TO HON. J. D. BLIGH AT PARIS.

August 19th, 1828.

I trust my very dear son has not for one moment imagined that because I have not written to him on this most melancholy occasion, that I have felt less for him than any of those who have. I desired Trefusis who first communicated to me the sad news, to write to you, for that I could not. In truth I was so astounded by the account itself, as well as by the manner of it, I was so well aware of the extraordinary weight with which the blow must fall on you, that knowing I could say nothing that could mitigate your sorrow, I thought it better for a time, at least to let it have full vent. My heart indeed was too full. I loved your friend on his own account, but still more on yours, for his attachment to you exceeded anything I had ever seen, and I am ready to admit the affection contained in your excellent letter to your mother that your loss is irreparable.

There are indeed very few Simon Taylors in the world, and when and how are you again to find one of them ? Still however you have friends, and dear ones, and they will exert themselves to alleviate your just grief, and as far as they are able to repair your great loss.

I feel that it is almost impertinent to write on any other subject, and yet you will, I am sure, rejoice to know that your aunt and cousin are as comfortably settled here as possible. We have passed three days with them, and have talked much of you, and your lost friend. There never was anyone so universally beloved and regretted. I believe I may say—

" Multis ille bonis flebilis occidit,
" Nulli flebilior quam tibi, etc."

the whole of this beautiful ode of my favourite is forcibly recalled to my recollection, and although we cannot admit the heathen doctrine of " perpetuus sopor," I am sure you will willingly adopt the sequel and say with me—

"Pudor, et Justitiæ soror,
" Incorrupta Fides, nudaque Veritas,
" Quando ullum inveniet parem ?"

Expect to hear again soon.

From your truly affectionate Father

D.

September 4th, 1828.

My dearest Johnny,

You will be pretty nearly sick of seeing my handwriting, and yet I am sure will prefer that to none belonging to the family and I cannot make out that you are likely to be supplied from a better quarter.

Papa is very busy cutting and sawing we think too much so as he opens views of the Martello Tower etc. as well as the Castle.

The Cliftons went to Eastwell yesterday, and propose returning Saturday, they will I think remain here during our absence.

The commencement of our journey towards you is likely I fear to be again delayed, for Papa has postponed his visit to Cobham till Monday, the day on which I expected we should set out.

You need not be uneasy on Mim's account, for, on the contrary from being injurious or disagreeable to her, I think the proposed visit to Paris even were you not the object would be beneficial to her, she herself says it agrees with her better than any other place, and I assure you I have been latterly rejoicing not merely in the idea of going to you, but likewise in the prospect on her very account, for (of late years especially) a stationary life suits her even less than Papa, in short I have often thought of urging them to make little trips and leave their incumbrances here with the dear Mary. In this case however the desire of seeing you my dear Brother overcomes my generosity and wish that

LADY ELIZABETH BLIGH.
From a drawing by Miss Kate D'Arcy.

they would enjoy themselves à la Darby and Joan.

I am sorry to say we are obliged to patronize a morning concert to-day and which will cut my scribble very short, and without much compliment to you I can say is not a little disagreeable to me.

I am glad you liked Heber's lines and I hope you will not dislike those I enclosed in my last, however, I will not try your patience with any more of my effusions lest I should end in disgusting you by my prosings. I have no reason indeed to think I have, or at least that you do not take my intentions kindly. And we are desired to try to " comfort one another with such words " by the " Father of Mercy and God of all comfort, who comforteth us in all our tribulations that we may be able to comfort them which are in trouble by the comfort wherewith we ourselves are comforted of God."

I have here unwittingly put myself on a level with St. Paul ! ! by apparently applying his words to myself.

This nasty Concert obliges me to conclude. And I believe I have nothing more to add. Dear Emily* is going on perfectly well, thank God. Frederick insists upon christening his little girl Emily Wingfield.

They have had a visit from Mr. Fiennes, the first he has ever paid them. Emily has never seen him yet. Poor Mrs. Fred Brownlow has been very

*Daughter of Isabella, Viscountess Powerscourt, m. Rev. Frederick Twisleton, who later took the name of Fiennes and became 16th Baron Saye and Sele. Their daughter Emily Wingfield, married (1) 1849, Thomas Guy Gisborne, of Yoxall Lodge, Staffs ; (2) 1872, John Harwood Griffiths.

near dying, but is better. John has another child. 1 forget whether I told you that Charles* made anxious and affectionate enquiries for you ; he and Jane seem very happy. He is going to pull down the old house immediately, and they are fitting up the garden house for their temporary residence.

God bless you, dearest John. Continue to love

E. B.

I am glad you are inclined to feel kindly towards P. Stewart. I was always inclined to like him independently of the character I heard of him from our dear (I will not call him lost) friend.

COUNTESS OF DARNLEY AT SANDGATE TO HON. J. D. BLIGH AT PARIS.

24th October, 1828.

My dearest Johnny,

I wish I could give you some intelligence to be depended upon from the Heath.† I scarcely reckon upon any by the last Coach, but your father wrote a line by post last night, saying that he hoped their going yesterday had done some good, and they have a lovely day. I am now going to make an experiment from what Hunter said, that a letter sent this evening to Dover would go to-night by Bag or Messenger. I thank you for No. 1 and Elizabeth has some parcels. We had several at Calais, and every box and parcel opened, and well taxed. I assure you my dearest Johnny, much as I always

*Charles Brownlow, afterwards Lord Lurgan.

†Lord Darnley had attended a great meeting on Pennenden Heath on October 28th, convened by the Earl of Winchilsea to protest against Catholic Emancipation.

feel your absence, I never did more, if so much as when I lost sight of your dear face last Friday. But my dear son, though I fear you cannot be so happy with us at dear Cobham as you have been, yet I do indeed look forward to blessings for you, that you may not at present expect ; continue to follow the path to as much perfection as human frailty will allow of, and that will bring peace at the last.

I have got into a disagreeable hobble about my bill to Mlle. Victorine, which I do not choose to tell Lord Darnley till I know whether I can get back what I have over paid. I hope that it will not give you much trouble to go to Mr. Daly and get him to arrange it if Mlle. Victorine will pay back as the bother arose from my mistaking the figures 5 and 9 according to the French which always appear the same, and I in my bustle and Beppy saying I ought to have so much more to pay than she had, most foolishly wrote the sum 9, as I think Mr. Daly will see plainly the mistake, and I hope be enabled to get back what is over paid, but I fear not without trouble, at all events I beg Lord D. may not be enabled to quiz me till it can be arranged.

I send the bills which were given to a young woman, who, when I paid the bill Thursday at Paris would not give up one frank for herself. I think you will have reason to say how unfit my mother is to pay bills.

God bless you.

Yours most affectionately,

E. D.

24th October, 1828.

My dearest Johnny,

The Cliftons are just gone to Hatch. He on horseback and she and Cawdell in the chaise, they return, I believe, Wednesday. The boy has been very well, but only from pain of teething and has not fever. Emma is, and is looking very well, and very portly, C. also.

The weather milder here than at Cobham consequently Dahlias, Geraniums, and Salvias are nearly as fine as at Paris.

We are all glad that you were not routed from your abode at Paris from the ineffectual row at Penenden. I think it might have been managed more successfully if Clifton had had the whole arrangement, and the odious Cobbets etc. could have been wheeled off, they certainly were out-generalled, not so victorious by numbers as was supposed.

Poor little Mary gets into frequent scrapes about her music lessons, but I think her a very good child, and she looks and is well. If James is not gone give my love to him, and tell him to bring the cloaks for Fanny de Vesci and Catherine.

I hope money will be paid back to Mr. Daly by Mlle. Victorine which I wrote to you about, that will pay, I believe, the three fur cloaks, for me, Emma and Elizabeth, I wrote to Ritchings to get the bill and tippet also.

I don't know whether this is finished, but I have put it up as it would otherwise be too late.

E. D.

LORD CLIFTON AT CLIFTON LODGE TO LADY CLIFTON
AT COBHAM.

November 17th, 1828.

My dearest Love,

Tho' I have written frequently it has only been by little scrawls, and I am happy to sit down and write to you from our dear comfortable little abode, having arrived here to dinner. I am glad to hear so good an account of dear little *Ta* whom kiss for Tata. I am sorry to say I did not see George in Dublin but I heard that he is well. I hope Uncle Tom will come down in the course of the week, but he would not promise. I hope I shall be able to get to Moore Abbey for a night or so, but my chief difficulty is Abbeyleix where if I did not go, being so far on my way, I should never be able to make my peace again. As I did not arrive till moonlight I cannot give you much account of the place and its looks, etc., except that I see the yards are full of immense clumps of turf, so that we need not fear cold. There appear to me to be near 2,000 bricks. The consequence is that I find the house (as usual) quite warm and dry, and Mrs. Eliza and Mr. Paddy Thornton very assiduous as Cook and Housekeeper, and Butler and Valet. I dined yesterday with Mr. and Mrs Cuming, and like what I saw of him. She is in good looks tho' thinner than in her maiden days, she has no appearance of sickness, etc. This morning I breakfasted with my old acquaintance Sir Joseph de Courcy Laffan. Elizabeth can tell you who he is, and how he dosed me in the days of

Lady C. M. A. G. O.*   I suppose you will be going to Cobham to-morrow.   I shall be busied here, with planting and various improvements.   I *did* give John Connor a douceur when I was in Town but I am sorry for it, for he is a great sot.

Adieu, sweetest darling love,

Your affectionate Husband,

CLIFTON.

LORD CLIFTON AT CLIFTON LODGE TO LADY CLIFTON
AT COBHAM.

My dearest Love,

I am sorry that I have not written in time for Post to-day, and that I have not heard from you to-day or yesterday, but I hope before this goes to have intelligence of your dear self and babe.   I received this morning letters from Moore Abbey and Abbeyleix, I suppose if I go to the one I must extend my trip to the other also for a couple of nights.   Do you give leave ?   I have had Mr. Hargrave the Architect here, and mean to put our building concern into his hands.   I cannot consent to have our dear pleasure ground cut up by the approach coming across it.   What do you think of coming out of the avenue opposite about the middle of the garden wall, and so creeping up to the house? Recollect there must be a return to the Stables. I have had Millie with me to-day, and have engaged him from the 1st of January.   Alas ! poor Gunning.   He will however continue for a time at least

*Dr. Laffan had prescribed for Lord Clifton in Paris, in the year 1823, when the latter was an admirer of Lady Charlotte Mary Anne Georgina Osborne, alluded to in Chapters II and III.

in a subordinate capacity. I fear that I shall be nearer a month than three weeks away from you as I cannot well finish here in less than ten days more. Kiss my darling little *Ta* for *Tata*. Take care of your precious self for your affectionately attached husband.

CLIFTON.

LORD CLIFTON AT CLIFTON LODGE TO LADY CLIFTON
AT COBHAM.

Nov. 22nd, 1828.

My dearest Love,

I have been made happy to-day by the intelligence of your safe arrival at Cobham, by your letter received yesterday. I was happy to find that you had been made comfortable by Mr. Hutchinson's advice. I hope you remunerated him for his services before you left Sandgate: if not we can send the money. I find a great deal to do here, more than I expected, and to-day my business has been increased by an attempt to resist task work, instead of day labour on the part of my men. However I shall easily get the better of this difficulty. I have engaged Millie as I believe I told you, and hope that when he comes things will go on better.

Gunning is a good-for-nothing overseer, and requires too much looking after himself. I have opened a quarry since I arrrived, and almost planned the Trim approach. By the way I do not know how Gunning will be up to making a Trim approach. The material is so convenient that I think this road will not cost much. I have almost determined (it is really almost heartbreaking) to give up our dear nursery Pleasure Ground, as I cannot imagine any way of getting up to the proposed entrance without cutting it up. It is really almost more than I can bear to do after all the trouble and expense it has cost. Such a nice walk too!!! When shall we have such another? Oh! dear, oh! dear, I shall cry over it. What do you say? Are you magnanimous enough to abandon our dear Pleasure Ground? It certainly will make a very pretty approach both from Trim and Athboy.

Oh! my walks—Oh! my evergreens, my dear, dear Pleasure Ground.

However I will make you other walks elsewhere of course. Kiss *Ta* for me. The sweet little creature, I hope he will remember me. God bless you my darling.

Your affectionate hubby,

C.

Sunday, November 23rd, 1828.

I add this to my letter written last night, dearest Love, to say that I have received your very nice letter and directions of Wednesday last, for which many thanks—also the Kentish papers pro. and con. from my father, and am now going to walk to Church.

May the Lord evermore bless and preserve you and yours,

Your affectionate husband,

C.

Nov. 24th, 1828.

My dearest Love,

I am still undecided about our approach. So much am I averse to cutting up our dear pleasure ground that I would prefer making it a little awkward, by coming into the old avenue, about opposite to the N.E. angle of the garden, and leaving it again about half way from that to the courtyard gate, and so sidling up to our new approach. I think I must stake it out some how or other to-morrow, as all future dispositions depend so much on the line of approach. You must know that I have quite altered my opinion of this place since I came here last, and now think it capable of being made quite pretty, at no great expense, no more indeed than I contemplate in the regular employment of workmen. I shall not develop my plans at present, but endeavour to mature them on the spot. I must stay here for a meeting of the Curate Subscribers next Sunday, and then I think of going to Moore Abbey on Monday, Abbeyleix on Wednesday, back to Moore Abbey on Friday, and to Dublin or here as I find it necessary on Saturday, so as to sail early in the next week and be at Cobham at the latest on the 15th. I have refused all invitations but those I have mentioned from Naper, Featherstone, etc., in order that I may lose no time. I am sure you wish me to go to Moore Abbey and Abbeyleix. Indeed I could not go to the one without the other very well, or without giving offence, nor indeed should I like to slight the dear people or the dear place that gave me my best beloved. How is our darling Ta? I long to see him and you, and all the rest. I have been looking at a pretty extensive plantation on the Bog to-day which looks well. We are going to plant about 8 acres also of Rathkeenan which Mr. Featherstone has taken. I met him there to-day. Kiss Tata's Da for him.

Ever your affectionately attached husband,

CLIFTON.

LORD CLIFTON AT CLIFTON LODGE TO LADY CLIFTON AT COBHAM.

Nov. 26th 1828.

My dearest love,

The monotony of a bachelor life here, spent as it is among our trees and flowers, does not afford much to interest you, except that I know you will find much pleasure in hearing that I continue quite well, with the blessing of God. I hope that you are so also and as comfortable as circumstances will allow of. With the exception of Mr. Hargrave (our architect) I have been alone. Uncle Tom will not, I suppose, come, as I received a letter from that kind odd creature pleading more important avocations; however it is not impossible that he may come to-morrow as I have offered to take him to Moore Abbey on Monday. I hope you approve, in principle at least, of my going there as I first thought of doing so on your expressing a wish that I should ascertain in person how Mary and child are going on. I hope from what I hear that there is not much the matter with the young heir of the house of Moore. I am served here in princely style, Eliza, cook and housekeeper; Peggy, kitchenmaid, Paddy Thornton, Butler and Valet and *garde de chasse*, and Johnny Lawless, foot-boy, Eustace, coachman and groom. I state these particulars as I think they will interest you. I have been laying out *our* Trim approach, and various plantations; I hope that they will be tolerably advanced this winter. I have determined not to sacrifice our Pleasure Ground, but rather enter in an awkward way : I fear I may repent but I was forced to fix on something. To-morrow I must pay some visits in and about Athboy. I believe the hounds are coming here, which I could dispense with. I am reading your Anderson's Domestic Constitution which interests me. Did you know that I had stolen it. The parcel about which the enclosed note is, is I suppose my Father's present to Bessy Cuming. I have not opened it, nor shall I. Ta Ta sends kisses to Ta and duty and love to Ta Ta Ta and Ma Ma Ma, and love to own Aunt and M. E. B. I am sorry to hear of Jane's mishap. I hope to be with you in little more than a fortnight. It is more than that time since we parted. Adieu! sweetest dearest wife, your own attached.

C.

LORD CLIFTON AT CLIFTON LODGE TO LADY CLIFTON AT COBHAM.

Nov. 28th, 1828.

My dearest Love,

How good it is of you to write so constantly such nice letters, for which my best thanks. There

U.

were indeed a good many commissions in your letter received yesterday, but I will endeavour to execute them. I gave Robert 10 shillings before I left Sandgate, but not anything to Harry or Thomas. I gave James the groom £1. I will give 10 shillings to each of our gate people for you, sweet love, and I am sure they will be thankful to my dearest wife. My Dearest love must excuse my staying so long away from her, but I think you wished me to see your sisters, which I hope to do on Monday. Abbeyleix could not decently be omitted. I will, with the blessing of God, write you a full account of those places. You may look for me about the 14th or 15th, but I fear I shall not be able to get over sooner. I hope Mr. Henry* enjoyed himself shooting at Chattenden; I did not even know he ever carried a gun. I believe I told him I would shew him some shooting, or give him some shooting at Cobham, and that he thought he might as well shew his shipmates some during my absence. I gave three of them leave to have a day's shooting about which I wrote to the keeper at Chattenden. I suppose Sir Henry will be over very soon : at least I hear he is to be at Moore Abbey the beginning of next month, and I suppose at Abbeyleix at Xmas. I have ordered your presses. I am delighted to hear that Johnny is to be home so soon. I suppose he will arrive before I do. Mr. Disney came last night as I believe I told you, and I believe returns to-morrow. I do not think he is improved and is more dilatory and unsatisfactory than ever. I asked him according to my Mother's message about the

* Henry Parnell.

matting, and he told me that it was gone long since : I however happen to know that it is in Athboy waiting for directions ! ! Kiss my darling little son, who gives me already great pleasure by the account you gave of his obedience. Dear little chicken how I long to see him, and the " ould hen " (as Gunning says). God Almighty in His mercy bless and preserve you and him prays

Your affectionately attached husband,

CLIFTON.

LORD CLIFTON AT CLIFTON LODGE TO LADY CLIFTON AT COBHAM.

From Dear Clifton Lodge,

Nov. 29th, 1828.

My dearest Love,

Before I go to bed Saturday night I must write you a few lines and tell you how dearly I love you, and long to be with you again. You are indeed a kind darling patient wife, for altho' I know you wish much to see me back you neither complain of nor chide me for my protracted absence. I hope to be able to bring you a good account of our dear relatives. I wish I could feel duly grateful for the great and manifold blessings I enjoy. I often think indeed that mine is a most enviable lot, and that I want but a proper sense of religion and a becoming worship of my Creator, to make me the happiest of men ; even in my solitude here I find myself surrounded with so many blessings that I feel how ungrateful and unworthy of them I am. My happiness is certainly damped by the constant scenes of wretchedness which I am doomed to witness, and my inability to apportion means of relief to their manifold wants. I hope when we are settled here that we may devise some way of sharing more than we do the blessings which the Almighty has lavished upon us with our indigent neighbours ; poor creatures, my heart throbs when I even think of them. It is very painful to refuse the poor creatures work when they come to supplicate for it, but I cannot find it for all. I must try and find some when I return from the Abbey. Mary expects me on Monday, and I have written to propose Wednesday to Aunt de Vesci, proposing to return to Moore Abbey on Friday and here on Saturday, to sail from Dublin not later than Wednesday evening. Uncle Tom will not come here I believe. I offered to take him to Moore Abbey but he says he has more important business and so I suppose he has. I hope you were amused with my conversation with the Lydd Landlord in the " Morning Post," except that it makes me tell a gross falsehood, which I hope I did not. The best part of it is where he soliloquises and talks about offering me sixpence to have my hair cut, which it really wanted at the time as well as baby's if you recollect.

I will make a pretty speech for you to Mrs. Hopkins to-morrow if I have an opportunity.

Adieu ! my dearest Love ! May the Almighty disposer of all events bless and preserve you and yours.

From your affectionate husband,

CLIFTON.

Nov. 30th, 1828.

My dearest Love,

As I must start rather early in the Morning towards Moore Abbey, I take up my pen to write you a few lines to-night; indeed I have almost ever since I have been here written my letters over night, as I am out all day generally. I have as yet projected more than I have done or even marked out: however I have a good many men at work every day, about 40, and 50 or 60 are employed on the Portlester side. I am levelling and planting and laying out the Trim approach, I hope you will see improvement when you return *home*.

Mr. Hargrave says we may inhabit this side of the house in June or July next, but I hardly think we shall be able. Dawson Court is still unlet. Mr. Chambers says he wishes his Mother to take it, and I think it would suit them very well. They only ask £80 a year; and the meadow and garden are worth £50 or £60 of it. The Martleys, Hopkinses, W. Hopkinses,' McVeaghs, Rotherams, and in short all the fashionables are now at home. We had a sort of half meeting of the Curate subscribers. Mr. Rotheram I am sorry to say again reduced his subscription from £5 to £3 3 0. It is a great pity Mr. Chambers will not write his sermons; every one wishes him to do so. He preached to-day from the beautiful text, "Come let us reason together saith the Lord" from the 1st lesson of the day, but failed to be impressive from repetition and want of connexion, still he is a valuable little man, and does a great deal of good. He certainly has the cause of Religion at heart, and is zealous in his calling, so that we must excuse his little defects. Father Tuite, the Priest of Kilbride (our parish) has got into a scrape for denouncing as a *Brunswicker* (because he had some Protestants to dine with him) Mr. J. Gannon, who has, I hear, complained to the R.C. Bishop, and so I suppose Father Tuite will be, as they say, sent *out of that*, he told his flock from the altar not to pay for their potato ground. Mr. Rotheram gave me as a reason for lowering his subscription, that he subscribed to 3 Brunswick Clubs, and the New Star of Brunswick Newspaper.

I hope to reach Moore Abbey in time for dinner to-morrow and to see your dear sisters. Uncle Tom is incorrigible ; he would not come either this week or last, but now says perhaps he may meet me when I return ; I do not think he will. Kiss my da Ta for Tata ; the sweet little thing how I long to see him and his dear Ma ma. Give my duty and love to Ta ta ta and Ma ma ma, and love to own Aunt and M.E.B.

Ever your loving and attached husband,

CLIFTON.

LORD CLIFTON AT MOORE ABBEY TO LADY CLIFTON AT COBHAM.

Dec. 1st, 1828.

My dearest Love,

I arrived here between 5 and 6 and found your sisters and Henry quite well. The latter grown quite stout. Car. has been indisposed, and says she

302

will write to you soon. She has received your letter, but says you are very sparing of them, altho' improved lately. Three of Lady Elizabeth Dawson's children are here and she returns to-morrow with another, so that with Agnes Erskine there will be a good party of children. They appear to be very comfortable here, and have got the use of a garden and a cow, but I believe contrary to your Papa's plan. I rode the bay pony to Almond Bridge, and drove the jaunting car horse in the gig from thence. I visited the school at Balliver to-day which does not appear to be going on so well as it should be. I intend however to enquire further as I go back. I had a very fine day for my journey which was performed pleasantly enough, in company with Paddy Thornton, who acts as my Squire. I have nothing particular to say in addition to the letter which I wrote last night, and which you will I conclude receive with this. Kiss *Da Ta* for me

Ever your attached husband,

CLIFTON.

Sisters send their love.

LORD CLIFTON AT MOORE ABBEY TO LADY CLIFTON
AT COBHAM.

Dec. 2nd, 1828.

My dearest Love,

Your sisters are very kind and good natured to me, and I should be very sorry to part with them so soon as I intend, were it not for the pleasure which I anticipate in returning so much the sooner to you. Henry is grown quite stout, and has plenty of beam notwithstanding what his Uncle Henry says, and stands up well under his canvas. How much I do wish sweetest wife that you were of the party and then I should not care about moving East or West. As it is I hope to go to Abbeyleix to-morrow and to return on Friday, and to C. Lodge on Saturday. I hope you and my dear child are quite well, and that I shall find you so and all our dear relatives in about 10 days. I was out shooting for an hour or two to-day, and killed 6 woodcocks, a hare and a partridge; I also supervised the plantations which I do not think in a flourishing state, altho' your Papa told me they were. I believe there is some idea of the planters having cheated in some late transactions, but I have not heard the particulars. The young trees are overgrown with the long grass, and do not therefore appear very thriving. I think both your sisters look rather thin, but they appear pretty well; Mary seems still delicate, but she says Dr. Adams did her good. Kiss my *Da Ta* for me. I hope you execute these commissions; ever dearest Love, your much attached and loving husband,

CLIFTON.

LORD CLIFTON AT ABBEYLEIX TO LADY CLIFTON AT COBHAM.

Dec. 4th, 1828.

My dearest Love,

I arrived here yesterday evening but had not time to write. I found all well. You are indeed a very dear Love for writing so constantly to your truant husband. I received a darling letter directed here this morning. There are no people in the house at present except Mr. Mcclintock, brother to

Car's. friend, who is I hear going to be married to a daughter of Sergt. Lefroy. I believe Mr. and Mrs. Walker, and Lord Ashbrook's son and his wife, are to come here to dinner to-day, and Mr. Cavendish brother to your friend Colonel (Henry) Cavendish. I left your sisters quite well yesterday about 1 o'clock at the Infant School, which is very nice. Mary seems to enjoy it much, and it must be of great use to the poor people. I drove over in the old dog cart and *Rooney* (*i.e.* the car horse) brought me very well. I mean, D.V. to take him back to Moore Abbey to-morrow, and the next day Eustace is to meet me at Clonard with the bay pony, and I hope to get home again. On Monday I hope to go to Dublin, and then to lose no time in getting to you, or at least to London, where I must perhaps stay to look out for a house. Indeed I must not defer, as you are in your seventh month, I think. Aunt De V. looks pretty well, rather thinner than she was but appears in good health. Lord De V. looks remarkably well. The Veseys from Knapton dined here yesterday and are quite well. Only think of the family misfortune that has happened. When they were in the North unhappy Fop was run over by Mrs. Eaton's coachman, and expired in Mrs. Vesey's arms soon after. I luckily heard this from Car. at Moore Abbey, and accordingly have made no enquiries which I should otherwise probably have done. I believe the subject is not mentioned without tears. I see Mr. Wood's paper is still full of the County meeting business ; and find that we have a grand dinner for the 22nd, which is mighty agreeable.

Adieu! my dearest Love. Kiss my sweet child for me. Hoping to see you both and all at Cobham soon.

I am my dearest Love's affectionate husband,

CLIFTON.

LORD CLIFTON AT MOORE ABBEY TO LADY CLIFTON AT COBHAM.

Dec. 5th, 1828.

My dearest Love,

I returned from Abbeyleix to-day and found your sisters quite well, as also the numerous children, and Lady E. Dawson who arrived yesterday. I have not heard whether Uncle Li. is to get anything from Lady C. Damer. I believe he is in London. Lord Portarlington went over on Lady C's. death. I have a letter from Uncle Tom about going to C. Lodge. I think however he will not go. I purpose going there to-morrow and leaving it about Tuesday on my way towards my dearest Love. How I long for the time to arrive when I shall again clasp you in my arms. Will they reach round you? I have a letter from my father to-day still about the County Meeting business—I fear I shall be a good deal engaged in it after my return. I think Car. has a fancy for coming over to us in London : I told her neither I nor you would ask her, because it was so stupid for her before. If you wish to have her I think she would come but I shall not press her. I am sorry dear little Ta wants correction. He is generally however inclined to behave well. Kiss him for me notwithstanding. Henry appears a strong healthy boy. Mary appears to be living very comfortably here, and wants us to inhabit a wing next Summer.

Your affectionately attached,

C.

Clifton Lodge,
Saturday Night,
Dec. 6th, 1828.

My dearest Love,

Now I am at our dear Lodge again after being absent since Monday morning, and when I consider that had I not gone on this expedition, I might ere now have been with you, I think I have paid your sisters, and our dear relations at Abbeyleix, no slight compliment by going to them. Rooney drew the gig, Paddy Thornton and me very well. I had the pony and chesnut horse to meet me at Clonard, and so got home in good time, having left M. Abbey after breakfast. You will receive no letter from me by this day's Post, but that you will, I know, forgive and account for, as I was travelling all day. Mary wants you to go and take a wing of the Abbey next Summer. It appears that she turned Miss Fowler away at last : I wondered how she had got rid of her, as I supposed she was to be a fixture at Moore Abbey. We are to have another meeting of the subscribers to the Curate to-morrow. I have got most of the Subscriptions renewed, but Mr. Rotherham has again reduced his from £5 to £3 3 0. The reason he gave was because he subscribes to 3 Brunswick Clubs and the New Star of Brunswick. I send you a letter just received from Pilcher : write me word to London what I am to do about the Villa, which I purpose looking at on my way through. I hope to start on Tuesday, and if the weather moderates (for it is now very stormy and has been so almost ever since I have been in Ireland), to be in London by Saturday at latest. Probably I shall hardly be able to reach Cobham before Monday, the 15th. It appears quite an age since I saw you, altho' the time seems to pass quickly too. You need not disquiet yourself about the weather as it rarely happens that the same storm extends from Kent to the Irish Channel. For instance I had none of the storm which visited you while I was last crossing ; how very fortunate to get over before these S.W. gales set in. It blows a hurricane now with rain, so that I ought to be thankful for being comfortably housed. God bless you, and my sweet child and all that are dear to us, and preserve you both here and hereafter. I will write to Pilcher to look about for more houses, send back his letter to Berkeley Square.

Ever my dearest love, your affectionately attached husband.

CLIFTON.

Lord Clifton returned to his wife and family at Cobham, on December 12th, 1828. John Bligh was there, on leave from Paris, and on the 22nd he records in his journal : "Drove to Maidstone where we dined at the 'Star,' with 300 persons who think that

Catholic Emancipation is necessary for the welfare of the country. My Father in the chair. Very satisfactory.'"

There were gay parties at Cobham throughout January, 1829, shooting almost every day, music and dancing in the evenings, and a large party for the Rochester Ball on January 15th. Lord and Lady Winchilsea were among the guests, so evidently the dissensions of Pennenden Heath and the House of Lords were not allowed to affect neighbourly intercourse.

On February 4th, 1829, the whole family went to London for the opening of Parliament, and the Cliftons to 37, Grosvenor Place, which they had taken for the season. John Bligh notes in his journal on February 4th, that at Brooks's he heard " agreeable rumours about the King's Speech," and on February 5th " heard in the House of Lords the King's Speech read by Commissioners announcing H.M.'s wish that the Catholic Question should be settled by Parliament. Much gratified."

The course of events in Parliament which now so rapidly led to the complete removal of the disabilities of Catholics may be rapidly sketched here to explain the following letters illustrating the intense excitement felt by all classes of society at that time. Before Parliament met Mr. Peel had resigned his seat. He stood again for the University of Oxford but was defeated. "An immense number of parsons came to vote of whose intentions both parties were ignorant, and they almost all voted for Inglis" (Greville Memoirs, I, 183). Lord Clifton and John Bligh actively supported Peel's candidature; after his defeat at Oxford he was returned for the Borough of Westbury in time to carry the Catholic Relief Bill through the Commons by large majorities. But the centre of excitement was the House of Lords where the result was doubtful till the last moment. Lord Winchilsea proposed to March with 25,000 men to Windsor to present a petition to the King, and his famous duel with the Duke of Wellington, on March 21st is alluded to in Lord Darnley's letter of March 24th.

The second reading of the Catholic Bill in the House of Lords was carried on April 5th, by a majority of 105, larger than was expected; the third reading on April 13th, and the Royal Assent given on April 14th.

Lord and Lady Clifton's second son, Edward Vesey Bligh, was born on February 28th, 1829, at 37, Grosvenor Place, and the letters show the delight and interest which

their grandmother, Lady Darnley, took in the
two little boys.

EARL OF DARNLEY AT 46, BERKELEY SQUARE TO HON.
J. D. BLIGH AT PARIS.

February 19th, 1829.

Dear John,

I own I was disappointed in receiving no letter
from Dover, where I hope those that came just after
your departure reached you in safety, or rather in
time.

I have remained here for the Catholic Associa-
tion Suppression Bill, which is read for the second
time in the Lords to-day, and I hope to join Mim
and Bep. afterward at C. H. where they seem to be
in health and spirits, though disappointed in the
expectation of passing four or five hours with you,
at least your Mother is, she agrees with me on this
point of feeling.

The best news here seems to be that the Duke
of Cumberland is at least neutralized, some say by
express and peremptory command. I repose perfect
confidence in the goodness of our cause, the empty
violence of our opponent, and the sincerity and
energy of our leader.

Your affectionate,

D.

February 23rd, 1829.

My dearest Johnny,

Finding that no letter from home is going to-night, I sit down though ordered by Mr. Beaumont " to do nothing " ; (pretty much as I fear has been the case) to tell you that last night was a very good night with me, having gone into bed at 10 o'clock had no cramp and slept well seven or eight hours, the night before having had no sleep, and very little any night since I returned from Brighton. Lord A. told Lord D. that though you are the fifth for promotion that you must go by gradation, he must make you Secretary of Legation before Secretary of Embassy, and more betoken, that Lord M. is not to be the latter, when you are ! Is this news to you ?

Aunt P. is gone I believe to-day from Addington, where she was in such a fuss to leave Brighton for last Saturday.

I regret not having known that Colonel S. was off for London, as Isa and Cat. might have come here. We go (D.V.) Thursday to meet Dear C. at No. 37 on his birthday ; that day he expects to come back from voting for Mr. Peel at Oxford.

I suppose the Brunswickers will try to make some confusion, at least breaking of windows, if the question is carried. I hope you approve of little Mary's remaining here till after March. She does not, but I trust it will be for the best, though not the pleasantest, I shall miss her sadly.

Charles came here Friday intending to stop till to-day, but he yesterday had a letter from poor

Jane at Long's Hotel saying had been bled and not well, so he was off of course à *l'instant* though not at all alarmed. He has bought a 21 years' lease of a house in Belgrave Square, not floored, etc., etc., and he pulls down poor Lurgan House directly he has fixed upon a plan, and pretty much on the same spot.

God bless you my dear Johnny.

I am truly your attached

E. D.

Lady C. is gone I believe to Boulogne, and Emma has invited Miss P. to No. 37 from Abbeyleix.

I am very desirous to pay my debts to you. Pray pay fr 110 for a cloak to the fur man.

Little dear very well. C. much pleased.

Mrs. Edm. Knox has another girl ! Remember me to Lady S. etc.

COUNTESS OF DARNLEY AT 46, BERKELEY SQUARE TO HON. J. D. BLIGH AT PARIS.

March 10th, 1829.

I am not in mourning, though I accidentally write on this paper. We are going to dine early, for business in the House of Lords. To-morrow go, (D.V.,) to visit dear Mary till Tuesday. We are, thanks to God, in good health, but almost all but in this house are complaining. At 37, Grosvenor Place poor dear C. is laid up with gout ; could not dine with the Papists yesterday, but he was here Wednesday at the Ancient Music which probably increased the swelling.

Ta improves much and comes here daily when making his first walk, and catches no cold.

We had a very pleasant dinner and till half-past eleven, all were much pleased with Patty,* who sung beautifully; little Great Duke liked not a little Charley Mr. Blake also, and Lord Killeen. My principal purpose in asking Patty was that Lady Bective should hear her, and she was really enraptured, said she had not given Edward Bligh sufficient credit for his good taste.

I am grieved to say that poor dear Clifton is in bed and suffered much all night, and does not choose to see anyone (Dr.) but Vance, and *malheureusement* obliged to send Madden off for drunkenness.

They are in great spirits about the House of Lords division, some say 50 majority, others 60, and Lord Rosslyn, who is pretty good authority, 70! In short Bully Win. will lose. The D. of W. speech great effect in answer to Lord W. and Lord D. delighted. The Duchess of Rutland keeps her bed, she is so ill with alarm about Bloody Mary, Guy Faux, and "Duke of Norfolk."

Thanks for the programme of the ball. I hear Berry made a bad attempt at Q. of Scots.†

God bless you dearest Johnny. Your father at division.

Yours,

E.D.

* Miss Siddons.

† Lady Stuart de Rothesay's Fancy Ball at the British Embassy at Paris. The Duchesse de Berry appeared as Mary Queen of Scots. A year later she was a refugee in Holyrood Palace!

Tuesday, 3rd.

Dearest Johnny,

I am at last commissioned by that long Visit
Maker, to make affectionate and best wishes to the
" Cher Bli."

He and Mrs. Webster have just dined off
Pheasant Pye, *pour passer le temps*, and now to give
me some to write to you, I have sent off the
Dame in my carriage, and he on foot.

Poor dear Beppy is, I lament to say, not yet on
this floor, having had one of her bilious headaches
which came on at Lady Clifton's, and she was sick
most of the night, but after her chicken broth I
hope she will feel quite well. Whether Lord D.
will dine at home or not I know not, as we have not
dined together since I came to town. He has
several Petitions to-day, one from Shoreditch which
particularly delights him, with many respectable
names, all with places of abode, and Lord Eldon
has one from the same place which Lord D. knows
has been signed in the streets by any passers by,
and schools, etc.

I am afraid Lord D. will not hold his tongue
till after Lord Eldon which would have better
effect.

The Duke of Norfolk has been here to-day in
great spirits, but says the Oxford business will have
a very bad effect which I think from the quantities
of unheard of parsons who will return to their
retreats hundreds of miles off, frightening all the
poor souls with Bloody Mary, Guy Fox, etc., etc.,

I fear it must end in some ways with noise and tumult. God preserve us from any great danger, and if He is with us who can harm us?

The Ancient Music begins to-morrow. The A.B. says Elizabeth and I must dine with him; I sent word not if the first Director does, but I am afraid the Duchess of Clarence dines there.

Tell M. Este my shawl has safely come to hand, and I much thank him.

I suppose Lord Hertford has really (as the papers say) made over his strength to the Premier.

Poor Mrs. Taylor has sent little Mary's kettle holder, and all her letters to me.

Elizabeth and I were quite overcome at the Rehearsal, though we did not sit in our places!!!

.Emma going on capitally except that I fear my second grandson will be starved, but Mr. Stone will not hear of his being fed. He was even a finer boy than John Stuart, who gets on in speaking,—little Mary also in French. I am delighted that I have not brought Mary.

C. and Jane better or well. Roderick gone to Scotland.

Aunt P. and Cata. went to Watton yesterday. Just heard that C. is writing to you.

COUNTESS OF DARNLEY AT 46, BERKELEY SQUARE
TO HON J. D. BLIGH AT PARIS.

March 20th, 1829.

My dearest Johnny,

I write as you did without time, and I hope the enclosure may please you, the emblem I think good, and the little glass when raised, you will of course have put in some hair.

Neither myself or Pip have been well, but he is much better, and I think perhaps will not be cupped, which had been determined upon but only 8oz.; tell Mrs. Warre's brother that he is very well, and dined here with her *Sposo*, the Cassillis, Amhersts, etc., etc., yesterday. Wednesday the Duchess of Clarence and Miss Fitz C. dined and went to Ancient Music. They are in wretched lodgings in *St. James' Place*.

I am getting the Doctor [Stokes] if Lord Darnley will let him to copy a list the Bishop of Derry gave me of Mr. Evelyn's (a *better*). I think nearly 120 Peers majority, but it will be above 70 at all events.

Lord Palmerston's speech reckoned very good.

Dr. Chalmers much admired at Edinburgh.

Yours dearest Johnny,

E.D.

Good accounts of Mary. The big boy and his nurse here just now, very well and little one better. Em well. Sir Henry Parnell dined here.

EARL OF DARNLEY AT 46, BERKELEY SQUARE TO HON. J. D. BLIGH AT PARIS.

March 24th, 1829.

Dear J.,

I do not know that I can tell you anything more than you will find in the Newspapers.* The Great Captain was cheered yesterday going to the House

*Duel between the Duke of Wellington and the Earl of Winchilsea.

317

where I saw and shook hands with him. His wild antagonist did not appear. There never was so offensive a letter, and on reading it the only observation that occurred to me was that the Duke of Wellington may overlook and despise this attack, but no other gentleman could. I do not think the briber " has succeeded in exciting discord in Kent." As to my " unlucky knack," I suppose you allude to some misrepresentation of Beppy's.

The great Question goes on well. In Ireland they are behaving like Angels, and I have always been very sanguine in my expectations of it and immediate favourable operation there. It is the only foundation and cornerstone on which the welfare of that hitherto unfortunate Country can rest.

When it is settled, I intend to call attention again to the state of the Poor, on which I send you a corrected copy or two of my last year's speech.

We are all pretty well. Your Mother better than I have seen her for some time in consequence of Dr. Holland's medicines. I have directed three Concerts in succession, and wish you could have heard them.

I will settle your account at Coutts's, after our first division in the Lords where we expect a majority of seventy or eighty, or shall I pay at once 337 francs ?

Yours,

D.

March 31st, 1829.

Dearest Johnny,

I have just now heard that no letter from this
house has been written to you, so here goes a few
hasty lines as Beppy is off to Mrs. Webster's for a
drive, and then to spend a couple of hours with
Emma.

I have heard little of the ending in the House
of Commons, but I send you the "Times" in my
great kindness, for I had intended keeping it for
Mr. Stokes to read to me this evening, as I expect a
tête-à-tête. Elizabeth and I were at Mrs. Legh's
last night at a Ball, and it was pretty good, and if
Beppy chose it I would go to Lady Hampden's
to-night, but she will not go to such things but with
an order from Papa, which I do not like, and from
laziness I am not at all sorry on my own account
when she refuses, though I wish she liked it a little.

I hope we shall have warmer weather soon, as
it now rains. Your Aunt P. will, I trust, get quite
well soon of a troublesome pain in the pit of her
stomach, as she has the last two days been much
better. Mr. Stokes was there and Lady Maria
Meade unluckily when she was ill, I intend to go
and return same day this week (to Watton).

All seem in good heart about the question and
I hear in Lord Eldon's long visit of four hours, the
King spoke three and three quarters ! ! ! God
Almighty will I trust and pray prosper it to the
end.

The Grosvenors dine with us to-morrow, but no Royals I hope, as the only chance is Cum.

Lady Cawdor is very near being confined. Bob Gro. has never come though we have often asked.

Adieu. I can no more.

Yours truly,

E. D.

Very glad you like the seal.

COUNTESS OF DARNLEY AT BERKELEY SQUARE TO
HON. J. D. BLIGH AT PARIS.

June, 1829.

My dear J.

I received your letter to-day, and the box with the *chapeau*, (which both Elizabeth and I like *very* much) Sunday; the messenger from Corfu having brought it safe. I hope Elizabeth will wear it *to-morrow*, as it is much prettier than one that she has had re-made by Mrs. Mackenzie's maid which will do for the horticultural on Saturday which I do not expect will be well attended by Company, tho' better provided for by Gunter : Lady Dartmouth has a *fourchette* on the same day. This day I have partaken of a very magnificent and Royal one at Grosvenor House, Princesses Augusta, Gloucester, Clarence, and Kent, Sussex, and Leopold.

I had not seen *the* Gallery this year, and like its interior much better than the exterior.

The three sons, Ladies Wilton and Stafford were there, Lady Taylor and the Ladies in Waiting, and there were very good things to eat, and plenty of Gold Cups.

The Great Rubens' look extremely well tho' Lord D. complained that they were so very coarse which such immensity must be methinks ; the quite new part is a cube of fifty feet where the four Rubens' are.

Lady Grosvenor dreads all their private comforts being altered, but no time is fixed.

Last night we were at Prince Leopold's who had Pasta and Sontag etc., etc. The Hall is now the Music Room and the Colonnade covered in and lined with scarlet cloth.

There is good chance I think, except we have a thunder storm, of a fine day for the Regatta which the Duke of Clarence gives. People, his own sons especially, are much given to laughing at this water party, and threaten us with at least 50 drowned ! I believe there is little, if any, danger, but it assisted in keeping me awake last night.

Lord D. is gone down to the House of Lords, and from that to the Opera. Sontag is gone to Oxford, and from that to Cambridge. Your Aunt P. is disappointed of going to Watton for a fortnight ; and I hope will come to Cobham the 28th, when we do (D.V.) or the 30th.

The Regatta is to be on the 7th, and if poor Lady Uxbridge is not dead before that, Sir William and Lady Cumming etc., etc., are to come to us.

Pickler intends celebrating your father's birthday at Cobham which he (Lord D.) does not yet know. The 30th is also Lady Londonderry's fancy ball, which causes already great sensation, and no doubt will be very good. Lady L. to hold a magnificent court ; she as Queen Elizabeth, Lady Ellenborough, Queen Mary. As a Show it will have good effect. Sir R. Gresley, Colonel Anson, etc.,

etc. Your Father spent Sunday at *sweet* Cobham ;
he says the roses, kalmias, etc., etc., are in perfection,
so I fear losing much of their beauty and perfume.
We intend going down for a day before the 30th if
possible.

Everyone surprised at the Irish Secretary. He
(in manners) will not much accord with the Irish.
I am really in great hopes that Mr. Bolton will
effect great things in your Father's health and
comfort. He adheres very closely to rules, and says
his occasional pain in his chest is better. He eats a
hearty breakfast ; to-day a roll, three or four bits of
toast, and two mutton chops, and cup and a half of
coffee *sans lait* ! He is a quarter of a stone lighter,
and looks very well, not so sleepy, though allowed a
nap by his doctor.

Poor dear Matt Forde is settled in the Hotel
Burlington in Cork Street, good rooms on ground
floor, but over the kitchen. He is much larger,
and Beppy who dined with him and the Bayleys
says he was not in good spirits, but eats a good deal.

A contrast to this chronicle of fashionable
society is afforded by Lady Clifton's Journal
of the same date.

LADY CLIFTON'S JOURNAL.

July 19th, 1829. [Cobham]. An excellent
sermon from Mr. Shepherd on the duty of education,
one point he dwelt on much, namely, that children
learn more from example than from precept, that
their characters are formed more by what they see
you do and hear you say every day than by the
lessons which you teach them. He also mentioned

the necessity of daily prayer on the part of parents for the spiritual improvement and welfare of their children. The greatest efforts of parents cannot succeed without the blessing of the Almighty. He pointed out the folly of parents in allowing the most extravagant praise to be offered to the child, and in suffering themselves to be deceived by partiality and by the flattery of their friends into the belief that their children are much better than they really are.

Mrs. Macrae gave me some good advice as to the best way of managing our children while we are here. She said we must adopt a system of counteraction. We must always be on the watch to counter-act the bad effect of the silly praises and compliments too freely offered to children by strangers, and of the well-meant but injudicious treatment of near relations and friends. For instance the female relations try to promote the good behaviour of children by promising them as rewards, lace frocks, smart ribbons, etc., thus doing their utmost to encourage and increase the vanity and love of dress and outward show which is naturally too predominant a passion in every mind.

The men of the family hold out as rewards to the little boy, wine and fruits, and horses and dogs, etc., thereby encouraging those passions which most perhaps (in boys) require to be kept in subjection. These are only a few of the many methods adopted by friends out of mistaken kindness to please the child and to stimulate it to a temporary obedience and submission. They gain their point for a time : the child is so strongly stimulated by the hope of a reward so suited to his corrupt nature, that he complies with the request made to him, be it what it may. But alas! corrupt motives are implanted and evil desires encouraged in the child's breast, which may be the cause of days and years of misery to the child and all connected with it. We must therefore while here or at Abbeyleix, etc., be continually on the watch to counteract the mischief done by such injudicious treatment. We must shorten as much as possible the time allotted for our children's intercourse with friends who indulge themselves in such unthinking and careless language, and we must endeavour to have them more under our own eyes than usual and in every way to counteract the evil done to them.

I feel anxious to adopt some plan when I go to Ireland for the religious improvement of our little groom (aged 15). Could not Mr. Chambers be prevailed upon to give him an evening now and then. There is the nursery-maid also, whom I mean to endeavour to attend to myself, and to give her a few texts to write out every week.

The Cliftons went to Clifton Lodge in August, 1829, and remained there for several months, perhaps the happiest in their lives as they both so much preferred a quiet domestic life to any other.

The chief family event of this autumn was John Bligh's appointment to the Legation at Florence to which reference is made in the following letters.

H.R.H. the Duchess of Kent at Broadstairs to the Countess of Darnley at 46, Berkeley Square.

Broadstairs, 8th Sept., 1829.

My dearest Lady Darnley,

I have just had from Sir John Conroy your's and Lord Darnley's very kind enquiries. It was indeed very agreeable to me, to hear of you again, it seemed an age since I had that pleasure ; and as usual in your own kind and friendly way.

. I should like to know about all your family— and I hope to hear soon from you.

I can congratulate you at last, on Johnny's promotion, which I was much pleased to read in the Gazette.

I have a delightful residence here, so very quiet that Victoria and I are charmed.

Victoria sends you and dear Lady Elizabeth, as well as her dear little friend Mary, her best love.

Pray give them mine also, and my most friendly regards to Lord Darnley.

Always believe me,

My dearest Lady Darnley,

Your sincere and affectionate friend,

VICTORIA.

Earl of Darnley at Sandgate to Hon. J. D. Bligh at Florence.

October 12th, 1829.

Dearest John,

We drank your health here yesterday with how much sincerity and how many good wishes I leave you to judge, nor will I attempt to do justice to the feelings of our hearts towards you by words.

I am so much provoked by the untoward circumstances of your present situation, that I cannot write about it with patience, nor indeed have I anything at present to say. I am however to pass a day this week at Walmer, and I am resolved to brush up the Great Captain. You shall have the result. I have neither seen nor written to Aberdeen.

The *Filles* are writing, and I conclude will give you all domestick news. You will be glad to hear that within these few days your Mother has been remarkably well, which she certainly was not before.

I have been obliged to dismiss Ling having found him myself in the ale house at Cuxton, and hearing that there is much poaching and little game in the Great Wood etc., the contrary being the case on the other side, I put T. Walls in his place. I think I shall look into the concern myself next week, and you shall hear again on the subject.

One of the most provoking features in your Florence expedition is that it should be as unprofitable in a pecuniary as in every other point of view, especially considering the very deranged state of my Finances. However I have ascertained that the Quarter in 1827 was never paid, and I will take care that it shall as soon as possible, together with your other claims against me. There is so extraordinary a stagnation in all markets here, that Stevenson can sell neither Cattle, Hops, nor even Corn. We are both considerably overdrawn at Coutts's and nothing comes from Ireland, where Clifton has found the dry rot in his new rooms. But things will, I trust soon mend, and I say to myself—Tu ne cede malis, sed contra audentior ito.

D.

Earl of Darnley at House of Lords to Hon. J. D. Bligh at Florence.

12th March, 1830.

Dear Johnny,

I take this opportunity to acknowledge the receipt of your letter from Rome of the 25th, which arrived last night, I found it together with Clifton at Berkeley Square after attending the House of Commons to hear Spring-Rice's Motion and Speech. Charles also spoke, but not as well as usual. He was the only one (as far as appeared) for unlimited English Poor Laws. Rice's views are sound, and differ so little from mine, that it is a most satisfactory result to see the House of Commons unanimously adopt in 1830 on his Motion almost the identical proposition that the House of Lords scouted in 1828 on mine! I shall remind them of that, and contrast the two.

Another Penenden Heath is at this moment going on. I refused to sign requisition or to attend. Stanhope, Winchilsea, Teynham, the only peers, Cobbett I hear is elsewhere, but there will be a fine mob, especially as it is a fine day.

I am told that they are very angry with me for having denied the exaggerated statements of distress. At all events I am sure this meeting can do no possible good, and may do mischief. I trust

I am not too sanguine, but I think everything is beginning to improve gradually, though at present I fear little progress has been made, at all events there is plenty of money, and I have borrowed some at 3½ per cent. But I am told Lord Foley has borrowed £300,000 at 3 ! In the City they lend for a short period at 2.

You will be glad to know that I am about to purchase out Prentis at Cuxton, and at the same time (I hope) to get rid of Higham which has been nothing but loss, and of no use whatever *quoad* game.

I have not said a word yet to your *Chef*, though as the year is wearing fast, I may as well sound him as to the mode of fulfilling his promise, but I will certainly do nothing to commit you in any way. I think the Government are quite safe especially as the Royal *Earwig* is under a cloud so dark, that I trust he will never emerge. He attempted to brave public opinion as a Director of A.M. but we have *cut him dead*.

Your most affectionate

D.

LORD CLIFTON AT 46, BERKELEY SQUARE TO HON. J. D. BLIGH IN ROME.

March 16th, 1830.

PRIVATE AND CONFIDENTIAL.

My dearest Johnny,

I really feel conscious of being so bad a correspondent as almost to warrant an observation of yours in a letter to Beppy "that I never write," or at least " very seldom." However I am very anxious that this letter shall reach you in due course, as I wish as soon as possible to know your wishes respecting its subject matter.

Imprimis I must, however, tell you that I left the *Filles* pretty well at Cobham, having been there for two nights, and returned with my father.

A variety of circumstances have contributed to render the representation of Canterbury not the same thing to me that it has heretofore been, and I am therefore desirous of giving it up if I can do so with a good grace. Before, however, I do so, or take any steps towards it, I am anxious to ascertain whether it would suit your views to succeed me there, if I can so manage it. Now the only way in which I think that can be done (at least without a severe contest), is for me to vacate my seat, and then I think you might come forward upon your own ground, and with your own views, and (by *management*) unopposed. With this idea of management I have not mentioned the subject to my father, nor shall I do so, at least till I know your wishes on the subject, and perhaps not at all till the matter is quite decided upon one way or other ; nor indeed to anyone else, so that I must request you to keep the thing a profound secret. It will not be necessary for either you or me to alter our course of proceeding in the least till I hear from you again ; but I may in the common course of my own business, pave the way for any future proceedings in your behalf, if they shall prove necessary.

It is satisfactory to me to find that this arrangement would be palatable to my father.

Yesterday on the road (I having previously determined to write to you this day on the subject), he of his own accord suggested that the seat I held appeared "irksome to me" (the very word I should have used to you), and "that perhaps I might like to make it over to you." I turned the conversation as soon as I could, feeling that any development of my real intentions at the present would but mar the design. I have a report of H. Cooper's having been over to Lord Sondes with two others, on the false report of a new writ being moved for Canterbury, confirmed by a letter from himself to-day, but I think the thing might be managed notwithstanding. This, however, I must search and investigate, and in the meantime I only wish to ascertain your wishes. Remember that it is anything but a sacrifice to me (on the other hand, the seat with an office under Government will be not a little troublesome), that if you take office while holding it, you must vacate, and abide the consequences. The time at which it should be done, if at all, is either at the close of this Session, or the opening of the next. I should prefer the former, but if your diplomatic engagements would interfere then, the last mentioned time might do. You must of course be on the spot and ready to take up the cudgels the moment I declare. In the meantime I shall pay as much attention as possible, which will be of use whether I continue or resign. I do not pretend to say at present whether the thing is practicable or not; I only think it so. But there is plenty of time to sound without suspicion, or trouble or inconvenience to either of us. All I wish to know is what your wishes are on the subject, and how far it would be practicable to shape your course accordingly. Independent of my own convenience, there are reasons for the preference of the earlier period mentioned, which will I daresay occur to you. The only one I can see for postponement is on account of vacating on taking office. The Under Secretary of State does *not* vacate. If you wish to stand, and provided that my father neither knows of our intention till the time arrives at which he must be made acquainted with it, nor has any scheme of his own in progress, I will take care that you may take the field with every chance of easy work, if I think it prudent to attempt it at all. I think it should not be left till a General Election, as *then* there would be probably a severe contest. *Now* I can resign handsomely and satisfactorily. This Session will probably last three months longer, so that nothing extraordinary need be done at least till I hear from you.

If Gascoigne is with you, I have no objection to your consulting with him, provided it is told him in confidence, and as a profound secret. Nor indeed with anyone else who is a real friend of your own.

I know not whether it may be agreeable to you or not ; nor will my having written to you make the least difference as concerns myself in any way if it is not. I shall consider in the meanwhile fully and deeply the circumstances of the case, and you will not, I am sure, be disappointed if upon reconsideration I have occasion to tell you that the scheme is impracticable.

I left Emma and her chicks at Moore Abbey

last week, and have good accounts of them since. I intend to return to Ireland if I can for a few days at Easter, but that is uncertain, as are also my plans. The "worthy and independent" are rather indignant on account of my absenting myself from Parliament, but a few votes, and some attention (as H. Cooper says) will restore all this, and it may, moreover, stand me in some stead.

How these votes may please my father and his *Rex* and *Dux* I cannot tell; but it is not my doing if they are unpalateable at the Treasury. I should be very sorry to do anything to hurt your prospects, and hope I shall not.

Write as soon as you can.

Interea·vive et vale !

Your affectionate Brother,

CLIFTON.

P.S.—It may be as well to let me know when you write, whether you could come if required about May or June, and what steps should be taken to that end, should I find it expedient or necessary to summon you. Of this, of course, I shall best judge by what I hear from you, and discover at home in the meanwhile.

Lord and Lady Clifton returned to Cobham in the spring of 1830, and by that time the plan for John Bligh's standing for Canterbury had been given up as impracticable by all parties concerned.

April 26th, 1830.

Dearest John,

Your weather in Italy may be much warmer, but it cannot be much finer than ours is here. I never remember so beautiful a Spring, and you may be sure we leave this place with much regret the day after to-morrow for the smoky city. Parliament meets again to-day, and there is so much before it, that it must, of necessity, sit late, but it must be something very extraordinary indeed that will keep us from our Roses in June.

No one seems to know the real state of the King, not even his Doctors, as they, I hear, as usual, differ. The fact of his being seriously ill cannot well be doubted, but there does not seem to be any immediate danger, and his tenacity of life is so very extraordinary, that it sets all speculation at defiance. At all events I do not think a new King would necessarily imply a new Ministry, but rather the contrary.

You write as if you were about to pass your life at Florence with your *maison bien montée*, etc. But the month of August is drawing very near. Some of the circumstances of your case have been very untoward and provoking, but I hope you may verify the old proverb " The worse luck now, the better another time." His lordship might as well have allowed you to remain at Rome till after Easter, but I conclude he will not have the face to delay his departure after having hurried you, and that he is off by this time.

I am sorry I cannot give as good an account as I could wish of your Mother's health. The fine weather seems to have done her some good, and at times she appears in tolerable health and spirits, but she is very often, especially at night, under much suffering from violent pain in the head, and various modifications of nervous irritability. This, as you may suppose, is a great drawback to Beppy's and my comfort and happiness, and we are both ourselves more or less invalids also.

Beaumont has done me, I think, a little good. The Quack, I fear, none, but I am not quite determined against giving him another trial.

Your ever affectionate,

D.

Mim. and Bep. send love. The former says she wrote to you by the last post.

After the death of George IV on June 26th, 1830, Lord Clifton did not offer himself for re-election at Canterbury. He also declined an invitation to contest the county of Kent, preferring to oppose the well-known agitator, Jack Lawless, in Co. Meath. Lord and Lady Darnley and Lady Elizabeth Bligh were invited to visit the new King and Queen at Windsor Castle in August, and part of a letter from Lady Darnley describing this visit has been preserved.

Monday, August 16th, 1830.

This moment arrived from that magnificent
residence of our Monarch, it is a fit abode for the
King of England, tho' with less gaudy gilding it
might have been quite as appropriate for William IV
and Adelaide! notwithstanding it is very beautiful, but the nation need not have had so much of
filthy lucre to pay, and William IV is really setting
about retrenchment. When all that is contracted
for already is done, he told me what he should wish
to have done would come under £10,000. The
Menagerie at Windsor, the King's Band, etc., are
to be done away with, but they are no doubt living
away at a great expense; when we were there we
were nearly 30 in the House tho' all were (except
we three) *the family* and their attendants, nothing
could be more kind and gracious than our being
selected in that way with only *the* family. St.
George's Hall is preparing in a sort of way, for the
banquet on his birthday, the 21st, and he told me
that there would be a much greater quantity of gilt
plate from Town for that day. We had a complete
service for 48, one or two days, for Esterhazy and
the Envoy who came to congratulate and condole
Saturday; and for the Prussian Prince, Sunday,
who is said to be a horror even worse than *Cum.*
who, by the bye, I was obliged to sit by at dinner,
etc. We had a good deal of rain especially at a
Review of Prince Leo's Regt., 5th Dragoon Guards.
Sunday was the only day fine enough for riding and

driving, but we (had) a very fine view of all the Pavilions about the Virginia Water, and Elizabeth and Olivia de Ros rode with the Queen, and we did (not) return till 7, long after the Seftons, Bagots, Poles, and Somersets had come to dinner. Lord and Lady —— were in waiting, they none, K. Q. or maids know their business.

I do not recover from my short breathing, and was sadly put out tho' I had no stairs to go up.

LADY CLIFTON AT COBHAM TO LORD CLIFTON AT CLIFTON LODGE.

August 17th, 1830.

My dearest Love,

I am very anxious for your next letter as are all here, but it appears from the paper that your going over has had some effect in causing Mr. Lawless to withdraw himself. I hope, dearest love, it will be settled in the way most agreeable to you. The party from Windsor arrived about 10 o'clock last night in very good spirits and apparently much pleased with their visit, they have I believe, been invited to come again. Elizabeth told me that the King would most likely come about a fortnight hence from next Friday, and only remain a day or two, but that the Queen was not coming. Chevalier Remoni comes here to-day, and I believe Dr. Longley is expected towards the end of the week. I am afraid the letter I sent you last night must have been too late and therefore charged double; I had it ready early in the day, but the letter-man was kept until your father's return. I need not say I long to see you, dearest love, for you know that I do. I look back with some regret to the many happy months we have spent together, and wonder whether such will ever come again. Notwithstanding this reflection I am not so selfish as to wish you to neglect your duties in order to be with me. I believe I am looked upon in your family quite in this light, and have no doubt but that they consider that I prevented you from standing for the county of Kent. But I know in my own mind that if you desire to be a senator from Christian and not from ambitious motives, that I should think it very wrong to dissuade you from so laudable a purpose. I hope it may please God to bless me with your dear society before very long, as I miss you much, and our little John's education would go on much better were you here to superintend. I do try to make him my chief object at present for I consider he is now at a very critical age, as regards the formation of good tempers and habits in his little mind. Little Ed. grows more and more like you.

Ever dearest love, your very affectionate wife,

EMMA CLIFTON.

I have just got your Athboy letter and am delighted to hear you are well, and nothing bad going on—I had some fears of a mob.

REV. JOHN STOKES AT COBHAM TO HON. J. D. BLIGH AT FLORENCE.

August 23rd, 1830.

My very dear friend,

As I know the interest you take in my happiness, I must inform you of a little reformation that has taken place in myself which (if I may judge by its present effects) is likely to add very considerably to my comfort, and I am more eager to communicate it to you, because it is part of that reformation which you have so often endeavoured to excite me to. In the first place I am become ashamed of my old sermons, and still more ashamed of the way in which they were prepared. I have given up my former maxim which you so often combated, that it was better to preach good sermons from the stock that has been published to the world than bad ones of my own composition. I now think that one original sermon made expressly for one's own parish, however inferior in quality, must be more useful. And after all usefulness is the only valuable quality of a sermon. I have determined therefore in future to preach my own sermons. This, perhaps, you will say may be of more advantage to myself than to my hearers. However it is your own advice. Another amendment I have to boast of is that I make my said sermons very early in the morning. I have roused myself for the last two or three weeks at five o'clock, and written for two hours before I commence my toilet. There I confess I have not made much progress towards reformation, but I hope in time to do it, I still lose nearly two hours in that operation. I see the absurdity of it, and yet (such is the force of long habit) cannot cure myself of this folly. I cannot tell you how happy I feel now. No bilious complaints, no blue devils, no fears of starvation, notwithstanding my increase of family. All goes on smoothly with me, God be praised, my treasures are all well. My wife is quite recovered from her accouchement, and my son and daughters are in perfect health and everything I could wish them to be. But this is quite enough of myself and my family, I will now turn to a better subject, the inmates of Cobham Hall. But I take it for granted that on this hand I can have nothing new to tell you. I suppose you hear from one or other of your family every post. I know you have an excellent correspondent in your dear sister. However I will just tell you the present party in the house, and leave the detail of particulars to abler pens. But first let me tell you what is of most importance. Your friends are all well. Lady Darnley is not at all the worse for her visit to Windsor, if anything the better, and appears to be gaining strength daily. The present *société du Chateau* in addition to the Host and Hostess and their lovely daughter and granddaughter, is as follows :—Lady Powerscourt and Miss Wingfield, Lady Clifton and her charming boys (your brother has not yet returned from the Meath Election), Mrs. Tighe, Mr. and Mrs. D. Tighe, Miss Crofton, and though last not least (as far as keeping up the ball of conversation goes) the valiant colonel and accomplished Chevalier Remoni. There is also an artist there at present, Mr. Fowler the painter of the portraits of Lady Elizabeth and Miss Brownlow. He is at present, I believe, taking one of Lady Clifton. Mr. Trefusis has been there for two or three days, but is off this morning. I shall not ask your excellency to write to me, but I wish you would find time to write a few lines to your amiable cousin Miss Wingfield. She wrote to you in two or three of my letters last winter, and from what she said, when I offered to leave her room in this, I think she is rather hurt that you have never acknowledged this. Besides you should, I think, have written to her or your Aunt upon the subject of their late dreadful anxiety for poor William.* Excuse these hints from a tried friend, and if you condescend to act upon this of course you will have tact enough not to say you received them.

God bless you. My wife begs to join me in love, (old women like to send their love to handsome young men) and I am, my own beloved friend,

Affectionately yours,

J. STOKES.

Pray give my kind regards to your friend, the gallant colonel, but I shall not allow my wife to send her love to him. I suppose you know the King intends to visit Cobham the beginning of next month. There is a chance, I am told of his being at Cobham Church. If the Church is to be so highly honoured do you not think the Vicar ought to become a "Dignitary."

EARL OF DARNLEY AT COBHAM TO HON. J. D. BLIGH AT FLORENCE.

August 26th, 1830.

Dearest Johnny,

I am beginning to grow very angry and impatient about you, seeing that Aberdeen's year has been more than 12 months and his week has already exceeded a fortnight. It is true they have been a

---

*Hon. and Rev. W. Wingfield.

good deal bothered, and their business much congested by the late events in France, which I suspect they do not relish quite as much as they ought. The language at Windsor seemed to be in favour of little Bordeaux, but I trust they will acknowledge with a good grace the same glorious title by which our King holds his crown, a compact with his subjects who have preferred him to their legitimate Sovereign, who had forfeited their allegiance by an attempt to subvert their liberties, to preserve those liberties inviolate.

Clifton is not yet returned from Ireland, where he has done good service by keeping out Jack Lawless, but failed in coming in himself. He has, however, in Meath as well as in Kent, done himself much credit. It is, I believe settled that Emma shall be confined in this house which I hope will make them all very comfortable. Nothing can be nicer than the two boys, and little Edward promises to rival little John.

The Tighes left us to-day, and Ball and Longley came, the latter fresh from Paris, full of admiration for all that has happened there. I go on Saturday, 28th to Sandgate for a day, and then to Margate to attend the Sea Bathing Infirmary so as to return on Tuesday, and I hope to take a few pats. with Clifton on the following day. I say a few, for I fear there are not many, as Wells thinks it the worst breeding year he ever knew. I am quite provoked that you cannot be here, but I trust I shall soon be enabled to announce your release, and that you will find enough to amuse you to the end of the season.

Your mother, though poorly at times is, I trust, getting quite well.

Your most affectionate,

D.

We have almost finished the most beautiful harvest I can remember. I never saw such fine crops and so well and easily saved. We ought to be thankful.

HON. CATHERINE WINGFIELD AT COBHAM TO HON. J. D. BLIGH AT FLORENCE.

September 4th, 1830.

My dear Johnny,

I do not like to be left out of the number of those who give you accounts of your dear relatives here. I am sure news on that subject is agreeable to you from any one, so I have determined to write you a few lines before leaving this dear place which we do the day after to-morrow. I am always so happy here that the day of departure must be a sorrowful one, but it is very salutary to us, " whose souls cleave unto the dust " to be often reminded that " all things come to an end," for then the conclusion of the matter (" but Thy commandment is exceeding broad ") is brought to the heart with delightful effect. Dearest Uncle D. returned from Sandgate with a hoarse cold, but I am happy to say he appears to have quite shaken it off, and were it not for his anxieties about Aunt D. would I think be very well, but they have a very visible effect on him, he is sometimes dreadfully depressed about her, she is certainly not as strong as she was a few

342

years ago, but that I think without the addition of her late severe illness, is not to be wondered at, and Mr. Beaumont who seems to have taken a sensible view of her case, declares most positively, that there is nothing essentially wrong about her, but that the unpleasant sensations complained of proceed from a diminution of muscular strength; that this does cause distressing sensations, no one who has had any experience of bodily weakness can doubt, but it is greatly to be wished that she would make the best of them to her devoted husband; dear Uncle D., I love him better every day. My dear Aunt seems in very good spirits to-day, and had a good night. There is a grotto in progress in her garden under the direction of Mr. Douglas Guest. I hope it will be an amusement to her; she drives her dear little Ponies very constantly.

I rejoice to say dearest Beppy has been pretty free from headache lately and looks very well. She rides very often and we have had many happy walks together. Dear little May's looks are still delicate, she grows fast. Dear Emma is unchangeably sweet and placid in spite of her disappointment at Clif's absence being so prolonged, there is a chance of his coming to-day, which for our sakes especially I hope he may. Dar. is a delightful boy, and Edward an interesting dear, fat as a porpoise. The dear Doctor is a much improved man, he does indeed appear to view his Saviour in a new light, and I trust He will enable him to shew that light to others, his humility is truly edifying, he does seem willing to receive the Kingdom of God as a little child, the only spirit, saith the scripture, with which

343

a man can enter that Kingdom, but we must not expect to see dear Mr. Stokes, or any child of God perfect while in the body, the work of the Spirit is sometimes a very slow work, but it is also sure.

Messrs. Sale, Pay, etc., are coming here this evening, so I hope there will be some good music.

Were Mama on the spot she would no doubt send you her love. I have the blessing of seeing her in good health, added to many other mercies lately vouchsafed to me.

With sincere good wishes to your companion,

Believe me always,

My dear Johnny,

Your faithful and affectionate Cousin,

CATH. WINGFIELD.

Monday, 6th. Clifton arrived late Saturday night, quite well.

EARL OF DARNLEY AT COBHAM TO HON. J. D. BLIGH AT FLORENCE.

September 7th, 1830.

Dearest John,

You will receive at the same time with this letter a short scribble I wrote last night. This morning's post has brought a letter from Lord Aberdeen, which I send with my answer, which I hope you will approve. Indeed under the circumstances I do not see how we could do otherwise. I trust the request of your immediate deliverance from Florence will be complied with, and that we may look forward with some confidence to the pleasure of seeing you here soon. The present state of the Kingdom of the Netherlands is most interesting and critical, and I think the situation inferior to Paris, certainly superior to every other.*

You will be glad to hear that the *incomidìtè* mentioned last night has passed off prosperously, and that I am (thank God), quite well to-day, though still keeping at home etc. The females (except Mim), are off for the Chatham Races. Clif. talks of looking at the Pats. Loves and blessings to our dearest *Sekepy*, as Da. calls Secretary.

Your ever aff.

D.

P.S.—Mim and I etc. go to Sandgate on Monday, leaving the Cliftons in possession, and expecting to return on the 27th in time for the accouchement.

EARL OF DARNLEY AT COBHAM TO HON. J. D. BLIGH AT FLORENCE.

Sept. 13th, 1830.

Dearest John,

I suppose by the enclosed that the fate of Europe is in your hands, and I doubt not will be taken good care of.** By the bye when I saw the Great Duke the other day, he said, " he has not had much to do, but that little he has done well." I trust nothing however material will now intervene to prevent your speedy arrival, as I conclude Sey-

*John Bligh was at this time appointed Secretary of Legation at The Hague.

**Letter from Lord Aberdeen regretting that it was not possible to give John Bligh leave.

mour, who I heard was tired of Constantinople, will not lose any time in relieving you.* I do not see how you can have anything more desirable than the Hague, where I am sanguine in my hopes that all will subside into a satisfactory, though very interesting state of things. I look forward to the hope of that I have long desired, a visit to Holland in the Spring if we live and do well so long. But alas both your parents feel more sensibly every day that (as Lady Spencer roars out) 60 will tell. Indeed your mother at times makes me very unhappy, and if I did not make some allowance for the exaggeration of nervous feelings, and the very variable nature of her complaints, I should think more seriously of them. Clifton and I have just been dining with the Justices at the Falstaff. Our Corps is to be reinforced by Major Day, Rev. Formby, and *Maître* Smith. We go (D.V.) to Sandgate to-morrow, leaving the Clifton family here to be augmented shortly, as we trust. Beppy said she would write to you, but prefers playing the organ. We intend to return before the end of the month for the accouchement. The Harvest here has been prosperous and abundant. Hops just begun. I have this day inspected Nellie R's, which are rank luxuriant, and mine are not bad.

Your ever aff.

D.

The Ladies desire their love to the Colonel and many thanks for his agreeable letter.

Mr. Fowler, who has been long here, has made an admirable and very like picture of Mim, with which she is much pleased, as we are all.

*Mr. Seymour did not reach Florence till December 31.

THE OLD HOUSE AT SANDGATE,
1826.

From a drawing in the author's possession.

September 13th, 1830.

At the eve of departure for Sandgate I sit down
to eke out a letter to you my dearest Johnny; the
Waggon and my Ponies are gone, and to-morrow
please God we leave this house and Emma is much
delighted in the idea of being allowed to remain for
the purpose of producing, I hope, a fine Girl,
nothing can be more excellent than those already
here who are both healthy and very dear.

My dear Johnny,

I wish you could see your godson, who is
sitting for his picture as Hercules. I think he will
be like you, and am sure you must like him whenever you see him, he is so good-tempered. Lady
Darnley would have written more but was
obliged to let Mr. Fowler alter her nose a little.
I wish I could write something more worth your
reading, but will only now add that I am very
affectionately yours,

EMMA CLIFTON.

LORD CLIFTON AT COBHAM TO HON. J. D. BLIGH AT
FLORENCE.

September 22nd, 1830.

My dearest Johnny,

I cannot say how much I feel ashamed of
myself having been so long silent, or how often I
have intended writing both to you and Gascoigne,
particularly since I have been released from
electioneering bustle which occupied me for six

weeks or so with no little trouble, although with no fruits to myself. I doubt whether I should so easily have resigned my seat at Canterbury had the pregnant events of the " three days "* transpired before I did so. I quite agree with you that the times require the exertions of upright and independent men, and that no one having pretensions to such a character ought to flinch from public business. I am inclined to think that although the uproar of this gallant achievement on the part of the Parisians so soon passed over, we have by no means seen the end of revolutionary movements in Europe and that, although hitherto of a much milder character than the Revolution forty years since, its consequences will be still more generally felt, and that its effects will be far different from those which led to a holy (or arbitrary) alliance. My electioneering has been curious, a brilliant triumph for my protégé at Canterbury, which might have been still more brilliant had we played the higher game, and thrown Watson back, as I would have done had I been on my own bottom, and I told Fordwich so the second morning of the Election, but that I would not advise another to play the bold but hazardous game. I am afraid the ancient and loyal City will have but an indifferent pair of representatives. The Hon. Richard has exchanged to half pay. As to the County of Kent I think that, had I deemed it compatible with other duties, I might have managed it, although Honeywood evidently played into Hedge's hand. I think

* The Revolution in Paris resulting in the abdication of Charles X and the accession of Louis Philippe.

348

he will make a good Member, particularly as he appeared on Pennenden Heath in leathers and tops, which is all right for a country gentleman. As to the County of Meath, I verily believe I might have turned out Somerville, had I been aware of the state of things in time, but unfortunately there is no one who can or will inform us of what is going on. Disney and family are so shilly-shally and sleepy. As it was, I made a splash, helped to send Jack Lawless to the right-about, and got into a scrape with a blackguard attorney who contrived to make out a most extravagant Bill which we are trying to remit, but I hope shall not go to law about. Moreover honest Jack* was half inclined to challenge me to help himself into the public favour again, but was content with a remonstrance to which I returned an answer which he was pleased to term polite and satisfactory, and which with his own letter he published, and you may perhaps have seen. The said Jack was clever and good-humoured at the hustings and rather won my favour by his deportment there. Poor fellow, he narrowly escaped being ducked in the Boyne or murdered; I found I was too late to do anything and so withdrew. On my return I found all pretty well here although my mother is not so stout as she was, and my father had a slight attack owing, I believe, to a turtle feast which took place the day I arrived. I hope Sandgate is doing them both good. I have been to-day to Cliffe, where I walked two hours and twenty minutes without seeing a bird, and then would only shoot a brace as they are so scarce. On the other

*Lawless, the Irish agitator.

hand there are more birds towards Cuxton than I ever saw, but they are very wild.

How melancholy is the fate of poor Huskisson. How curious that he should be the victim of the Trading and Mechanical Juggernaut, and crushed in celebration of the Triumph of the Steam Idol.

My paper warns me that I must conclude. What is the " Great Captain " to do with the new Parliament ?   I think he will find it somewhat unruly, although Billy Holmes knew how to take care of himself on the late as well as all other occasions.

Pray remember me most kindly to Gas. I hope both he and you will come and shoot some pheasants. I do not think there are a great many, but no doubt more than are seen. Boghurst is dead.

Your affectionate brother,

CLIFTON.

CHAPTER VI.

The Sundry and Manifold Changes of the World.

THE birth of a much desired granddaughter marks the close of a
singularly happy and peaceful period
for the family at Cobham. Lord and Lady
Darnley had suffered much from the loss of
four dearly loved children (three in childhood and one in the first year of her married
life), but in their later years they were blessed
with much love and affection from the three
remaining, who, with the pretty gentle
daughter-in-law and her two fine boys were
their constant companions. A little girl was
the one thing wished for to complete the
family happiness, and Lady Elizabeth Cust
was often told that her grandmother cried
for joy when she was born. In the evening
of the 30th September, 1830, Lord and Lady
Darnley were sitting alone in the library at
Cobham after dinner, unaware of anything
happening in the North wing, when about
11-30 p.m. Mr. Beaumont, the family doctor
opened the door unexpectedly, and said,
" your Ladyship has a granddaughter," and

Lady Darnley was so startled as well as delighted that she burst into tears.*

October 1st, 1830.
8 a.m.

Dt. Jy.

I write in much haste to inform you that our dear Emma produced a fine girl last night at 11, before we knew she was ill, and is as well as possible this morning after a good night. The *Filles* only arrived from Sandgate the night before, and C. and I yesterday from Canterbury from a very brilliant feast of H. Cooper the Mayor. I was happy to find by your letter to C. that your Elba expedition had been prosperous and satisfactory. I begin to fear the place of your next destination** will be extinguished in the flames of bloody civil war. I suppose C. and I will look at the Pheasants presently ; you shall hear more soon on this and other subjects.

Your ever aff.   D.

EARL OF DARNLEY AT COBHAM TO HON. J. D. BLIGH
AT FLORENCE.

October 28th, 1830.

Dearest J.

I am sorry to say our *Cordon Sanitaire* appears

*Elizabeth Caroline, the third child and elder daughter of Lord and Lady Clifton was baptized at Cobham Hall, October 29th, 1830. She married December 13th, 1855, Sir Reginald John Cust.

Lady Elizabeth Cust and her eldest daughter, Evelyn Georgiana, who married April 30th, 1879, the Hon. Arthur Pelham, are the joint editors of this book.

**The Hague.

to be ineffectual, and I much fear we (especially in Kent) have been inoculated from the opposite shore. I think indeed the most likely explanation of the present lamentable state of this County is the constant smuggling intercourse carried on with our neighbours on the continent. Fires every night, and stacks, barns, etc., destroyed in various parts of the County. On Sunday night I had my share, in the partial consumption of a barley stack which, however, does not appear to have much connection, if any, with the other outrages, and my people all exerted themselves and behaved well. I returned suddenly from Sandgate on hearing of it, and we are taking every possible precaution against any further mischief. By far the worst feature in the case is the fatal pusillanimity of some farmers who have been frightened into raising wages, and other coaxings of the labourers.

As I trust you may have left Florence before this letter can reach you, I do not write more at length, but unless we succeed, as I trust we soon shall, in discovering some of these atrocious incendiaries, and exhibiting them on Penenden Heath, the worst consequences may be apprehended. Sure I am that no human wisdom can avail, if it is decreed by Providence that this hitherto happy country is to be the scene of civil war. But this I trust God in His infinite mercy will forbid.

The *Filles* are just returned from Sandgate. Mim at least not worse.

Yours,

D.

November 9th, 1830.

Dear John,

I send the *Camer Gazette*, and with it (to my shame be it spoken) a letter that I have this day discovered, which I fear has been long *fourni*, together with other papers, in my box. I trust it is not of very material consequence, so that I shall be forgiven this piece of *unofficial* negligence.

We are here in a most unpleasant state of things, and *my friend* Wellington has proved himself the most powerful *Bear* the Stock Exchange has ever known, for in a week he has lowered the Funds 7 or 8 per cent. This last exploit of putting off the grand affair in the City which was to have taken place to-day, has filled us all with consternation, and many with disgust. I hear Wellesley (the Marquess) says it is the boldest piece of cowardice he ever heard of. The cry is, they must go out, but the report is he means to brave it, and to all appearance he retains his hold on the King, to whom, however, I had an opportunity of stating my opinion the day before yesterday, and of reading a letter I have written to his Minister withdrawing all support on account of his strange and uncalled for declaration about reform.

I have just seen Lord A. at the House, who says the only reason your name is not in the last Gazette is your not having yourself announced your acceptance, but as I undertake to answer for you, I conclude it will appear in the next. I hope your

Mother is better, and she seems pleased with her new Dr. Farre whom I have also consulted, and he pronounces my complaint the *gastrick* angina pectoris which he says is not dangerous if well managed. He is certainly a clever, sensible man, but I do not much rely on any medical opinions in so obscure a case. You see my Quack has been housed.

Yours in haste,

D.

Although neither Lord nor Lady Darnley were really old, he being at this time 65 and she 60, they had both for some time been failing in health, and the Cliftons did not leave them during this autumn and winter. In January, 1831, Lady Darnley became seriously ill, and Caroline Parnell who was staying at Cobham wrote to her mother, Lady Caroline Parnell, in Paris: "This house is in great state of affliction just now; poor Lady Darnley is dangerously ill, and Mr. Bligh, one of her sons who she has wished much to see is not yet returned from Florence; the doctors think if he came it might be of great service to Lady D., and that perhaps she might recover." Lady Clifton adds on the same sheet: "I am now fully employed in attending I fear, the last hours of my dear mother-in-law."

John Bligh had been detained in Florence until the arrival of Mr. Seymour, his successor as Chargé d'Affaires at the Court of Tuscany. He left Florence on January 5th, and travelled to Paris with his friend Colonel Gascoigne. He describes his journey by " the new road, along the sea-side, which is very beautiful and remarkably well managed;" to Marseilles, Arles, Nismes, and Lyons. On his arrival in Paris he heard of his mother's dangerous illness, but was detained there by diplomatic business, and did not reach Cobham until January 23rd. The following letters show Lord Darnley's anxiety for his son's arrival, and describe his own and Lady Darnley's precarious state of health.

EARL OF DARNLEY AT COBHAM TO HON. J. D. BLIGH AT PARIS.

January 13th, 1831.

Dst. Jy.,

I hope this letter will meet you at Paris on your happy return to your friends here who have so long anxiously expected it. I wish I could add that you are likely to find them all as well as you left them, but our anxiety about your dear mother still continues, and has indeed lately been augmented, for although the steel prescribed in London has appeared to agree, and flattering prospect of permanent advantage had arisen, I grieve to say that these two last days have obscured them by what seems to be a new feature in the disease, and has induced me to send for more medical advice. My complaint seems also to be progressing as the Yankees would say, so you see your poor old parents are in need of the comfort of your presence.

Our political situation is indeed critical and alarming, but I am too much engaged by my domestick cares to write much, and at Paris you will hear all the news. You will also, I hope, order for me on your account 600 bottles of any very good French wine you may fancy. I should also be glad if you feel yourself sufficiently at home with Lord Granville, to urge your pretensions to him, (who, I believe, has much weight in the Government at home) to succeed to Hamilton at Paris if he can be removed, and the Hague Mission is *cut down to a Frigate*, which is, I believe, in contemplation.

Things go on badly in Ireland, and Sir H. Parnell contends that nothing short of the recall of Lord A[nglesey] can save us from a repeal of the Union, and a Mobocracy under King O'Connell.

All join in love and good wishes with
Your most affectionate,
D.

LORD CLIFTON AT COBHAM TO HON. J. D. BLIGH AT PARIS.

January 13th, 1831.
My dearest Johnny,

It is provoking that we should have been so long in expectation of your being on the road and therefore have written so seldom ; I believe it is about a month since I addressed a few lines to you at Paris, requesting you to execute some commissions for me ; I now write to say that we cannot spare you for a moment longer than necessary, and that I do not wish you to execute them ; indeed Emma says she does not wish to have the books.

We have a series of ups and downs in rapid succession with our dearest mother. At one moment she is apparently in a sinking state, and the next is walking and driving about. Dr. Smith has again been called in to-day to the horror of all here except my father and Mr. Beaumont, and gives an opinion as before at direct variance with those of Drs. Farre and Holland and Tupper. I believe Farre is to come down soon to consult, the system of flying from one doctor or a set of doctors to another is indeed most vexatious, and must if persevered in be pernicious. We want your presence very much for many reasons, but above all to assist in restoring dearest Mim., which I think it would contribute to more than anything else. We have not shot much. Red Wood afforded a very good day. Cobhambury very fair. Mount, R. Heath, Norwood, Lodge Wood, M. Grove, Coal Wood, Merrills, Birch Wood, etc., still intact.

I shall hope for you in about a week.

Your affectionate brother,

CLIFTON.

EARL OF DARNLEY AT COBHAM HALL TO HON. J. D. BLIGH [TRAVELLING TO ENGLAND.]

January 15th, 1831.

Dst. Jy.,

My letter of last night was too late for the

down mail, and you will probably get it together with this. In the chance, however, of your arriving to-day, I have sent one to Sittingbourne.

I am sorry to say I cannot give a better account of your dear mother, though Farre, who left us this morning assured me that he thought she would recover if she adhered to all his directions. Her complaint has been of such long duration, that you must expect to find her in a very reduced state. Your arrival will, I am sure, do her good, but she is in a very weak state. Your other dear friends are well.

My complaint *progresses*, but I am in other respects well.

EARL OF DARNLEY AT COBHAM TO HON. J. D. BLIGH.

January 16th, 1831.
Evening.

Dt. Jy.,

I wish I could give you a better account of dearest Mim, but she continues in a very unsatisfactory state, and God only knows what may be the result. It is most distressing to reflect that after your long absence, you should have to meet such a drawback on your happiness. But God's will, whatever it may be, must be done. Your presence will, I am sure, be a great comfort to the dear sufferer at all events. Your other dear friends are all as well as can be expected. Poor dear Beppy's watchful anxiety must of course affect her. My malady is more or less affected by anxiety. Little Mary and the two very fine boys are most flourishing. Adieu, dear Johnny, I am too much engrossed by one subject to write on any other, though our painful attention is much called for to publick as well as private sources of anxiety and regret. Ireland, poor Ireland, is worse than ever.

D.

EARL OF DARNLEY AT COBHAM TO HON. J. D. BLIGH.

January 18th, 1831.

Dt. Jy.,

I think you *must* arrive to-morrow, and under that impression I believe I shall send my fast trotting mare to meet you at Sittingbourne that you may lose no time. You will find the Knights Place gate open.

Would to God I could send you a better account of your poor dear mother, but I grieve to say it goes from bad to worse. Oh how I pity my poor dear boy's feelings on account of such a return after so long an absence, but God's will be done, and if it be His will to take her hence, I have the consolation of knowing that in the state of health and nerves into which she had fallen, she never could have been happy in this life, and I have the consolation of knowing that no means of human care have been neglected.

Your afflicted and affectionate

D.

On January 23rd John Bligh at last reached his afflicted parents. The sight of her favourite son helped Lady Darnley's illness to take a favourable turn, and though still confined to her room the immediate anxiety was much lessened. Lord Darnley was also much better, and on January 29th he was able to go out shooting with his sons and other friends. He went to London and attended the House of Lords several times, and on March 1st attended a meeting at Sittingbourne for promoting Parliamentary Reform. Lord Clifton was summoned to attend the Grand Jury in Co. Meath at this time and felt sufficiently at ease about the health of both his parents to leave for Ireland on March 3rd. Colonel Gascoigne accompanied him.

LORD CLIFTON AT HOLYHEAD TO LADY CLIFTON AT COBHAM.

March 4th, 1831.

My dearest Love,

We arrived here at half-past 9 by Spencer's Coach from Shrewsbury where we slept last night, tho' we only stopt from half-past 11 till half-past 5 this morning. All went off prosperously however. I hope you and our dearest children continue well, and also that my dearest Mother is better, and going on satisfactorily. We are about to sail at 12 o'clock. I will write from Dublin.

Your attached and loving husband,

C.

LORD CLIFTON AT DUBLIN TO LADY CLIFTON AT
COBHAM.

5th March, 1831.

My dearest love,

We arrived this morning safe and well, praised
be God. I have nothing to communicate except
that Meath is quiet. My father will tell you about
my interview with his XLNC. I will write at
length from C. Lodge and tell you all about it.
I am going there immediately. Kiss my sweet
children for

Your attached and loving husband,

C.

Thanks for your letters of the 1st and 2nd.

LORD CLIFTON AT CLIFTON LODGE TO LADY CLIFTON
AT COBHAM.

March 6th, 1831.

My dearest love,

I arrived here before 9 yesterday evening and
found everything sufficiently comfortable, altho'
they had given me up. The country is quiet and
peaceable, and this place is in as good order as I
could expect considering that so much has been
going on. It looks pretty well except that alas!
all the Laurestinus plants are killed by the Frost,
which is not a little annoying and disfiguring. I
do not see that one has escaped. The rubbish is
nearly cleared away but not quite; some of the
old vaults still remain and must be packed off
immediately. I long to hear good accounts of you
all, particularly of my Mother; I shall be anxious
to hear that she uses her legs; send me some

account of Tiny Baby,* and the Das. Mr. Hargrave is arrived but I have not seen him, and shall not for some time if I can avoid it, as the rain kept me from Church this morning, and I wish to be alone a little. Adieu, dearest. Kiss my dear children for

Your affectionately attached hubby,

C.

Love to all.

LORD CLIFTON AT TRIM TO LADY CLIFTON AT COBHAM.

March 7th, 1831.

My dearest Love,

We are busily engaged here with the Criminal Cases and shall be kept some time as the calendar is heavy. Tom Bligh and Edward came too late for the Grand Jury. Lord Langford has written to announce his brother as a Candidate for the County, the more the merrier. I really cannot write for there is so much going on. The country is quiet. I am rather disappointed not to hear from Cobham to-day. My love to all. Kiss the dear children for

Your attached and loving husband,

C.

LORD CLIFTON AT TRIM TO LADY CLIFTON AT COBHAM.

March 8th, 1831.

My dearest Love,

I have received two dear nice (1 long) letters from you to-day for which many thanks and for the good accounts they contain. Business goes on here but slowly ; as to Politics nobody seems to know what they are about, all are scheming one way or other ;

* Lady Elizabeth Cust.

I am afraid I am too honest to make the way I ought with the Freeholders!! I have got most wretched ink and pens, and the postman has sent to say he will only wait 3 minutes. So Adieu dearest love. Kiss my sweet children.

From your loving hubby

C.

LORD CLIFTON AT TRIM TO LADY CLIFTON AT COBHAM.

March 10th, 1831.

My dearest Love,

I really am so perplexed and bothered by business of various kinds here that I cannot write a collected letter but as Gascoigne has written to Johnny at my request you must get the news from him. The business is unprecedently protracted and I think we shall not be discharged before Saturday possibly before Monday; the trial has lasted all yesterday and to-day and will last probably to-morrow. It is about a conspiracy against a young lady accused of writing threatening letters to her own Father; I am quite tired of it all, and so must be Gascoigne who is here, and now returning to Clifton Lodge with me.

Kiss my Das for your attached hubby

C.

LORD CLIFTON AT CLIFTON LODGE TO LADY CLIFTON AT COBHAM.

March 13th, 1831.

My dearest love,

I have been much distressed by your's and Johnny's account of my dearest Father's health, and

shall be most anxious to get Dr. Bree's opinion
to-morrow, which I fear I shall not if the letter is
directed as the last was to Dublin as they are not
delivered there on Sundays, but might pass through.
I am sorry to find that you and the dear children
(including Mary) are unwell. May God in His mercy
grant that these sad things may pass away and
leave a due impression of the nothingness of human
affairs. We are now going to Church. Pray thank
Johnny for his letter and say I will write to him
to-morrow. Kiss my dear Babes for

Your attached and loving husband

C.

LADY CLIFTON AT COBHAM TO LORD CLIFTON AT
CLIFTON LODGE.

March 13th, 1831.

My dearest love,

I felt quite grieved to receive no letter from you
this morning and am told that there cannot be one
to-morrow. But I am more inclined to admire you
for writing so often, than to blame you for once
omitting to write, knowing you must be very busy.
I am happy to tell you that our dear children are
pretty well and we ought to be thankful to our good
and merciful God who daily poureth out benefits
upon us. Oh! what a blessing in this stormy
weather to have a comfortable home and a blazing
fire-side for one's dear children. Having mentioned
the storm I must add that it is tremendous just
now. I hardly know what account to give you of
your dear father. I cannot say that he is well, and
yet he is certainly better than he was yesterday.

The fact is that he was not so well yesterday evening and I fear suffered much pain, but he is certainly better, although low and weak. Mr. Beaumont desires that he should be kept very quiet, and it appears that the greatest possible attention must be paid to diet etc. He has a bed put up in his little breakfast-room,* and Elizabeth slept in his study** last night. It is truly distressing to see him suffer, at the same time I should tell you that he is more free from pain to-day and I should hope that he is somewhat better, but I feel so ignorant about his case, and so perplexed that I really am not sure that I am giving a right account of him. If I can I will get Johnny to write a few lines. I hope dearest love, you will not fail to take all care of yourself, and may He whose mercies fail not, but Who renews them every morning, take you under His protection and bless you with temporal and spiritual blessings for His dear Son's sake.

Pray remember me kindly to Colonel Gascoigne. Mr. Stokes sends his love.

Ever your very affectionate wife
EMMA CLIFTON.

Pray write a few lines to dear kind Uncle Tom Parnell, and appoint a time to see him on your way through Dublin. He seems hurt at your not enquiring for him when you went through.

[Postscript by Hon. John Duncan Bligh.]
Dearest C.

As Emma tells you that she will get me to add

*The small room on the way to the South Library.
**The South Library.

a few words I do so, not that I have anything essential to communicate to you upon the *now* most interesting subject to us all. As far as I can make out Dearest Father has been without positive pain throughout this day, but uncomfortable from apprehension of it, from debility and lowness, the natural consequence of the remedies which the *faculty* deem it necessary to apply in order to render the secretions what they ought to be as the proper foundations for all after proceedings. I hope we shall be able to keep him quiet, but the impatience of his nature is much against that. Aunt P. I fear will go to-morrow, if she does she shall take a letter for you to Town.

Ever yours,

J. D. B.

My Mother walked into her dressing room to-day.

Lord Clifton at Clifton Lodge to Countess of Darnley at Cobham.

March 15th, 1831.

My dearest Mim,

In addition to the improving accounts of your health your letter written by your own hand has indeed given me unfeigned pleasure, and I rejoice to hear that you are now walking about your room. I hope it may soon be about your garden, if the weather is more favourable than the present, which, here at least is wretched. All our laurestinus shrubs have been killed here, which we could ill spare. The Frost was very severe on this side of this channel. It has rained so much that we have scarcely been able to get out, and the roads are in a swimming state. I heard to-day from Abbeyleix Aunt de V. presses me to go there but I cannot. I, have also been asked by M. Forde. They all rejoice to hear of your convalescence dearest Mim,

Your dutiful affectionate son,

CLIFTON.

LORD CLIFTON AT CLIFTON LODGE TO LADY CLIFTON
AT COBHAM.

March 15th, 1831.

My dearest Love,

Look at the date of this and consider whether you made any acquaintance 6 years ago of which you have since repented. I have not, and the sound of Aunt De V's voice still rings in my ears pronouncing the fatal words of introduction to "Miss Parnell, *Miss Emma Parnell*, Mr. Ross of Bladensburg and Mr. Thomas Nugent." No dearest wife I do not repent but on the contrary every revolving year contributes to assure me how inestimable the treasure is, of which that introduction led me to the possession. Your account of the dear pledges of our love is not so satisfactory as I could have wished, but I pray to the great and good giver of all things for His blessing upon them and us, and that He will preserve them in health and safety till I return, and for ever. I have only as yet seen Mrs. Hopkins and others at Church as yesterday I was busy at home and to-day it is so wet that I can scarcely get out. The Colonel* is writing you a witty account of our mansion and its accompani-

*Colonel Gascoigne.

ments. I hope that it will be tolerably comfortable when you come here which will I hope be early in the Summer. Bars and bolts are putting up which will I hope make it secure. Below stairs I think you will like the Kitchen, Housekeeper's Room, Butler's Pantry and Servants' Hall. I will not mention anything above but leave it to your imagination to picture the variety of sitting and bed rooms. I will enquire into the state of the Glove and other schools and let you know. Kiss my darling boys and girl for their affectionate Papa.

Ever dearest love,

Your affectionately attached hubby

C.

LADY CLIFTON AT COBHAM TO LORD CLIFTON AT CLIFTON LODGE.

March 16th, 1831.

My dearest Love,

I begin now to look out for your coming back, and trust it will not be long before, by the blessing of God, I shall enjoy the great pleasure of seeing you. Your dear father seems much better to-day. Elizabeth is also better and is down-stairs again to-day. Little Mary is better but still keeps her room I believe from prudential motives. Da has not lost his cough, and as the weather is so changeable and the ground so wet, Mr. Beaumont has not advised their going out. I am very sad and lonely without you, and I much regret to find by your letters that you are engaged in what I consider must be very annoying, the contracted politics of a county, and the jealousies and party-feelings which take up so large a part of the hearts and heads of country gentlemen. If there was no high wall of bribery and corruption to be climbed over before the most pure-minded individual can serve his country in the House of Commons I should say most cheerfully, " go on, and prosper," but I own I should not think you justified in committing even but a slight offence against the law of honesty, were it to save your country. We are not to do evil, that good may come. Will you oblige me by reading a short article in the Record which I have marked with double lines, on this subject ? I long for a letter, but still more so for your return. Mr. and *Mrs. Cole** are in town so you might write to her to ask her to look out for rooms.

Ever dearest Cliffy,

Your very affectionate wife

EMMA CLIFTON.

When you have done with the Record pray send it to Miss Bagot

Nurney House,

Kildare,

Co. Kildare.

(In Lady Elizabeth Bligh's writing).

E. B.'s best love to dear Cliffy. Emma seems very well I am happy to inform you and her cold I hope going.

[This letter was franked by Lord Darnley. He died unexpectedly between 9 and 10 a.m. on March 17th.]

*Lady Henry Moore who had married in 1830, Edward Henry Cole, of Stoke Lyne, Oxfordshire.

Clifton Lodge,

March 17th, 1831.

My dearest Love,

I am not at all satisfied with the accounts of
my dearest father which this day's Post has brought,
and I have hardly resolution to remain here as
long as private and political interests would seem
to require, so anxious am I to ascertain on the spot
the extent of his illness. I rejoice however to find
that the other invalids are convalescent. The
workmen are to be *out of this* by the 15th of May,
and I have told Mr. Hargrave and Mr. Laughlin
that the house must be finished by that time, and
they assure me that it will be done. Pray continue
to write your dear affectionate letters which give me
so much pleasure. I am sorry to say that yesterday I again neglected to write and to-day's Post will
not reach you till Tuesday, so that I shall be in the
same scrape as last week, I will tell you whence it
arises. On Wednesday there is no Post from
London, and so I have neglected twice on Wednesday to write to you. I send this only to shew that I
am thinking of you, but will write again to-morrow
to give you later news. The wind may perhaps
delay to-morrow's Post and this might arrive a day
sooner tho' I do not expect it will. There is a
Reform Meeting talked of here which, and one of the
Magistrates, I must attend if I can stay. I begin to
feel it very long absence. Kiss my darling children
for me and give my affectionate love to all the rest.

I am sorry you have at last lost Aunt P. and Cata.
Ever dearest Wifey,
Your attached hubby,
C.

LORD CLIFTON AT CLIFTON LODGE TO LADY CLIFTON
AT COBHAM.

March, 18th, 1831.

My dearest Love,

I am disappointed not to hear something of the dear invalids to-day altho' I ought not to be so in consequence of having had a line from Johnny of Monday's date.   It makes me however very uncomfortable and I am not sure whether I shall not start on Monday instead of waiting for the various meetings here.   Do not however expect that I shall do so, as I must stay here if possible and may have to return immediately if I go over now.   I find the letter I wrote yesterday did not go. Kiss my Das for your attached hubby
C.

My duty and love.   I must defer writing to Johnny as we are going to Ardbraccan to see the Bishop etc.

During Lord Clifton's absence in Ireland the state of Lord Darnley's health and more especially his sufferings from angina pectoris had caused great anxiety and distress to the family at Cobham, still a fatal result was not anticipated, and Emma, Lady Darnley in later days described to her children the consternation which fell upon the house on the morning of March 17th, 1831, when Lord Darnley was found dead in his bed at about 9 a.m. John Bligh records in his journal that he had some pleasant conversation with his father on the previous evening and left him about midnight hoping that he was going on well. It was fortunate that he was there to give orders and break the news to his mother who was still confined to her room. Letters took some time to reach Ireland, and it was not until 1 a.m. on March 22nd that Lord Clifton reached his sorrowful home. The funeral took place at Cobham on March 26th.

Edward, Lord Clifton, who now succeeded as 5th Earl of Darnley, on going into his father's affairs found that it was necessary to make economies at Cobham Hall. In a letter addressed to his wife, from which an extract follows, he explained matters fully to her.

EDWARD EARL OF DARNLEY TO EMMA COUNTESS
OF DARNLEY.

Cobham Hall, 1831.

My dearest Love,

As you appear to agree with me so entirely as to the necessity of economizing and managing our affairs so as to enable us to live not only within our income, but so also that I may gradually liquidate my debts, I will endeavour to state to you as clearly and fully as I am able the extent of those claims

upon me, and the probable means I have of satisfying them. I am likewise desirous of shewing you
that I am not wholly inattentive to these matters,
or incapable of calculating my resources, as well as
the demands upon my purse; and I may at the
same time put you in possession of facts which will
at once give you some idea of the matter, prove to
you that I wish to conceal nothing from you, and
give you an opportunity of assisting me, by giving
you some knowledge of the actual state of things. . . .

The details given in this statement can
hardly be of interest at a later date, but the
result of Lord Darnley's calculations was to
reduce a nominal income of £25,000 to one
not exceeding £8,000, and one half of this
latter sum Lord Darnley expressed his intention of setting aside as a sinking fund for
payment of debts charged on the estate. It is
not surprising therefore to find that Lord and
Lady Darnley settled down to a very quiet
and uneventful life, which was indeed the
most congenial thing possible to the tempera-
ment of the new Lady Darnley.

Lord Darnley took his seat in the House
of Lords on June 21st, 1831, and describes the
occasion in a letter to his wife. He was
obliged to go to Meath in July to support his
brother John, who stood unsuccessfully for
that County at the General Election which

followed the introduction of the first Reform Bill.

EDWARD EARL OF DARNLEY TO EMMA COUNTESS OF DARNLEY.

London,
June 22nd, 1831.

How vexed am I, my dearest Love, that I did not write to you yesterday. The fact is that I did not forget it, but I was so strange and so uncomfortable in the House of Lords, as a member of it for the first time, that I did not venture to avail myself of the means which its purlieus would have afforded of writing to you. I fear you have been disappointed. I took the oaths and my seat in the midst of the most crowded House of Ladies you ever saw. The whole place was full of Feathers and Diamonds, into the centre of which I was ushered to take the necessary oaths etc., and when I got there I found that the Chancellor's Clerk had put John instead of Edward upon my Writ. This however by the kindness of Mr. Courtenay the Clerk, who is a friend of mine, was set to rights, and with dishevelled hair, and in a state of melting from the heat I read through the Allegiance, Abjuration, and the rest, and subscribed my name as a Peer of the Realm. I staid in the house till about 9 or 10, but was absent during the King's Speech as I thought the fatigue would be too much for me. Only think of all I did. There was such a crowd by the Horse Guards that I could not get on in a carriage, so Johnny and I got out, and I intended to take a boat at Whitehall Stairs, but finding that

I walked well, went on to the House and afterwards walked back by myself to the Horse Guards, where I saw your Papa and George, and saw the King pass from the windows. I then got a boat and went to the Temple Stairs and then walked again up Chancery Lane to a place which Mr. Robert Disney had appointed to make an Affidavit that I intended going over to give evidence if the business of the House and my health did not interfere. I am thank God quite well to-day, the better for my walking and therefore I intend setting out this evening to go a couple of stages on my way to Ireland. Alas! I dislike it amazingly but I do not think it will hurt me to go in this quiet way. I promise you if I feel inconvenience that I will not persevere in my journey. I will write and hope you will do the same constantly.

Kiss my three darlings.

From your loving husband

C.

EDWARD EARL OF DARNLEY TO EMMA COUNTESS OF DARNLEY AT BRIGHTON.

Dublin,

July 26th, 1831.

My dearest only Love,

Unfortunately we were out of Dublin to-day till after the Post had gone, or I would have assured you by it how truly happy I am in the reflection which this anniversary brings to my mind most forcibly. Yes, dearest Love, it was this day six years that gave me to your fond arms as a loving husband, and in the warmth of my heart I declare that every hour since has added to the gratitude which I feel for such a blessing, and to the love I bear you now the dear Mother of my three darling babes whom with your dear self may God in His mercy bless and preserve for Christ's sake. This much dear wife, on this our marriage day. I will add more to-morrow, when we hope for a better account from Brighton.

Kiss my sweet children, from your attached and loving husband

C.

Wednesday. Johnny is gone to canvass, and I am off for Clifton Lodge. In all probability he and Naper will not both stand.

Colonel Gascoigne has just now called. He desires me to thank you for your letter, which he owns was more than he deserved, and which he promises to answer by the next post.

All here are well, and I left my own treasures at Cobham well also.

You have heard of course of the rejection of the Bill* by the Lords. I am quite astonished to find London so quiet. Adieu !

Ever affectionately yours,

J. STOKES.

The failing health of Elizabeth, Countess of Darnley, was the chief care of her children during this sad year. She rallied to some extent from the illness which preceded her husband's death, but though able to go out,

---

*The second Reform Bill.

she never recovered any measure of health. Her devoted daughter, Elizabeth, was always with her and the beloved granddaughter Mary Brownlow, now eight years old, with her governess Mrs. Hutton.* Emma, Lady Darnley and her children were with her at Brighton and Eastbourne in July and August, and in September she settled at Leamington where Lady Powerscourt and Catherine Wingfield joined the party. Mr. Stokes, Vicar of Cobham, visited her there, and writes a report to John Bligh at the Hague.

REV. JOHN STOKES AT 46 BERKELEY SQUARE TO HON. J. D. BLIGH AT THE HAGUE.

October 11th, 1831.

I cannot let this day pass without scribbling a few lines to my dear and most loved friend. It is

---

*Mrs. Hutton was in after years well-known in the family as governess to Lilla Bligh, John Bligh's only child, who married Walter, 4th Earl of Chichester. Mrs. Hutton writes in 1868 to Lady Elizabeth Brownlow after a visit to Stanmer :

" Can you call to mind the route taken by your Ladyship's Mother to the seaside in the autumn of 1831. One of its various stages was from Tunbridge Wells to Brighton. She had been suffering more than usual and as the day was closing in, the question arose how far there was still to go. She pointed to the right hand side of the road saying "We shall soon be at Brighton, there is the gate of Stanmer, then spoke of Lord Chichester, etc." How little could I then suppose it would be my lot to enter that gate an invited guest taken there in his carriage by a Granddaughter then unborn, so many many years after her honoured head had been laid low."

thirty years to-day since I first wished you many happy returns of it. Our friendship was then in its infancy, and was merely a liking of four and twenty hours standing on my part, for a little saucy good humoured boy in petticoats; what it was on your part, I know not, but I remember at the time you took very kindly to the cross-looking tutor just imported from Oxford. What yours has ripened into, I do not venture to say. If I may judge from its fruits I should say into a friendship as warm as my own; of which I will venture to affirm that a more ardent and a more sincere one never existed. God bless you my dear fellow, may you live to see many many returns of this day, and may every new year of your life bring with it a new store of blessings both temporal and spiritual. I left the dear party at Leamington on Friday the 23rd ult, and fully intended writing to you as soon as I got home. Why I did not, I hardly know, except that I found myself dreadfully in arrears in everything when I got home, and my time was very much occupied. I am again a run-away for a few days, having come to town yesterday to work a little for Clifton. I left Lady Darnley wonderfully improved from the severe attack of which you heard the particulars at the time. And Dr. Jephson assured me that if her Ladyship will but strictly obey his rules, he is quite confident he shall work a permanent cure. At the same time, he says there is great danger of effusion, and consequently of a sudden death, if she deviates from the regimen he proposes. As Lady Powers-court and Miss Wingfield were both there, I left my charge with less reluctance. Had that not been the case, much as I wish to return home, I could not have felt easy to leave your poor dear sister. Nobody knows what she has to go through, poor dear, at times. It is almost too much for her.

On the 9th of November Lord and Lady Darnley with their children arrived at Leamington with Caroline Parnell, who had lately become engaged to Dr. Longley, Head Master of Harrow and later, Bishop of Ripon, Archbishop of York and Archbishop of Canterbury. They were married at Leamington on December 13th, 1831.

The following letters show the gradual progress of the Dowager Lady Darnley's illness; she died on December 22nd, and was buried at Cobham by the side of her husband.

EDWARD 5TH EARL OF DARNLEY AT 16, UNION PARADE, LEAMINGTON TO HON. J. D. BLIGH AT THE HAGUE.

November 10th, 1831.

My dearest Johnny,

I write from my mother's house, knowing that you will be glad to hear from me as soon as possible what I think of her. I am really astonished that she should appear so little altered after the severe attacks with which she has been visited, but I cannot say that there is much change in her countenance since you and I saw her at Eastbourne. She is, however, in bed, and has a sore on her foot which I have not yet seen: it is, I believe, on account of this last that they keep her as quiet as possible, and object to her getting up. I have not yet had an opportunity of talking privately with Dr. Jephson, although I have seen him, and had a flying parley with him two or three times : he is gone to Leicester this afternoon so that I cannot report this afternoon what he says of the case. I will, however, make him explain very particularly his ideas on the subject and write you word if he tells me anything remarkable.

The rest of the ladies whom we found here in great health and looks, have been walking about to-day with Emma, and Mrs. L. elect,* and M. E. B. has been doing the honours to her cousins, who arrived here well with us yesterday evening about half past six from Dunstable where we slept the night before.

Beppy has shewn me your last letter which contains reflections upon the irreparable loss we have sustained, very much in consonance with my own feelings on the subject. I, too, cannot imagine how it is that I look upon this privation with so much apathy and indifference as it would seem ; how for instance I can bear to visit each well known spot, and look on any of the shrubs and trees he knew and loved so well, without shedding tears for the loss of a Father whom I prized above all men, and loved most tenderly, and with the utmost reason, for never had any sons a more truly kind and indulgent parent, whose only happiness seemed to be to consult the best interests of his family, that is of his family properly so-called. Dear, dear man, I cannot think of him (and think of him I do at

*Caroline Parnell, engaged to Dr. Longley.

every turn) without affectionate regret *tam cari capitis*, and yet I cannot but at the same time feel how little the awful change affects me. But enough of this. Our sentiments on this painfully interesting subject sufficiently correspond to ensure a mutual understanding of each other's feelings. Dr. Jephson is decidedly of opinion that there is no organic disease in my Mother, and that everything depends upon the control of her mind, which alas ! it is difficult to accomplish. I expect to go on to Ireland in a few days. Our friend Naper is in this neighbourhood at his father-in-law's, as I heard this afternoon from *Pig Barnard mini* whom I met returning from hunting. We have not got a house, and I believe Emma and Co. will remain at the hotel where we have comfortable lodgings. Aunt P. and Cata are here. Emily etc. at Stoneleigh.

My mother desires her love and to say she wishes you were here. All the rest send their loves. The wedding is to be in about a month.

· Your affectionate brother,

C.

Let me know if you would like any game to be sent over to you, or else write to Wells to send you some. I hope you will not fail to kill some of them before the season is out, and so hopes he. I think we shall be obliged to return to Cobham, and London for Parliament. I now can hardly reckon on settling at Clifton Lodge before the spring. Pray let us know what probability there is of your coming over. I expect to be in Ireland about three weeks.

December 1st, 1831.

My dearest Johnny,

I was much disturbed when I recollected in the middle of Monday night, that I had neglected to write to you in the day, but I hope you considered no news good news, especially as I had been sending you such favourable bulletins of late.

I have received your last with more than usual pleasure as I began to grow very fidgety at not hearing. Your letters of the 4th did not reach me till the 25th, or had I heard since the 1st or 2nd, Dr. Jephson promised, and I believe really intended writing to you last post and this, but he is so much engaged, I do not wonder that he forgot his promises as he often does.

Mamma had a slight attack of erysipelas in her face which although disagreeable to herself, I believe was not considered an unfavourable symptom as proving a natural tendency or habit of body. They talk of a seton in her poor side (just under the heart) when her foot heals, to which she has consented, but which I fear will be very trying.

She caught a little cold the day before yesterday, sitting up on the sofa and had a very slight attack of lumbago, but it appears to-day much relieved by sudorifics and opiates. The latter have rather affected her head during this day, but as she is now much more inclined to sleep I think all this will soon pass off. She speaks occasionally with much anxiety about seeing you, but much less so than I have known her do, not so I mean as to make your absence more particularly distressing.

The last thing she did on that Sunday night we were so much and so reasonably alarmed about her, was to desire Jones to pack up two paper weights she had bought for you (diamond engravings upon black marble) and direct them to you, which of course would have been as great a melancholy gratification to you, had she been as we so fully expected *called away* that night. I have them in my possession packed up as she desired, but being bulky and weighty I have not attempted sending them to you. Clifton is not returned. I believe E. expects him about the 6th. I believe she would think it highly improper to have the Dr. [Longley] in the Hotel with them unless C. is come. He comes the 7th if E. does not put him off, and I fancy the wedding is likely to take place about the 13th. Caroline Parnell has been much pleased this morning by receiving your congratulations. I wrote a few lines to the Dr. in his letter and have had a letter from Dr. L. I think him a very fortunate man, besides her amiableness, he might have sought long in her line of life for so useful or befitting a wife. His family are much delighted as you may suppose.

I have seen with great grief the account in the papers of the dear Bishop of Calcutta's death! I had no expectation of seeing him again, but I hoped his career of usefulness in his diocese might have been prolonged. The Lord of all knows best. As to our loss and that of his friends, I have learnt to look upon this passing scene as so very transitory that a few years more or less makes but very little difference.

Oh, dearest Johnny, what happiness when we shall all meet around the throne and centre of all happiness, the fountain head and source of what we in the meantime for want of better call happiness. I am certain after the intercourse which God condescends to hold with those who worship Him in spirit and in truth, none approaches nearer to heavenly joy than family and friendly intercourse on Christian principles. What a delight to think that this felicity will be perfected to all eternity ! and that to a degree beyond all we can form any idea of here !

This place is full of people but is still very quiet to us as we know no one. I was not aware till now that it is a centre of attraction to fox-hunters, and red coats are flying about two or three days in the week. The country appears in a tolerably tranquil state, and I trust the King's Proclamation will succeed in crushing the odious political unions. There was one here even. Your intelligence respecting your Russian Embassy grieved me. I cannot willingly give my consent, and I do not think if our dear mother lives she could at all.

Your letters are all cut through and through, now Adieu, dearest Johnny. I am late for post.

Yours truly affectionately,

E. B.

8th December, 1831.

My dearest Johnny,

I have taken time by the forelock to-day being very anxious to write you a comfortable letter, and expecting the Bride and Bridegroom elect with Clif and Em to luncheon at my and Molly's dinner at 2 o'clock.

What would I give to transport my dearest John into our little Society, were it but for an hour? But this is talking nonsense and it is *well* that we cannot gratify every wish even those most like to those desires which will be gratified to their fullest extent hereafter.

These are indeed " awful times " and I trust we shall not only individually, but as a Nation be enabled to lay them to heart.

I have for these two or three years looked with intense interest at the world and the kingdoms thereof, feeling sure that the period was near at hand when that Kingdom should be set up which is to endure for ever. I am afraid of talking much upon the subject for fear of being thought enthusiastic and visionary, and indeed my poor little mind has been so engaged by other things, that I am sorry to say, those things in the Word of God which were essential to my salvation have been but much too little studied, but I did feel an intense and overwhelming interest in the contemplation of prophecy—both fulfilled and unfulfilled and I found it most practical, not only as being elevating to the mind and tending very much to raise it above the joys and sorrows of this present state, but also as giving an increased interest to the Bible, indeed throwing a new light upon the whole book, and on passages which before had appeared most obscure. Oh ! how I wish my memory and other talents had been better cultivated and I could name to you where you might find most striking passages, and also cease to forget as I do the very titles of the books I read. I remember that " Newton on the fulfilled prophecies," I read with intense interest ; that is a work which no one can account visionary and it prepares the mind wonderfully for the very interesting occupation of watching the operations of the Ruler of the Universe in our own day. It is a very common error to imagine that there is no fulfilment of prophecy in action at present—but can anyone on reflection doubt that there is and will be to the end of time.

I believe there is scarcely a prophecy in Scripture which has not a double interpretation, for instance those referring to our Redeemer's First Advent, having an equal reference to His Second, which glorious and blessed event, and which is looked upon by many as visionary is, I believe, the end and object at which the revelation of God points.

His humiliation was a blessed event to us, but will not His return without humiliation but in unspeakable majesty and glory be infinitely more so ! When the kingdoms of this world shall become the kingdoms of the Lord and of His Christ, and when Satan, the former Prince of it, shall be bound and " the knowledge of God " (without any temptation to forsake Him ; consequently the unbounded happiness of creation) "shall cover the earth as the waters cover the sea."

I have been led away though, and launched into depths which I fear will induce you to think me enthusiastic, but I should indeed rejoice if I could turn your mind dearest John, (which I see with great pleasure is contemplating with religious feeling the events that are passing in the world) to consider them as all subservient to one *great* end, which I believe to be hastening its approach. I found this impression give an increased interest to the study of the book of life in my own case, and therefore I am always anxious to impart it to others. If you feel inclined to begin the study I would give a good deal to send you some books which might throw some light upon it, but you need no man to guide you dearest John, when the Spirit of God is with you, which by prayer through Christ He ever is, for " He will guide you into all truth."

You may guess from the tenor of my letter that I have good news to give you. Dr. Jephson positively intends writing to you, but he is particularly busy to-day, in short, 1 doubt his doing so. Her changes are so rapid that I hardly dare tell you how very well I think our dear parent to-day is, especially when I look back on but the day before yesterday, when I really believed her sinking. Her mind is much more tranquil which gives me my best hopes for her, as it will you I daresay.

I have sometimes been tempted to think both the tranquillizing of that, and consequently her restoration to health *impossible*, but is not this doubting the omnipotence of the Almighty.

Clif arrived on Monday night, went to Town Tuesday morning, and returned here yesterday evening, having distanced the Lover, who was anxiously expected till a late hour, and I believe was not welcomed last night, not having arrived till after midnight.

I grieve at what you tell me of the steam boats. I fully believed Sir C. Bagot in London, many papers have affirmed it confidently.

Excuse this hasty letter, written against time, and believe

Your truly attached,

E. B.

LADY ELIZABETH BLIGH AT LEAMINGTON TO HON. J. D. BLIGH AT THE HAGUE.

December 9th, 1831.

My dearest Johnny,

I am sorry to say I cannot send you a very favourable report, indeed our dear Mother's existence is, I cannot hide from myself or you, hanging by a mere thread, and when I reflect that according to human foresight she could never be a source of comfort to her poor self or friends, I ought to be satisfied with this decree but, as you most justly observe there is something in the idea of being bereft of a parent, and that an only one, which rends the heart, spite of what reason may suggest. She had another bad attack of palpitation and syncope, which required so much stimulus to overcome it, that she has not yet recovered the effects of it, and at times I feel very despairing about her ever doing so, especially as her left side has a slight paralytic affection, and her mind has not at all recovered itself although the attack was some nights ago. I know you wish me to give you an unvarnished statement, indeed when there is so little prospect of a happy termination it is much kinder to do so, even if, as I fear it will, keep you in increased anxiety.

Poor dear Clif too is laid up with severe attacks of gout in feet and hands, but I trust it will lead to his and Emma's more serious attention to his general health. The Doctors, Mr. Pritchard and Jephson are horrified with the extent of his ailments, but alas he is too careless about himself to attend to their advice when he is temporarily better. They think it may be of the most fatal kind if not properly attended to, and that he ought to live by weight and measure.

He has no faith you know in any medical practitioner and has a prepossession against Dr. J. especially, but I trust he may be induced to give more attention to his case than heretofore.

I am not surprised that you did not give in to my prophetic letter, and I believe it was ill advised to write such, but the subject happened to be present to my mind very much at the moment.

Well dearest Johnny it signifies little what our views on those minor points are, if we keep those essential to salvation (such as the utter alienation from God by nature, our being brought near by the blood of Christ and the impossibility of being so by any other means in any degree, and being justified, sanctified by His spirit, and redeemed from the power of sin, presented by Him to a God of justice and perfect holiness, clothed in His righteousness, pure and spotless, and only thus possibly accepted in His sight) if we keep these things steadily in view, all the rest may be taken or left alone as suits our various dispositions and fancies.

God be ever with you, dearest Johnny,

Yours affectionately,

ELIZABETH BLIGH.

Mamma sent her love to you the other day. She often speaks of you as you may suppose, though she takes but little notice of any that are not presented to her view.

Mary continues perfectly well and the cousins much benefited by being here I think.

EDWARD EARL OF DARNLEY TO THE HON. JOHN DUNCAN BLIGH.

Leamington,
Dec. 22nd, 1831.

My dearest Johnny,

I have been almost in bed for a week, and written only one letter during that time, having had the Gout (but slightly) in both hands and feet. They are however getting better together very quickly hitherto, and I am happy to make the first use of my recovering fingers in an attempt to write to you and your long and kind letter of this morning makes it very *à propos*. Many thanks for it, I wish it held out a better prospect of your coming over. My immediate object in writing is to repeat what I understand to be a very unfavourable change in our dearest Mother whom I now cannot but consider in a dying state, from the accounts I hear, altho' I have not seen her for a week, having left my room to-day for the first time, I hope to do so to-morrow. She had two palpitations last week from which altho' not apparently severe she has not recovered as heretofore, and from the account of the Doctors there is effusion on the Brain, and she is in fact sinking fast. Dr. Jephson said this morning that it might be momentary or last for weeks or days or hours only. She hardly knows anyone as I am told, and her eyesight is very dim ; and they say that there are appearances of paralysis on one side—she asks for no one that she has not seen immediately before, nor do I think that your presence could be of any comfort to her, but I think it right to write in this desponding strain, as in case you wish, as wish you must to see her again, you have not, (as I now think for the first time), any time to lose. It is my purpose nevertheless to go to Cobham for the 29th (as a matter of duty) if I am well enough, to sit in our dearest Father's place, at the head of his Tenantry that were so lately. It is quite necessary that I should be there if possible, as I want the various accounts to be settled. They have been much in arrears and I have not been yet able with frequent urging to get the balance between us from them.

You will be happy to hear, as a set off to this melancholy account on the other side that our dearest Mother's mind is in a wonderfully improved state by all accounts : tranquil, composed, no worldly wanderings, and I sincerely trust in God's mercy, renewed by Grace unto Life everlasting. I was exceedingly anxious to have seen her to-day that I might report thereupon, but I was ordered not to attempt it, and it would have been I believe imprudent. I have written a line to Lord Palmerston to ask him to send you if possible leave of absence, should you think it right on the receipt of this letter to come over.

Ever dearest Brother,

Yours most affectionately,

C.

Edward 5th Earl of Darnley at Leamington to Hon. J D. Bligh at the Hague.

December 22nd, 1831.

My dearest Johnny,

I wrote to you this evening and also to Lord P. to send you leave of absence as I thought our dearest mother worse, since that time it has pleased the Almighty disposer of all events to close her sufferings in this world of woe, and between 8 and 9 she was taken away unseen by me. Of course the event was sudden at last though not unexpected.

Dearest Elizabeth has cried a good deal since and is now tranquil and in bed. I send this by express in order that you may not hear accidentally of our additional bereavement. When I wrote this evening I rather expected that you might have been to see her; but think of me for a week within 200 yards, and not seeing her. She died without a struggle, and we must all rejoice in the release which was the more to be desired as her sufferings were prolonged and increased.

We shall all, I suppose, move to Cobham shortly, where I hope it will not be long before we have the comfort at least of seeing you that we may lay the cold remains beside those parted now for 9 months after 40 years passed together. We have every comfort from the marked alteration in all our dearest mother's religious deportment. It appeared latterly to be truly pious and to show a lively faith.

I have no time to spare, forgive inaccuracies my dearest Johnny.

From your affectionate brother,

C.

THE GILT HALL AT COBHAM HALL.

CHAPTER VII.

Mors Janua Vitæ.

THE years from 1832 to 1835 passed
quietly, the time being divided between
Cobham, Berkeley Square and Clifton
Lodge. Edward, Lord Darnley often attended
the House of Lords and occasionally spoke on
subjects of local interest connected with the
county of Kent or with Ireland. He voted
for the Reform Bill in 1832, and was present
when the Royal Assent was given; his portrait
appears in a contemporary print of the scene
in the House of Lords.

Some interesting meditations written by
him during this period seem almost as if he
had some presage of his early death.

MEMORANDUM BY EDWARD, EARL OF DARNLEY, WRITTEN
ON HIS OWN BIRTHDAY.

Cobham Hall,
Feb. 25th, 1832.

Another, the most eventful, year of my life has
passed ; and in its course has swept away both my
beloved parents. A small vault in the Churchyard

now contains their bodies, for whom this day last year this house was not too large. This house with all about it is now mine : how fearfully is my responsibility increased, and have my will and power to fulfil it increased with equal pace ? Alas ! I fear not—useless has been my life during the last, as through all other years of my existence. Year after year slips away without shewing any fruits of a holy and religious life. There must be something peculiarly unsuited in my nature for the reception of Divine grace ; for with the many and awful warnings I have of late experienced, with the immense advantages I enjoy in the possession of my inestimable wife, whose example might well move me, I remain the same heartless cold and reluctant professor of a Faith of which my actions afford no fruits to prove it to be genuine.

What makes my conduct worse in my own eyes is, that I know, or seem to know what is right, yet practise it not ; because my heart minds not of the things that are of God.

Altho' by no means addicted to the fashionable vices of the world, still worldly objects appear to engross my thoughts, and I much fear that the accession of the good things of this life during the year past, has caused a still greater devotion than before to the perishable concerns that are before me. Daily experience teaches me that I am unmindful of the goodness of God, incapable of appreciating the blessings I enjoy. Within the short passage of this very day I can lay to my charge, circumstances in proof of this. May I so far obtain the favour of Divine Grace as to enable me to pray fervently for amendment of life in all particulars in which I err; and many, very many, they are, beside those secret faults of which I am not aware. This day last year I accompanied my beloved Father to a Reform Meeting at Sitting-bourne; on the 1st of March I heard with him the plan proposed which has since created such a sensation*. The next day I saw him for the last time, and before the fatal year 1831 has closed, I saw my dearest Mother's coffin laid beside his. May we not disregard this warning. Public events of no small interest have followed in quick succession, and we are still in uncertainty how the storm that has been raised may be appeased. My father was too much absorbed in Politics—too little am I— Ambition was his bane—Indolence is mine. I cannot but feel that with application I might have made my talents, such as they are, useful. Ignorance the fruit of idleness, shuts the door for ever against me—A wide field of action is however before me. May I hope to devote myself to the service of God in my attempt to benefit my Country. May He mercifully guard me from the temptations that surround me, and guide me in the way of truth. May He enable me to apply the good things I enjoy to His glory, and to the support of my fellow-creatures in distress. I feel, deeply feel, how much will be expected of me, how great my responsibility. My possessions are ample, but happily riches are not my lot. I must live economically to enable me

*The Reform Bill, introduced for the first time in the House of Commons by Lord John Russell. Lord Darnley and Lord Clifton were both supporters of the Whig Government and in favour of the measure.

to live within my income, which I am determined with God's blessing, to do, and I hope very soon to be out of debt and to pay ready money for everything, and at the same time to establish a fund for extinguishing gradually the encumbrances on my estate I only fear being over much occupied by the consideration of these matters which are as snares in my way. At all events I have no time to lose, 37 years have escaped me, and but a short period will bring me to the age at which my parents have died. We are not a long lived race, and who knows whether a term such as theirs may be allotted to me.   Already have I felt infirmity unusual at my age, which may rapidly increase and perhaps carry me off before my time. Oh may I be ready when the Lord knocks, and may He in mercy before that hour grant me the truly inestimable privilege of a penitent heart. I humbly pray for the blessing of God on my beloved wife and children, my brother and sister, and all my relations and friends, for Jesus Christ's sake.

Half past 11 p.m.

Cobham Hall.
Monday Morning, half past 2 a.m.
July 30th, 1832.

My Mother's Birthday ! !

Oh ! my God ! what are my sensations, while in traversing this house, in momentary expectation of my beloved wife's delivery, on this day too, I find the cloak I used to sit in, and the chair I used to lie in, when in attendance upon my dearest Mother in her very severe illness in the beginning of 1831 ; before the end of which fatal year she was no more. Without looking for it too I find her portrait, beside that of my Emma, and Elizabeth (now far from us). In this place my Father's image is ever before me—that best of Fathers, who while we watched my Mother's sick bed, was taken off before her. How inscrutable are Thy ways oh! God—with Thee are the issues of life and death. Oh! may my precious wife be mercifully preserved and comforted in this her trial; and should it please Thy Divine Providence to bless us with another dear child, enable us we beseech Thee to bring it up in the nurture and admonition of the Lord, as a faithful soldier and servant of Jesus Christ ; in Whose Name and through Whose merits we venture to address Thee. Oh ! may the manifold sins of our lives be pardoned for His sake. . . . .

Another dear little daughter is born to me at a quarter before three.

[Lady Emma Bess Bligh, married in 1854, Arthur Perceval Purey-Cust, Dean of York. She was named Bess after her grandmother Elizabeth, Countess of Darnley, on whose birthday she was born.]

January 1st, 1833.

I never remember to have been in lower spirits than during this day. I can hardly account for it by the alarming illness of my dear eldest child ; or by the recollection of the last New Year's paper written by my beloved Father two years since, in which, under circumstances of mental and bodily affliction he predicted events too truly fulfilled in the melancholy 1831 : nor can the expectation of seeing but little for the future of my only sister,* nor the absence, at a fearful distance of my only brother** afford in themselves a sufficient reason for this depression of spirits. To what must I then attribute it ? Surely to the want of that healing influence of the Grace of God to instruct me in all my thoughts and actions, and to lend a tone to my life. I am entèring upon another year without amendment, as I fear. In what particular does 1833 find me better than did 1832 ? Alas ! I fear in none, but rather must I feel accountable for having spent another precious year unprofitably. I hope that I am sensible of my utter inability unassisted by Divine Grace, to lead a new life ; but that I shall by it be enabled to do so—God grant it may so be. With every worldly advantage I ought doubtless to be grateful, and to shew my gratitude by the faithful discharge of my duty towards God and my neighbours. Alas ! I do neither one, nor the other. Too indolent to take proper pains about my fellow-creatures wants, I content myself with cold and formal almsgiving, and that not with sufficient liberality. I do flatter myself (vainly perhaps) that I feel an earnest desire to correct my evil habits. May the Great Disposer of all events grant me strength of mind to enable me to carry my wishes into effect.

*Lady Elizabeth Bligh who married in July, 1833, her first cousin, the Rev. John Brownlow ; a marriage which, though not promising from a worldly point of view, turned out most happily.

**Hon. John Bligh, Secretary of the British Embassy at St. Petersburgh.

In 1832 he was appointed Lord Lieutenant of Meath and in the following year was offered the Ribbon of St. Patrick. This honour he declined, not relishing the idea of receiving a reward for his votes, nor desiring to be too much beholden to the Whig Government.

MINUTE AND COPY OF LETTER TO EARL GREY.

Feb. 4th, 1833.

On going into the room, to dine with Lord Grey, he took me aside and in the handsomest manner offered me the Ribbon of St. Patrick. I told him he had taken me by surprise, but that my present impression was to decline the honour and to take the will for the deed ; adding that I thought I could appreciate the kindness of His Majesty and himself, and the motives which had influenced them. He proposed to me to allow him to recommend me for the King's approbation, and I requested a few hours to consider the matter, and wrote this letter on the morning of the 5th.

D.

PRIVATE.   Berkeley Square,

Feb. 5th, 1833.

Dear Lord Grey,

Although I was somewhat staggered by the sudden offer of the Ribbon vacant by the death of Lord Conyngham which you so handsomely made me last night ; I feel upon consideration that I was right in the wish which I immediately expressed to decline the honour if I could do so without disrespect to the courtesy from which the proposition had emanated on your part.

I esteem the offer as a tribute of respect to the memory of my Father, and were his services to Ireland my own, should have no hesitation in accepting this distinction. As it is, I do not feel conscious of having done anything to merit it, and therefore should regard it merely as an empty badge ; except inasmuch as it would indicate my Sovereign's favor, and your kindness, which I can appreciate in the offer as much as in the acceptance.

I remain, etc.

On his next birthday Lord Darnley continues his self-examination.

Feb. 25th, 1834.

No one can enter his fortieth year without reflecting (if he thinks at all) that a most material part of his life is past : it is almost beyond the limits of human existence that his term should be doubled. With us, short lived as almost all of my family are it is next to impossible that I should see thirty-nine more years ; it is more than probable that in addition half as many years should not be told ; and the changed state of health which I have experienced during this winter, makes me remember that it is not unlikely that I may not have even one year more to live. Is it possible then that I should still go on in that thoughtless indifference to eternity, and that clinging to things of this world and of time, which have marked my progress through life hitherto ? When sickness is upon me;

when I feel the chastisements of a merciful God, my heart is softened, and I reflect on these matters, in a better spirit : but alas ! no sooner does health, or even an approximation to it return, than vanity again occupies its old station, good intentions are scattered abroad, and the old man gets the better of the tendency (which I hope does exist) to a renewal of Spirit within me. Fervently then may my humble prayers be addressed to the giver of all good, on this anniversary of my nativity and all succeeding days that may be allotted to me, that I may be delivered from this great temptation—that I may be not, (should it please God to restore my health) led astray by the vanities of this life, particularly of my station which presents many temptations. That I may not abuse the innumerable blessings I under the blessing of Providence, enjoy, but use them all to the Glory of God. That whether I live, or whether I die, I may live or die in the name and for the sake of my Saviour Christ, and through Him (as I alone can) become at the last an inheritor of His blessed Kingdom—the thoughts of such an inheritance pass all understanding, and cannot be well considered together with worldly things ; and yet I cannot but recollect the very many blessings connected with this world's enjoyment which I have. My dearest and best of wives and my four sweet children, (with the expectation of another) all in the enjoyment of health, ease, comfort, affluence, the absence of those pressing ills which are upon so many of my fellow creatures (Oh ! may I seek to relieve their wants both spiritual and temporal)—these and numberless other blessings I gratefully acknowledge and enjoy. Besides I may say for 39 years, health, or only such exceptions as may mercifully serve to make me appreciate it, and what is more important still, to make me think of eternity and things above. Oh ! may I do so daily more and more. May the good work which, I hope, is begun in me go on through God's mercy in Jesus Christ to a perfect work. May my insufficiency vanish before the all-sufficiency of my Redeemer's sacrifice ; of the benefits of which I hope (humbly I trust) to become a partaker. That I may apply myself in a proper spirit to this great end is my fervent hope. That the one thing needful may be my object of desire and longing, that all worldly considerations may give way before it, and that it may be my most unfeigned wish so to live or so to die that I may become a partaker of the atonement wrought for fallen man by Jesus Christ.

D.

In 1834, Lord Darnley writes to his mother-in-law, Lady Caroline Parnell, in Paris, announcing the birth of his third son, Henry, on June 10th.

We are approaching now the end of the story of this happy married life. On Wednesday, February 4th, 1835, Lord Darnley was walking in the woods at Cobham with his cousin Charles Bligh and his brother-in-law Henry Parnell, when near the Mausoleum they came on a woodman cutting down a tree.

Lord Darnley took the axe in his hand to shew his companions the way to cut off branches ; unfortunately the axe slipped and nearly severed his little toe.

No danger was at first apprehended from this accident and Lord Darnley wrote cheerful letters to his aunt Lady Powerscourt and to his friend Dr. Longley making light of the affair. On Monday evening symptoms of tetanus appeared. Doctors were summoned from London and Lord Darnley sent an express to Harrow for Dr. Longley requesting him to go to Coutts' Bank to fetch his will, believing that he had not provided for his son Henry, born in 1834. Full accounts describing his last hours follow, written by the Rev. John Stokes, Dr. Longley, G. W. Rich, Esq., Henry Parnell, and Sophy Bligh, also by Lady Darnley herself. To the grief of all those who knew him, Edward, Lord Darnley died at 3 p.m. on Wednesday, February 11th, 1835.

EDWARD EARL OF DARNLEY AT COBHAM TO VISCOUNTESS POWERSCOURT AT ABBEYLEIX.

Feb. 5th, 1835.

Dearest Aunt P.

I have forwarded your letter to the Infant School, and having always forgotten it before, enclose an order for my £20.

We are all well here, *barrin* that I almost cut off a little toe with an axe yesterday : providentially it is a matter of no consequence, but might have been a serious accident. I was walking out with the other boys, and was shewing them how to cut down a tree.

The Queen's County Election has pleased me much, except that I cannot understand Sir Henry's conduct. I am summoned to dinner, and the letters now go before it.

Love to all from your affectionate

C.

REV. JOHN STOKES AT COBHAM TO HON. J. D. BLIGH AT ST. PETERSBURGH.

Feb. 10th, 1835.

My very dear Friend,

I know not whether you have been told of an accident your dear Brother met with last Wednesday. In his walks he took an axe from a woodman he saw at work intending to give a few strokes for exercise ; and unfortunately the axe glanced from the tree, and cut his right foot so as to sever the little toe, except a bit of the skin, and to cut off a slice of the next. All however seemed to be going on well, and he made light of it till yesterday evening when symptoms of Tetanus (or locked jaw) began to appear. To-day they have increased to an alarming height and he is consider'd in considerable danger. Brodie, Bolton, and Beaumont are in attendance, and Dr. Farre is sent for. As this cannot go till Thursday I shall continue it to-morrow, and conclude it on Thursday. So adieu ! for the present. I can write on no other subject.

Wednesday, Feby. 11th. Dr. Farre came in the night. Great danger is still apprehended. He has had this morning a frightful paroxysm. To any but a medical eye all appeared over with him. But he has rallied, and is now sleeping quietly ; ($\frac{1}{2}$ past one) I will write again as changes occur. I shall merely say now that you would be delighted to witness the beautiful state of mind shewn by the dear, dear, Patient. Such fine faith, and such genuine humility ! Dr. Longley is here and has kindly undertaken to carry on the account for me, as I am desired by Lady D. to answer all Letters of enquiry ; which you may suppose are very numerous. Let this be my excuse then if I do not fill my Paper. And I will only add my prayers that God may support you, should you be called to the trial of losing such a brother.

And before you open Longley's Letter put up such a prayer for yourself ; for from present symptoms I cannot but fear it may contain such trial for you. I must also just tell you that your dear Brother has shewn great anxiety that you should be inform'd of his state. Even in his paroxysm, when he could scarcely articulate, he tried to talk of Petersburgh and his dear brother.

God ever bless, and preserve you, my dear Friend, prays your faithful and affecte.

J. Stokes.

I will write again by the next Post.

February 18th, 1835.

Dear Lady Elizabeth,

Although you may possibly have heard every
particular which I can relate as to the last hours of
your very dear Brother, I am still willing to believe
that a few lines from one whose heart bleeds as well
as your own for the loss of an object of tender
affection will not be unacceptable to you. First
then let me express my deep gratitude to God for
the support which He graciously afforded the dear
sufferer in his hour of need. It was an unspeakable
comfort to me to learn from Henry Parnell
immediately on entering the house that his frame
of mind was most delightful, that he was fully
aware of the awful change which soon awaited him,
and was looking forward to it with calmness and
heavenly composure. O how completely does this
take away the sting of death.

But I will relate all I know in the order of
events. The accident, as you know, occurred on
the Wednesday, and on Saturday morning I received
a letter from him mentioning it, and treating it very
lightly. On Tuesday morning again I had a letter
from him (the last, dear fellow, I believe he ever
wrote) in most cheerful spirits, speaking of it still
as a mere trifle. You may judge then of my feelings when I received an express at nine o'clock that
same evening, containing a letter from Mr. Bean-
mont stating that alarming symptoms had come on,
and that he had expressed a wish to see me,
requesting at the same time that I would call at

Coutts' for his will, and bring it down with me. I was happily enabled to procure it, late as it was, and left Town for Cobham at twelve. By a little after three in the morning of Wednesday I arrived there, and found that Dr. Farre had just arrived, and that he, Brodie, and Bolton were just going to see their patient. It was thought better that he should not see me till after the consultation, and meanwhile I received from Henry Parnell those delightful assurances which will be a source of comfort and gratitude through life. In half an hour I went to our dear Brother's bedside, and found him entirely collected, and fully able to go through the business on which he wished to see me. When that was finished, we prayed together, and at the conclusion I repeated to him our blessed Lord's reply to the prayer of St. Paul, " My Grace is sufficient for thee, for my strength is made perfect in weakness"; his words were, " Yes, my dear fellow, not in my own strength, not in my own strength." Utterance was not easy to him, and he spoke but little. He then expressed a wish to receive the Sacrament, which Mr. Stokes administered to him and which his dear wife, Henry Parnell, C. Bligh, Miss Bligh and myself, besides several of the servants who were kneeling at the door received with him. After he had received the bread and wine, he expressed a wish that I would again pray with him, which I did, and it being then thought better that he should be left quiet after his exertion, I left the room. I then had an interview with the medical men, who had expressed a wish to see me before they separated

409

(as Brodie was returning to Town directly), and they told me that they could hold out but very little hope, that from their experience not above one in a hundred ever recovered. About seven o'clock I lay down for two hours, and at nine got up, hearing that he was worse. Convulsions had come on, which were alarming, and he felt himself so much worse that he wished to see his children ; he saw them all but the baby, and gave them his blessing. Dr. Farre observed that he never saw a more perfect example of resignation to the will of God than he displayed during this trying scene. A painful struggle continued till eleven, and many and fervent were the prayers successively offered up aloud by those who were around his bedside. Oh, if you could have seen his dear wife during these two hours of awful suspense ; such an example of the power of grace, and of the faithfulness of God to his suffering people ; her holy composure and self-possession, her unvarying confidence in the goodness of God during her dark trial were most sublime. Dr. Farre's presence was a great comfort, he has a truly religious mind, and was most kind and judicious in his application of Scripture Truth to the dear sufferer. Henry Parnell was at his head during this period, and his wife kneeling on the bed supporting him. At eleven we thought he must have sunk, but we were rejoiced to find that he presently subsided into a sweet slumber, and there were other symptoms which gave us a reason to hope the best. The Doctors said that if he continued in that state till five o'clock, they really should think the crisis was passed. He seemed so tranquil that all left the room but myself and the nurse. I remained at his head for about an hour-and-a-half, during which he slept with scarcely any interruption; now and then, in an interval, he spoke of himself as feeling better, and his countenance was more at ease. At about three, by a most remarkable coincidence, though all had still appeared to be going on as well as I have described, Dr. Farre, Mr. Bolton, Lady Darnley, Henry and myself were all in the room at once; I say a remarkable coincidence, because the Doctors had only come up for two or three minutes every half-hour, and his dear wife, having never quitted his bedside for twenty-four hours, had been in the dressing-room for a little while at her toilet, but at three we were all in the room, and she was in the act of blessing God for the apparent answer to our prayers which He had given, and I was just saying to her how we should rejoice in His Name hereafter, and praise His mercy, if our dear sufferer should still recover, when our attention was called to the bed by hearing that there was an appearance of another convulsion beginning; a difficulty of breathing in the dear patient induced Dr. Farre to order that he should be raised up in his bed, but the hand of death was upon him, and in one more instant his spirit had fled to the bosom of his Maker; the spasm had seized the organs of respiration, and he expired instantaneously, and without the smallest struggle.

And now, my dear Friend, what is our consolation under this deep affliction? Is it not that our dear Brother died in the Lord, that his warfare is accomplished, and that he has entered into his eternal rest? He evidenced in his last hours a simple and undivided Faith in the merits of his Redeemer, trusting in no righteousness of his own, but in the precious blood which had been shed for his sins. His patience under very great suffering was most beautiful, and the scene that his dying-bed presented was the most solemn, and at the same time the most elevating I ever witnessed. Never was the nothingness of this world more strongly manifested, or the incalculable value of the Gospel and its precious privileges. Blessed be God, we need not mourn as those that are without hope, but the memory of so dear, so affectionate a friend will ever be cherished in my inmost heart. He requested me to communicate with his brother on this sad occasion, which I did immediately, and I earnestly hope that he will be able to return to England speedily, as dear Clifton has left Johnny and myself as the two guardians to his bereaved children. May God give us both grace to discharge that important office to His glory, and to the benefit of those who are committed to our charge.

May God bless you, dear Lady Elizabeth, and bring His comforts home to you at this trying period.

Believe me your faithful and affectionate friend

CHARLES T. LONGLEY.

Febry. 18th, 1835.

P.S. I should very much like to write to Lady Powerscourt, if I knew where she was. If she is near you, perhaps you could communicate the contents to her of this letter, if there is anything she is not likely to have heard before.

London Dock,
17th Feb., 1835.

How to begin this letter to you, my ever dear Friend, I know not. You will have received from Mr. Stokes the melancholy detail of the awful event of the 11th which will be indelibly impressed on my memory to the latest moment of my existence. That I should in my letter of the 3rd inst. have been able to give you such a delightful acct. of your dear departed Brother, and witness his dissolution within ten days of that period, still would appear to me to be impossible ! but such are the inscrutable decrees of an All-Wise Providence and we ought to bow to them with implicit obedience however diffi-cult the task. The Doctor will have told you (what will afford you some consolation in the agonizing distress you must have felt in reading his letter) how thoroughly he was prepared for the worst, and impressed with the fullest conviction he should not recover. He told Mr. Bolton as soon as he saw him, that he would not be able to save him this time, altho' he was convinced that all that human means could devise would be done for him.

When I would describe to you Lady Darnley's conduct throughout this scene of distress I am utterly at a loss for words to do so. I never witnessed such truly Christian-like pious resignation mixed with sufficient firmness of purpose to enable her to take a prominent part in rendering every possible assistance throughout, and when at the moment of his departure from this World for a better, she looked up while hanging over him and whispered to Dr. Farre " May I kiss him ? " and on his assenting, did so repeatedly, I could compare her to nothing less than a perfect Angel, and was obliged to quit the scene immediately, being unable to suppress my feelings any longer. You will also have been told how perfectly easy the Soul separated from the body. I will repeat what you may not have heard, as being of comparatively less import- ance than other details, viz : the manner in which the accident occurred, as I had it from Charles Bligh, who was with him. They were walking near John Wells's house by the Mausoleum, where some Woodcutters were at work, and while looking at them, your lamented Brother saw a Root that had grown along the surface and said " Now I'll shew you how to cut a root in halves " and took the Woodcutter's Axe and struck hard upon the Root, when the Axe glided off and just caught the little toe of his foot and a part of the next, thro' his Boot. He started and said, " I have lamed myself I fear ! but it might have been worse and I ought to con- sider myself fortunate." He then leant on the arms of C. Bligh and the Woodcutter and went into John Wells's house and they fetched the Pony chaise in which he rode home and Mr. Beaumont was with him in less than an hour and a half, who wished to take off the little toe, which hung only by a piece of skin, but he desired it might be bound up altogether which was done accordingly, and every symptom as *regarded the foot* continued favourable *to the end*, so much so that Sir B. Brodie told Mr. Bolton after examining it he would not disturb it on any account. On the following Monday he came downstairs on his crutches and dined off roast Beef and drunk a glass or two of Wine, but in the evening felt symptoms which made him uneasy, and wrote to Dr. Longley and also to Mr. Bolton, describing his case in a jocular manner as having occurred to a young friend of his, and concluded by saying " the real sufferer is yours to command." You know I presume that Mr. Beaumont sent off for Mr. Bolton on Tuesday night and desired him to bring Sir Benjamin Brodie or some other eminent surgeon, and when they arrived, that they found it necessary to send off for Dr. Farre who your dear Brother had always told B. he should like to see with him, if he should think him very ill. I went down on Wednesday night and have already told you the rest. Oh! my dearest Friend! what would I not give if you were now in England, that we might console each other, for you cannot feel this lamentable and awfully sudden event more than I do.

I am expecting to hear what day is fixed for performing the last sad offices for my best and dearest departed friend, in which I hope to be able to assist, and then I shall indeed feel a sad and dreary blank that nothing can replace till I have the opportunity of folding you in my arms. Forgive me my dearest Friend, I am afraid I am selfish in thus indulging my feelings at the expense of yours, but you have brought it upon yourself by your uniformly kind and affectionate treatment of your old and faithfully attached but now heartbroken friend.

May a merciful God bless and support you !
always prays

Yours unalterably.

G. W. RICH.

Lady Darnley wrote a touching account
of her husband's last hours, and at her request,
Mr. Stokes, and the members of the family
who were in the house at the time wrote
their recollections of the details of the sad
event; these were added to her manuscript
and preserved in her desk with her husband's
letters.

ACCOUNT BY EMMA COUNTESS OF DARNLEY.

I remember that on the last night on which
my dear Clifton came up to his dressing-room after
he had been there some time he called me out of the
next room, and when I went to him I found him
lying on his sofa looking pale and tired, but I
remarked immediately that he had a particularly
sweet, placid, calm and happy expression of countenance. He wished me to pray with him, and
before we began he said pray for me " that God
may send his Holy Spirit to enlighten me," and I
think he added, " that I may know more about the
Lord Jesus Christ," but I am quite sure that he
finished his sentence with these words " about
Christ Crucified " and I clearly understood that he
wished me to pray that he might know more about
Christ Crucified. I prayed with him, and afterwards while I helped to settle him in bed and to

give him a little salvolatile and water, I again remarked to myself how particularly tender and affectionate he was in his manner, words, looks and voice to me, and I recollect now with great pleasure that both he and I seemed to enjoy great comfort and happiness in praying with each other, and in speaking to each other that night. He did not acquaint me that night that he had any symptoms of danger. He did not tell me till the next morning I suppose between 5 and 6 o'clock, when on my waking up he told me that he feared he had very unpleasant symptoms coming on, and asked me to ring the bell in the dressing-room which I did, and then I ran up-stairs for Mr. Beaumont. When I came down again I entreated him to tell me what he felt, as I could not persuade him to do so before. He then told me that he had known the night before that he had symptoms of lock-jaw. I asked why he did not tell me then, and he answered so tenderly, "because I could not bear to spoil your night's rest." Some time was then spent by Mr. Beaumont in making arrangements about sending for Sir B. Brodie and Mr. Bolton, and in getting coffee made for him. He took a cup of coffee from me, he said it was very good, but seemed unwilling to drink much of it but I remember with pleasure that when I made a point of it and begged him to drink it for my sake, that he drank it apparently with great pleasure. After Mr. Beaumont had made his arrangements and was gone out of the room, I read passages of Scripture to him and prayed with him. I cannot now remember which passage I read first, but I know that he asked me if I had noticed the

Psalm which he had read the last evening at family prayers. I said that I had, and that it was the 141st Psalm, something about cutting wood. He asked me to read it to him, and pointed my attention when I came to the verse as I read—it was "Our bones are scattered at the grave's mouth, as when one cutteth and cleaveth wood upon the earth." He remarked upon it as applying to his own case. I went on and read the 142nd and 143rd Psalms—then I think I began the 10th of John and read to the 18th verse. I passed over the following verses and began to read again at the 25th. I think I had read down to the 30th verse, and I was trying to remark upon the blessed portion of Jesus' sheep, and dwelling upon the words "My sheep hear My voice and I know them, and they follow Me, and I give unto them eternal life: and they shall never perish, neither shall any man pluck them out of My hand," and the two following verses. He listened with great attention, and with a calm, serious look. I had begun to turn the verses into prayer when Mr. Beaumont opened the door rather suddenly, and began to advise to take something or do something immediately which was to do him good. I begged Mr. B. to come in but my dear Clifton said to him as nearly as I can recollect, "if you please, Mr. Beaumont, I had rather that we should go on with what we are about just now : I feel myself better while Lady Darnley is speaking to me : I find that it soothes me and does me good."

I felt much pleased at hearing him say this, and upon trying to resume the employment which Mr. B. had interrupted, I felt a little uncertain as to what passage of Scripture I had been dwelling upon, and asked him to remind me ; he said, was it " He that cometh to Me I will in no wise cast out ? " which passage I had not read to him, and therefore it was a sweet proof to me that the truth contained in those words was in his mind.

I soon found my place and went on. I think then I turned to the 4th chapter of Romans, and read from the 20th verse to the end, and then I read the 5th chapter of Romans down to the end of the 5th verse, when I think I stopped and said "now I am going to read to you what has often given me comfort, listen " : I then read with emphasis the 6th verse " For when we were yet without strength, in due time Christ died for the ungodly." He immediately answered in a sweet and tender and solemn tone of voice " yes, that is precious comfort indeed. Christ died for the ungodly, therefore he died for me." I wish I could describe the earnest, fixed and thoughtful expression of his countenance when he said this. It seemed to me that his inmost soul received and sweetly rested upon this truth. He then said " read that verse again." I did so, I think three or four times. 1 went on a little and tried to pray for him, chiefly requesting in my prayer that he might be enabled to believe in the Lord Jesus Christ with all his heart, that he might believe that Jesus had borne his sins in His own body on the tree, that He being dead to sin might live unto righteousness, that he might indeed believe that Jesus had loved us and given himself for us and more to the same purpose. He seemed to join in my prayer with fervour, and when I paused he took up the prayer and went on with it. I cannot remember all he said, but I trust I shall never forget the intensely fervent manner in which he exclaimed " Lord have mercy upon me ; Christ, have mercy upon me ; Jesus, have mercy upon me," and during the whole time we spent that morning in conversation and reading and prayer, his countenance had such a. sweet, calm, solemn, thoughtful expression that it gave me the idea that his whole soul was occupied and absorbed by the subject of his salvation. He said to me in the most earnest manner " Oh ! if I were quite sure that I was a child of grace, I should be quite willing to go, I should not have a wish to stay." (I cannot distinctly remember when it was that he said something to me about his wish that he might be "accepted in Christ" and that he might give up "his idols.")

Then I think he said something to this effect, how could he know that his faith in Christ was real ? I think that I said in reply that all that we were required to do was to believe in the Lord Jesus Christ with all our hearts and that God could see into our hearts and know whether we really did believe, even if we had no power or opportunity to do one single thing to shew that we did.

He immediately replied, " yes I know very well that if we truly believe in Christ, we shall be saved, even although we should not have time to do one single work to prove our faith, but how can I be sure that my faith in Christ is real ?" I then spoke to him about the thief upon the cross who was only able to acknowledge his Lord by saying, " Lord ! remember me when Thou comest into Thy kingdom " and to reprove the other malefactor for his railing, and was answered " this day shalt thou be with Me in Paradise." I have since remembered that I told him he must pray for more faith : and I turned to the 2nd chapter of Ephesians, verse 8, and read the words " For by grace are ye saved through faith ; and that not of yourselves, it is the gift of God" and there I stopped ; and I felt surprised and pleased at hearing him go on immediately with the words which come next with marked emphasis, "not of works" because I remembered well that some years ago he used to cavil at that passage.

I cannot remember more of what passed just then, but have since recollected that during that long time that we were alone, which was indeed our last season of private conversation carried on for any length of time, I cannot recollect that he even once mentioned or referred to his children whom he doated on, or his place of which he had been too fond, or his business, or even myself. As he then distinctly knew his own danger I consider this circumstance as a sweet sign of grace. I then left him for some time, indeed he asked me to go out of the room before my brother Henry came in, and then took place that most tender proof of his affection to me which is described in Henry's written paper.

ACCOUNT BY HENRY PARNELL.

Taking hold of my hand in a most affectionate manner, he said " Will you take care of Emma." I answered that God would. " I know He will, I am sure He will, she is one of the faithful I am certain.

Pray for me dear Henry." I knelt down and prayed, and in mentioning some promise of salvation through Christ which I cannot recollect, be repeated it several times, and said I do, I do most firmly trust in God. Some one came in and he stopped.

ACCOUNT BY THE REV. JOHN STOKES.

The following is what I can recollect of the sentiments expressed by my beloved friend and *Benefactor* in the short conversation I had with him the day before he died. When I first saw him, he said—" My dear Friend my days are number'd." And on my saying—" as I know where your reliance is placed,—I trust your mind is easy," he answer'd —" I hope my Faith in my Redeemer is steady and firm. All that gives me uneasiness is that the Evidences of my Faith were not more satisfactory to myself ;—that my Life was not more completely what a Christian's life ought to be."

Soon after he said—" Should it please the Almighty to raise me up again, O ! may my Life be more devoted to Him ! May He increase my Faith and my Charity ! " He soon desired me to pray for him. When I asked him if I should use set form, he said " just as you please, only let the Prayers be from your heart." He then said—" if you have no objection I should wish my dear wife to join us." Soon after he desired me call his Cousin Sophy, and when she came he said immediately, " dear Sophy pray for me." And he pressed her to pray audibly for him then. While she was praying, and while we were reading and repeating Texts of Scripture, he more than once, upon any strong expression of the Saviour's power and will to save to the uttermost, said—" aye—that is right "—" repeat that "—or something to that purpose.

In speaking of his children he said to me—" In regard to them I feel happy, knowing in what hands I shall leave them. They will not be worse Christians from my being removed ; probably better." "Perhaps it may be for that it is ordained." Again to Miss Bligh and me he said—" I am happy in leaving my dear children in the hands of such a mother. O ! my dear friends, strengthen her hands in bringing them up as she will, I know, wish to do."

CIRCUMSTANCES RECOLLECTED BY THE REV. JOHN STOKES SINCE WRITING THE FORMER ACCOUNT.

When his friends read to him the 53rd of Isaiah—he said " Ah ! that is the thing"—" read all that again " ; and several passages he repeated after them—especially I remember " He was wounded for our transgressions, He was bruised for our iniquities," &c.

In like manner, when Miss Bligh was reading the 12th of St. John—when she had come to the 6th verse, " I am the way, and the truth, and the life, etc."—he interrupted her with some such words as these—" Ah—that will do"—" begin that chapter again."

On one occasion, either just before he spoke of the satisfaction as to the hands in which he was about to leave his dear children, just before he

utter'd the prayer that God would (if it pleased Him
to raise him up again) increase his Faith and his
Charity; he said, "I have indeed been blessed
above most men."

In the last solemn rite,—after receiving the
consecrated Elements—though his articulation was
indistinct, I heard him say—"Oh! my Saviour's
blood!"

ACCOUNT BY CHARLES BLIGH.

Dear Clifton said to me—" Charles I have been
very much pleased to see the change that has
taken place in you—persevere in the new course
you have entered upon. I have watched with
pleasure your evident endeavours to improve yourself. Pray for me dear Charles. You little
thought that so slight an accident would have
ended so." I said that I trusted he would be
restored to us and added that " He that believeth on
Him shall not perish, but have everlasting life."
"Yes dear Charles" he answered, "he that *believes*
truly believes" and this he seemed to say with a
calm confidence and perfect assurance that his
faith was of that saving sort. I heard him say
afterwards (when Emma was reading to him) with
peculiar emphasis " Yes the *precious blood* of *Christ.*"

ACCOUNT BY SOPHIA BLIGH.

On my going into dearest Clifton's room he
said " is that dear Sophy?" and kissed me several
times in the most affectionate manner and added
" Pray for me Sophy darling." Mr. Stokes being in

the room, I begged him to begin, and after he had finished I tried to offer up a short prayer, which he said he liked and kissed me again. He afterwards desired me to read to him and I began the 14th of John and when I came to the 6th verse he stopped me and desired me to read it over again. He seemed to take great comfort from it and also from the three last verses of the 11th of Matthew "Come unto Me, etc." Soon after he repeated with great emphasis the verses in the 33rd of Isaiah " He was wounded for our transgressions, He was bruised for our iniquities, the chastisement of our peace was upon Him and with His stripes we are healed." I asked him whether he was happy in his mind. He answered in a decided tone "yes, I think I am." Upon another occasion he said " Pray for me that I may have strength and patience to bear whatever pain may be appointed for me." I remember his saying to Mr. Stokes, who had been giving him some salvolatile " My day is over."

SOPHIA BLIGH AT COBHAM HALL TO VISCOUNTESS
POWERSCOURT AT ABBEYLIX.

Thursday, 12th.

Indeed my dearest Lady Powerscourt I have a painful task to fulfil, and would that I could by any means lessen the grief that I am sure will fill your heart at receiving the account of the awful calamity with which it has pleased the Lord to visit us. He has in His infinite Wisdom seen fit to take from us our much loved and valued Clifton—the blow has been so sudden, so unexpected, that I can hardly bring myself to believe that it has really happened, but it is even so, and lest you should not be acquainted with the particulars of the fatal accident which has deprived us of one, so dear, so deservedly lamented, I will relate them.

Last Wednesday week, dearest Clifton, with Charles, and Mr. H. Parnell went into the Great Wood, to cut down trees, and he was in the act of topping off a branch when the axe slipped and cut through his thick boot, severing the little Toe and taking off a great piece of the next; for the next 4 days he seemed to be going on pretty well, tho' of course with occasional pain from the Wound, but on Monday Eve. symptoms of Locked Jaw came on, and on the following morning his poor dear Teeth were almost closed.

Sir B. Brodie, Mr. Bolton, and Dr. Farre arrived in the course of the day, but together with Mr. Beaumont gave very little hope, pronouncing it to be the worst species of that most formidable malady, his sufferings all this time were most intense, and yesterday morning about 10 he had a most agonizing fit which lasted some time, and in which many thought every breath would be his last. He, however, survived this and slept for two or three hours. He awoke and a slight paroxysm came on. He desired to be raised for a moment, and then leaning back, peacefully and without a struggle breathed his last. We were all present at this awful moment. And now dearest Lady Powerscourt the most cheering part remains to be told. The dear sufferer had from the beginning a full persuasion in his own mind that he should not recover, and delightful was it to witness his sweet

426

patience and entire submission to the Divine Will, with his strong Faith, and trust in his blessed Redeemer's merits and righteousness. His mind was indeed kept in perfect peace, free from all doubts and fears, and we have every reason to take comfort from the blessed hope that he is now with his precious Saviour in everlasting happiness. Dear Emma has been wonderfully supported, her fortitude and calmness have never forsaken her throughout these trying scenes. She is indeed a bright proof of the value and power of true religion.

I must leave off now as Mr. Parnell is going to Town and will take this as we are anxious not to lose to-day.

Ever my dearest Lady P.,
Yours most affly.,
S. B.

Pray excuse the hurry, and I will write again by Post.

SOPHIA BLIGH AT COBHAM HALL TO VISCOUNTESS POWERSCOURT AT ABBEYLEIX.

Friday, Feb. 13.

My dearest Lady Powerscourt,

I was obliged to send my Letter to you yesterday in a very unfinished state, as we were anxious that you should have the earliest possible intelligence of the late sad event, and the opportunity of sending it by Mr. George Parnell to London, was not to be thrown away, as thereby a day was saved.

Dear Emma continues in the same delightfully composed and resigned frame of mind feeling deeply her great loss but at the same time most

wonderfully strengthened and supported and proving to all who witness her beautiful submission to
the Divine Will what blessedness and happiness
there is, in having a firm, unwavering Faith, in the
precious promises of the Gospel, especially in a
season of affliction. We have several times visited
the dear remains, there is a sweet placid smile upon
the countenance, an emblem of that perfect peace
and happiness, his precious soul is now enjoying,
and oh! dearest Lady Powerscourt what cause for
thankfulness we have that the dear creature's
sufferings were not protracted and above all for the
many undoubted proofs he gave of being prepared
for his great change, no worldly thought seemed to
cross his mind, no hint about this Place to which we
all know he was so much attached, no distress
evinced at leaving his Family, but his whole soul
seemed to be absorbed in the contemplation of that
Eternity into which he was so soon to enter, and in
satisfying himself that he was really a true believer
in Jesus—his was indeed a happy Death, undis-
turbed peace, built upon the true foundation—upon
one occasion he said with emphasis " That precious
blood of Christ"; but there are many other
delightful observations he made which we are all
trying to recollect and to write down for they will
be most valuable relicks. I have written to poor
dear Beppy, I fear her tender heart will receive a
very grievous shock, may the Lord strengthen her
mightily to bear it, indeed we have all, in a very
awfully short space of time, lost a most invaluable,
deservedly beloved Friend. May the solemn event
be abundantly blessed to all our souls, that we may

really prove by our future lives, that we have profited by the awful Lesson the Lord would teach us, by this afflictive dispensation. As I have Letters to write for Emma, I must conclude this my dearest Lady Powerscourt and believe me to be

Yours very affecly,

Sophia Bligh.

Many many thanks for your very kind letter.

We all took the Sacrament with him between 6 and 7 o'clock in the morning of the day he died.

Since I wrote the above his dear remains have been screwed down.

The dear Children are quite well. John seemed the first night to feel very much his dear Papa's Death. Emma took them all in after the event, and talked to them upon the subject.

The spot fixed upon in the Church Yard is close to his dear Parents. Mr. Stokes is as you would imagine most deeply affected.

The Rev. John Stokes at Cobham to the Hon. John Duncan Bligh at St. Petersburgh.

Feby. 25th, 1835.

My very dear Friend,

On this day I have been accustom'd for many years to write to your beloved brother (if not enjoying his valued society) words of congratulation and good wishes for his future health and happiness. And is it possible (for I can hardly yet realize it to myself) that I am now sitting down to give you some account of the melancholy ceremony which yesterday consigned to its parent earth the mortal part of that dear, that excellent creature? Oh!

how my heart aches when I think what a friend I have lost,—what a brother you are doomed to mourn over! But how unavailing is our sorrow! Let us rather look with the Eye of Faith to those blissful mansions, where he now rests in his Saviour's arms, and check the selfish wish to have detained him longer in this world of sin and woe. Such have been the thoughts that have often restrained the mournings of myself and my poor wife under our bereavements of last year; and such are the sentiments that make me now ashamed to feel so deeply the removal of your dear brother from such a world as this to a state of perfect happiness and serenity. The strong Faith and simple reliance upon the Saviour which he shewed in his last hours leave us not to doubt whether this was the nature of the change in his existence or not. With this in view then, my beloved friend, you may contemplate with composure the sad train that attended his poor perishable body to its last home. Everything was conducted precisely in the same way as in your dear Father's funeral, with this only variation; the remains were carried in a plain, unadorned hearse, instead of being borne on the Labourers' shoulders. This mode was adopted, from a recollection of the inconvenience suffer'd by the bearers, and the interruption it occasion'd to the solemnity. The following members of the family attended your sister-in-law and her three eldest children (forming a Picture that will not soon be forgotten by those who saw it). Your two uncles, Miss Bligh, Sir H. Parnell, and his two sons, Henry and George, Lord Castlereagh, Mr. Vesey (who I suppose you know is now the representative of Queen's Co.), Edward and Charles Bligh and Dr. Longley. Then came, as at your Father's funeral, the Tenantry, and a numerous train of friends and neighbours who wished to shew their respect and esteem. I will give you some of the dear deceased's more intimate friends who were present :—Our dear old friend Mr. Taylor (late of Bifrons) who happen'd to be in England, Sir Brook Taylor, Sir J. Lambert, Colonel Gascoigne, Mr. Berens, Mr. Robt. Baxter, and poor old Rich. There were nearly twenty clergymen present, three of whom officiated ; your poor old friend, with a half broken heart performed most of the service, in the Desk, and at the Grave ; Mr. Bowman (my Milton Curate) merely read the Psalms, and Mr. Graham of Rochester preached a beautiful and most impressive Sermon. I hope he may be prevailed upon to print it, in which case I will take care you shall have a copy. The spot where the dear remains are deposited is immediately adjoining the grave of your excellent parents, in a bricked grave capable of holding only two coffins. This is to be enclosed in an iron railing including the same space as that enclosed in 1831. And I believe a railing will be continued (at my suggestion) to the old ruined arch. This will appropriate a space for a family vault, should one at any future period be wished for. I understand from Edward and Charles Bligh that their Father is not expected to live. I shall look anxiously for your answer to my letter of last week, which I hope may contain your permission to me to fly to you. If you have granted that permission of course you will not answer this, as I shall have probably left England before your letter could arrive.

God bless and preserve you dearest Friend,
Ever affectely yours,

J. STOKES.

DR. C. T. LONGLEY AT HARROW TO VISCOUNTESS POWERSCOURT AT ABBEYLEIX.

27th Febry., 1835.

Dear Lady Powerscourt,

Often, very often, have you been in my thoughts since the afflictive visitation of Providence which has so suddenly deprived us of so dear a friend ; and I have been much wishing to write to you, as I thought that some details from one who saw so much of him during his last hours might not be unacceptable to you, but I knew not where you were, until I heard from T. Vesey that you were at Abbeyleix.

The great consolation we are permitted to enjoy in the midst of our grief is that as he lived in the habitual exercise of those virtues which most adorn the Christian character, so he gave the most convincing evidence in his latter moments that He with whom he had daily walked in the time of his health and strength did not leave him or forsake him when he lay on the bed of languishing, but upheld him by His free Spirit, and shewed how the strength of Christ was to be made perfect in our weakness. His entire resignation to the will of God, his firm conviction that it was better for him to depart, to be with Christ, his heavenly patience under the most distressing sufferings, proved most

432

emphatically that he was a true disciple of his suffering Saviour.

As I expressed a hope in my letter to Lady Elizabeth that you might be made acquainted with some of the particulars which I communicated to her, and as I think I understand from T. Vesey that you were going to join her, I think I need hardly trouble you by repeating exactly the details there mentioned. You have heard how wonderfully Lady Darnley was supported through the scene of awful suffering she was called on to witness, and you will be glad to hear that she continues to receive the same succour from above. She was enabled to follow the remains of her dear husband to the grave, and to go through the whole of the solemn ceremony without being overcome by it. The few previous days had been boisterous and churlish, but Tuesday morning was one of those days of bright and still and serene sunshine which are so rare, but so soothing to the feelings at this time of the year. It seemed really an emblem of that heavenly rest into which our dear friend had entered after the fiery trial to which he had been exposed. For miles before we reached Cobham (T. Vesey and G. Parnell accompanied me from London) we saw crowds of persons flocking towards the Park, and I doubt not that by every other approach there was the same influx of strangers, for by the time the procession set forth there must have been many thousands assembled. Of the family, and of his own friends, there were present Sir Henry Parnell, General and Colonel Bligh, Miss Bligh, Edward and Charles Bligh, Lord Castlereagh, Henry and George Parnell, R. Berens,

R. Barter, Colonel Gascoigne, Mr. Rich and his two sons, and Sir John Lambert ; T. Vesey I have mentioned before, also Sir Brooke Taylor and Mr. Taylor.

It was half past two before we reached the Church, Lady Darnley following on foot with John, in her right hand, supported by Henry Parnell. An admirable funeral sermon, which I very much hope to get printed for private circulation, was preached by Mr. Graham, a Minor Canon of Rochester ; the Church was crowded to excess ; and I think it was an address calculated to make a very deep impression upon all who heard it ; I will not fail to send you a copy, should I succeed in my object.

I was obliged to return hither very soon after we had paid the last earthly tribute to our dear departed friend, and with a very heavy heart did I take leave of dear Cobham, with the recollection of all the many hours of happiness I had passed there, of all the kindness I had there met with in my earlier life, of the many warm hearts which had so often greeted me there, may I not say with affection too, many of which have now ceased to kindle with the glow of feeling. The loss of these, whom it has pleased God successively to take to himself, were truly lamented by me, but the loss of none so deeply as of him who was the friend of my youth, and the brother of my maturer years. His memory will be most affectionately cherished by me to my latest hour, and the blank his departure has left in my existence can never be filled up, but he has also left us all a bright example of Faith and Patience, which I earnestly pray may be blessed to us, and may quicken our steps in running the race which is set before us, and further our progress towards that Heavenly rest, in which those who look for and love the appearing of their Lord shall meet never more to part.

Believe me, dear Lady Powerscourt, with much regard,

Yours most faithfully,

Charles T. Longley.

Harrow, 1835.

Recollections of her Father and Mother by Lady Elizabeth Cust.

I was about four and a half years old when my father died, I have an indistinct recollection of him walking with crutches in his last illness, and a vivid recollection of being taken into his room after his death and being lifted up to kiss him, scarcely understanding why, but feeling a vague awe. Although I was so young I remember my father on several occasions; I was a favourite of his and often as a child when I imagined myself slighted or less favoured than others, I have pictured to myself how different it would have been had he lived.

I will now try to recall my few remembrances of him. I used to go to his dressing-room every morning, and I remember watching him shave with great astonishment. I remember also at the time my youngest brother Henry was born I always went down stairs with him to his breakfast, and how kind he used to be to me, feeding me with grapes carefully skinned and the stones taken out. Another time we children went to the Surrey Zoological

Gardens with him and my mother and how terrified I was at the tiger. I can also remember walking home from afternoon church with him, he carrying my clogs across Berkeley Square; I had a dear little red prayer-book in which I used to read and remember how grand I thought the prayer beginning " Almighty God, King of Kings and Lord of Lords."

I remember once going to Ireland with my parents, and long after when I again crossed the Menai Bridge the rattling of the chains vividly recalled to my mind this former journey. We had little gardens at Clifton Lodge, mine was in the form of a T for Tiny, my pet name.

One other sad recollection I have, after my father's accident to his foot, he recovered so far as to drive out with his foot supported on the opposite seat of the carriage, the footman seeing a lump of blue cloak, gave it a violent blow to smooth it and came down with violence on the poor injured foot. I believe, from what my mother has told me, that in his own mind my father looked on this blow as the immediate cause of his death. When receiving the Sacrament the last day of his life he sent for the footman to receive it with him in token of his forgiveness. I have no recollections of my father's countenance, I remember him only as a tall large man ; his funeral I can picture to myself as if yesterday ; the long melancholy walk of a mile up the avenue following the hearse, the crowds of people lining the pathway, especially the old women in their red cloaks.

I remember that I walked with my Aunt Sophy, daughter of Colonel the Hon. William Bligh, who married my uncle Henry Parnell in the following May. I have been told that I much comforted my mother by repeating constantly to her the first verses of the fourteenth chapter of St. John's Gospel.

My father was very generally and sincerely lamented by all who knew him ; he appears to have been of a quiet and retiring disposition, with the kindest of hearts and a strong desire to do his duty. He was sincerely religious and most deeply attached to my mother, and his death was a crushing blow to her as she was one of those gentle natures ill fitted to stand against the world alone. Her spirits never quite recovered the terrible shock of her sudden bereavement though at the time her fortitude and resignation were remarkable.

My mother continued to live at Cobham, devoting herself to the care and education of her children, until the marriage of my eldest brother in 1850. She then made her principal home in London and after the marriages of her daughters in 1854 and 1855 she devoted herself entirely to religious and charitable interests. In the latter years of her life she lived at Norwood and at Brighton, where she died. Shortly after her husband's death her brother, Henry Parnell and her friend Miss Rushout persuaded her of the truth of the doctrines of the "Catholic Apostolic Church" (the members of which are usually known as Irvingites) and she remained a member of that body until her death. We were however carefully brought up according to the principles of the Church of England under the direction of our other guardians, my uncles John Bligh and Dr. Longley, afterwards Archbishop of Canterbury.

My mother's chief characteristics were her almost morbid conscientiousness and her very great kindness. She was never heard to speak unkindly of any one. She retained much of her beauty all her life and the following description of her written by her cousin Fanny Erskine (Mrs. Linwood Strong) in 1843 gives a good idea of her character and appearance.

"I really don't think there is her (Emma's) equal for real goodness in the world, and she is so gentle and beautiful and good natured, it is impossible to help liking her.

She is always thinking what she can do to amuse us, and Mrs. Gascoigne told me that she told her that she meant to try and make it pleasant for me as I was to stay the summer with her.

She has left off caps this last few weeks even in the morning and with her long black curls and rosy cheeks and red lips and laughing eyes she looks about 20. Mrs. Browne* says she looks exactly the same as she did when she was a girl.

She says, I am her daughter while I am with her and tries to make out that she is very old, which is a complete failure."

Up to the time of her death in her 80th year her delicate complexion and dark curls were quite remarkable and recalled the descriptions which I have heard of her girlish charms.

Nearly 50 years passed away before my mother was laid beside the husband of her youth in Cobham churchyard. My two elder brothers and I, who well remembered walking with her on that

· *Mrs. Peter Browne, who died June, 1884.

EMMA, COUNTESS OF DARNLEY.
From a painting by William Fowler, at
Cobham Hall.

first sad occasion were present, also the other brother and sister who were, at that time, too young to know their loss.

Our father's dying prayers and blessings have been fully granted, for we have all lived to see our children's children in peace and prosperity, and three of us have celebrated our Golden Weddings.

In my 83rd year I recall the memory of my parents with loving gratitude to them and to " God before whom my fathers did walk, the God which fed me all my life long unto this day." (Genesis xlviii, 15).

APPENDIX.

LADY CAROLINE PARNELL.
(PAGE 21).

A FTER the events related in Chapter I, Lady Caroline Parnell remained in Paris and refused to meet any of her family or other relatives, maintaining however, a constant correspondence with her children. She even adopted a feigned name to secure seclusion, her letters being addressed to Madame Elizabeth Pearson at the Post Office. This continued after she became Baroness Congleton in 1841, when her husband, Sir Henry Parnell, was raised to the peerage.*

Emma, Countess of Darnley, was particularly assiduous in her endeavours to bring about closer relations with her mother, and after Lord Darnley's death in 1835 she made her a special allowance. In 1850-51 although Lady Darnley and her daughters spent some months in Paris, Lady Congleton still refused to see them but continued to keep up a correspondence by letter, in which she seemed to take an interest in their pro-

* Lord Congleton died in 1842.

ceedings. It was not until October, 1860, that Lady Darnley succeeded in seeing her mother, after waiting in Paris six weeks before she was admitted.

She found her in a poor lodging, her only attendant being Ferdinand d'Eisenach, a German journalist of about 40 years of age. He was the son of a humble friend whose mother had commended him to Lady Congleton on her death-bed. Lady Congleton had educated him, and he now managed her affairs and waited upon her with faithful devotion. Lady Darnley found good reason to place confidence in him, liked him and befriended him until his death.

She described her mother as a very stout old lady with a large white face, sitting in an armchair unable to move, but full of vivacity and talk. During the next three weeks she visited her for some hours every day and made good use of her opportunities for bringing her to a happier frame of mind, finally leaving her in the same rooms but with better provision for her comfort.

Seven weeks later, on February 16th, 1861, Lady Congleton was sitting before the fire, Ferdinand d'Eisenach having left her for a few minutes to post a letter, when she accidentally set fire to her clothes and was unable to extinguish them before his return. Though not severely burnt, her already enfeebled frame could not recover the shock, and a few hours later she passed peacefully away supported in Ferdinand d'Eisenach's arms. Her last words were : " Mon pauvre ami, ne pleurez pas—je pars tranquille, dites à ceux de mes enfants que vous verrez que je les aimais bien tous ; à cette chère et bonne Emma donnez mes bijoux, qu'elle les distribue selon son bon cœur. Quelquechose m'étouffe, laissez moi me reposer."

Lady Darnley wrote the following paper after the death of her mother.

Saturday morning, February 16th, 1861.

" Saved, yet so as by fire."—1 Cor. iii, 15.

The first Sunday after I had seen her (December 2nd, 1860), while in Church at the Rue de la Madeleine during the worship, I had a solemn, strange and delightful impression on my mind for some minutes that there would yet come a time when that mean room where I had seen my poor mother would yet be filled with glory, and that in that place there would be joy among the Angels of Heaven over her, when she should repent. I had a strange consciousness of glory and joy in my spirit by anticipation.

How pleasant it is to remember now, that the one portion of Scripture which she seemed to have had treasured up in her mind during a long life, was the history of the Prodigal Son, which she spontaneously asked me to find and to read to her, and that the verse which she wished to refer to (and on my reading which she stopped me and said that was the verse which she wished to put me in mind of, for a reason which she gave) was, "I say unto you that likewise joy shall be in heaven over one sinner that repenteth, more than over ninety and nine just persons which need no repentance. (Luke xv, 7.)

WS - #0048 - 210423 - CO - 229/152/25 - PB - 9780243269297 - Gloss Lamination